CONTEMPORARY MUSIC THEORY
LEVEL ONE
BY MARK HARRISON

ISBN 0-7935-9881-8

HARRISON
MUSIC
EDUCATION
SYSTEMS

HAL•LEONARD®
CORPORATION
7777 W. BLUEMOUND RD. P.O. BOX 13819 MILWAUKEE, WI 53213

Visit Hal Leonard Online at
www.halleonard.com

Welcome to *Contemporary Music Theory Level 1*. I have personally taught these concepts to **hundreds of students** in Harmony classes held at the former **Grove School of Music**, and this book is now used in many schools worldwide including our own **Harrison School of Music** in Los Angeles. As such this book represents a proven and 'battle-tested' approach to the subject matter! The internationally-acclaimed Grove School provided a unique learning experience for the contemporary musician, and in this exciting environment I was responsible for a significant amount of the school's musicianship instruction. During the years I was teaching Harmony & Theory at the Grove School to students from all over the world, I had the best possible opportunity to determine what the music theory needs of the contemporary musician were, and what the best method was to communicate these concepts! This process has led to the creation of our *Contemporary Music Theory* book series - *the most thorough music theory courses available for the pop and jazz musician!*

Whether you are new to music theory, or are finding your 'classical theory' background inadequate for pop and jazz applications, this *Level One* course is an ideal starting point. In here we completely derive and explain major and minor scales, keys and key signatures, all intervals, triads and four-part chords, diatonic chords, modes, suspensions and altered chords. Everything is presented *from the viewpoint of the contemporary musician* and is information you can then *use right away* in your playing or composing/arranging! If you've ever labored through some college music theory course that looked like it was written in Greek (and which had zero relevance to your musical needs and aspirations) then I think you will especially appreciate the uniquely useful and practical approach contained in this book!

Today's pop and jazz styles are very 'ear-oriented' - in other words they tend to follow a set of rules and expectations that an 'educated ear' will understand. You may have already seen or used our *Contemporary Eartraining* courses (see page *vi*), which were a fundamental component of the musicianship program at the Grove School. For music theory instruction to be of value to the contemporary musician, the concepts *must be presented in a way that is consistent with how the ear works* - this is the whole philosophy behind our *Contemporary Music Theory* courses. For students wishing to strengthen their overall musicianship, the combination of our *Eartraining* and *Music Theory* methods represents the most efficient and 'targeted' contemporary music program now available!

Each chapter in this book is divided into three main sections:-
- **Textbook**, containing a complete explanation for each subject area addressed, with various examples of how to apply the theory concepts
- **Workbook Questions**, containing written exercises for each subject area
- **Workbook Answers**, containing answers for all of the written exercises.

AUTHOR'S FOREWORD

This book is ideally suited for self-study, one-on-one music tutoring, and group classes. At the **Harrison School of Music**, we typically cover this material in a ten-week class 'quarter', although the material can of course be adapted for use within different course lengths (i.e. a different number of weeks), at the discretion of the teacher or educational institution. There are hundreds of written exercises throughout the book, all with answers provided - a perfect way to cement your understanding of how today's music really works!

At the back of the book, I have provided appendices listing all major and minor scales (both with and without key signatures) and all diatonic triads and four-part chords in every key. These are followed by a complete glossary of terms used in the book, for your reference and convenience.

Good luck with your study of **Contemporary Music Theory** - and I hope it opens many doors for you as a musician!

Mark Harrison
Harrison Music Education Systems
Los Angeles, California

MARK HARRISON is a keyboardist, composer and educator with over twenty years experience in the industry. Before moving to Los Angeles in 1987, Mark's musical career in his native London included appearances on British national (**BBC**) television as well as extensive club and studio experience. As an active composer for television in both England and the United States, his work is heard internationally in commercials for clients like **American Express** and **CNN**, as well as in **A & E**'s popular **American Justice** series.

Mark was commissioned by the music equipment manufacturers **Roland** and **Gibson** to compose and arrange music for their trade shows, and in 1996 Boston's renowned **Berklee College of Music** invited Mark to showcase his composition **First Light** with Berklee's faculty orchestra. Active in the Los Angeles music scene, Mark has also performed with top professional musicians including **Bruce Hornsby**'s drummer John Molo; **Yanni**'s bassist Rick Fierabracci; and **Ray Charles**' bassist Adam Cohen.

After teaching at the internationally-acclaimed **Grove School of Music** for six years, Mark founded the **Harrison School of Music** (a successor institution to the Grove school) in Los Angeles. His groundbreaking keyboard method **The Pop Piano Book** is endorsed by Grammy-winners **Russell Ferrante** and **Mark James**, as well as other top professional musicians and educators. **Keyboard Magazine** calls Mark's presentation style "warm, humorous and clear", and names The Pop Piano Book "the most accessible and valuable keyboard method available for those interested in popular styles".

Mark has authored numerous music instruction books (including comprehensive methods for music theory and eartraining), and the **Harrison Music Education Systems** product line is published internationally by **Hal Leonard Publications**. Mark's methods are also used at many educational institutions (including the internationally-famous **Berklee College of Music**) and his books & tapes have been purchased by thousands of students in over twenty-five countries worldwide. Mark continues to be in demand as a uniquely effective contemporary music educator, both in the classroom and in his private teaching studio in Los Angeles.

Here are some other books available from

HARRISON MUSIC EDUCATION SYSTEMS:-

Contemporary Music Theory Level Two

This intermediate pop & jazz theory course covers 'II-V-I' progressions in major and minor keys, five-part chords, substitutions, harmonic analysis of pop & jazz tunes, voiceleading, use of 'upper structure' voicings, and pentatonic & blues scale applications. Includes hundreds of written theory exercises with answers!

The Pop Piano Book

A complete method for playing contemporary styles spontaneously on the keyboard. This **500-page** book includes application of harmony to the keyboard in all keys, and then specific instruction for playing in pop, rock, funk, country, ballad, new age and gospel styles. Endorsed by **Grammy**-winners and top educators, this book is available with cassette tapes and MIDI files of all 800 music examples!

"This is the most accessible and valuable keyboard method available for those interested in popular styles. Going through the method is just plain fun!"

ERNIE RIDEOUT
Assistant Editor, **KEYBOARD MAGAZINE**

Contemporary Eartraining Level One

A modern eartraining approach to help you hear and transcribe melodies, rhythms, intervals, bass lines and basic chords (available with four cassette tapes of vocal drills and exercises). Developed at the **Grove School of Music** in Los Angeles.

Contemporary Eartraining Level Two

A modern eartraining approach to help you hear and transcribe chord progressions, modes and key changes used in pop and jazz styles (available with three cassette tapes of exercises). Developed at the **Grove School of Music** in Los Angeles.

...and we're working on the following book for Fall '98 release:

Contemporary Music Theory Level Three

This more advanced pop & jazz theory course covers chord extensions, alterations and scale sources for **all** major, minor, dominant and diminished chords, and the application of this information to composing/arranging/playing situations using the **contemporary shape concept**. More advanced harmonic analysis of jazz tunes is also covered. Includes hundreds of written theory exercises with answers!

If you would like to inquire about these products, please call toll-free (in the U.S.):

(4 6 3 7)

1-800-799-HMES

(**H**arrison **M**usic **E**ducation **S**ystems)

or check out our website at:

www.harrisonmusic.com

or you may write to us at:

HARRISON MUSIC EDUCATION SYSTEMS
P.O. BOX 56505
SHERMAN OAKS
CA 91413 USA

- *The HARRISON SCHOOL OF MUSIC (based in Los Angeles, CA) is running group Music Theory classes using our Music Theory books!*

- *The school also offers Keyboard and Eartraining classes based on the acclaimed methods from HARRISON MUSIC EDUCATION SYSTEMS (see page vi), as well as guitar, bass, rhythm, arranging, songwriting, improvisation and ensemble classes.*

- *School founder MARK HARRISON was on the faculty at the internationally-acclaimed GROVE SCHOOL OF MUSIC for several years. The success of the Grove School proved that there was a need for high quality pop & jazz education taught by working professionals - this is now being provided in the Los Angeles area by the HARRISON SCHOOL OF MUSIC!*

If you would like to inquire about the school, or about private instruction with Mark Harrison, please call toll-free (in the U.S.):

(6 8 7 4)
1-800-828-MUSIC

or check out our website at:

www.harrisonmusic.com

or you may write to us at:

HARRISON SCHOOL OF MUSIC
P.O. BOX 56505
SHERMAN OAKS
CA 91413 USA

I would like to gratefully acknowledge the contributions of the following important people:

DICK GROVE

During the period from 1988 until 1992 I had the pleasure and privilege of teaching a wide range of courses at the **Grove School of Music**, in Los Angeles, California. From the time that **Dick Grove** founded this school in 1973 until the school's closure in 1992, his unique perspective on contemporary music influenced literally thousands of musicians and students from all around the world, as well as those of us on the faculty who were fortunate enough to work in this exceptional institution.

My experience on the Grove School faculty provided an ideal environment for me to develop and fine-tune my own concepts of how contemporary music should be taught, which in turn has helped me create my own series of instruction books and methods. Dick Grove's overall philosophy and concepts of contemporary music have been very influential in this process - and in particular during the creation of my *Contemporary Music Theory* series.

I am very proud to have been an integral part of the Grove School educational environment and 'music community', and this experience has inspired and influenced our own *Harrison School of Music* here in Los Angeles. Dick still remains very active in the music education field from his new base in Las Vegas, and we wish him continued success in his career!

SUE HERRING

We were very saddened to hear that **Sue Herring** lost her battle with cancer in June of 1998. An enthusiastic musician and student, Sue had taken time out from her busy television career to proof-read the first editions of my *Contemporary Music Theory Level One* & *Level Two* books. She worked with me in many private lessons as well as in group classes at the Harrison School of Music. Sue will be very fondly remembered, and her kind and gentle spirit will live on in the hearts of everyone who knew her.

Mark Harrison

x

TABLE OF CONTENTS

Contemporary Music Theory Level 1 by Mark Harrison

Notation basics, major scales & key signatures

Note-naming conventions and the music alphabet

First of all we need to familiarize ourselves with the 'music alphabet'. This refers to the alphabet letters **A - G** which we use to label different notes in music. These letternames are shown on the following keyboard diagram:-

Figure 1.1. Keyboard diagram #1 showing white-key note names

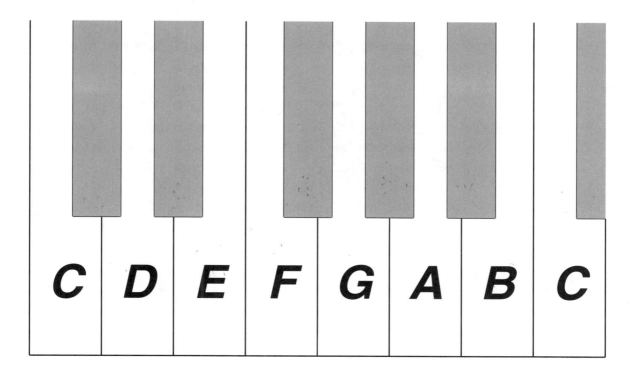

You'll notice that this diagram starts and ends on the note **C**. This is done for convenience, as the 'white keys' on the keyboard collectively make up a **C major scale** - more about this later on! Also observe that when moving from left to right in the above diagram, after we use the lettername **G** we 'wrap around' to the beginning of the music alphabet again to use the lettername **A**. By the way, it is of course **not** necessary to be a keyboard player in order to learn music theory and harmony - however, when we are first getting acquainted with the music alphabet and with note names, I think it is easier to initially visualize these concepts using a keyboard - this can then of course be applied to other instruments of your choice! From a keyboard perspective, we use the position of each white key **relative to the black keys** to determine which lettername to apply in each case (see following page):-

Note-naming conventions and the music alphabet (contd)

- The note **C** is always to the left of the group of 2 black keys.
- The note **D** is always in the middle of the group of 2 black keys.
- The note **E** is always to the right of the group of 2 black keys.
- The note **F** is always to the left of the group of 3 black keys.
- The note **G** is always between the 1st and 2nd key within the group of 3 black keys.
- The note **A** is always between the 2nd and 3rd key within the group of 3 black keys.
- The note **B** is always to the right of the group of 3 black keys.

Now we need to consider the note names for the black keys on the keyboard diagram. These use the same range of letternames, but are qualified with a 'sharp' or a 'flat' sign:-

Figure 1.2. Keyboard diagram #2 showing white-key and black-key note names

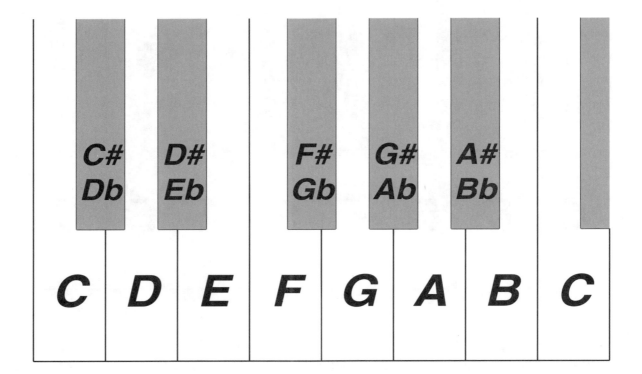

Note that each black key has been given two names - for example, the black key in between **C** and **D** can be called either **C#** (C sharp) or **Db** (D flat). In other words we can **sharp** (or raise) the pitch **C** to get to **C#**, or we can **flat** (or lower) the pitch **D** to get to **Db**. The term **enharmonic** is used to describe the same pitch having more than one name - for example, the note names **C#** and **Db** would be considered **enharmonic equivalents**.

At this point we need to learn our first music interval term - the **half-step**. The half-step is the smallest unit of interval measurement in conventional Western music. If we move from

Note-naming conventions and the music alphabet (contd)

any note in the diagram on the previous page, to the **nearest note** on the right or left, then this movement will be a halfstep interval. For example, if we start on the note **C**, we have already seen that the next highest note (i.e. nearest note on the right) is **not** the note **D**, but is the black key **between C** and **D** (i.e. the note **C#** or **Db**) - this black key is therefore a half-step higher than the note **C**. When we **sharp** a note (by appending the *'#'* suffix to the note name), we are **raising the pitch by a half-step**, and when we flat a note (by appending the *'b'* suffix to the note name) we are **lowering the pitch by a half-step**.

Another interval term that we will learn is called the **octave**. This is the distance between any note and the next-occurring note of the same name, either to the right (higher) or to the left (lower). For example, our diagram begins and ends on the note **C** - the interval between the **C** on the left and the **C** on the right is therefore an octave. If you count starting from the **C** on the left of the diagram to the **C** on the right, you'll find that there are **twelve half-steps in one octave**. This is a fundamental relationship upon which Western music is generally based!

Also you'll notice that certain pairs of white keys on this diagram don't have a black key in between them (just as well really, as then we'd have a problem identifying the notes on the keyboard)! For example, if we start on the note **E**, the next highest note (i.e. one **half-step** higher) is actually the note **F** as there is no black key between **E** and **F**. This situation is the reason why alternate note names (enharmonics) exist for the notes **E, F, B** and **C** as follows:-

Figure 1.3. Keyboard diagram #3 showing white-key enharmonic note names

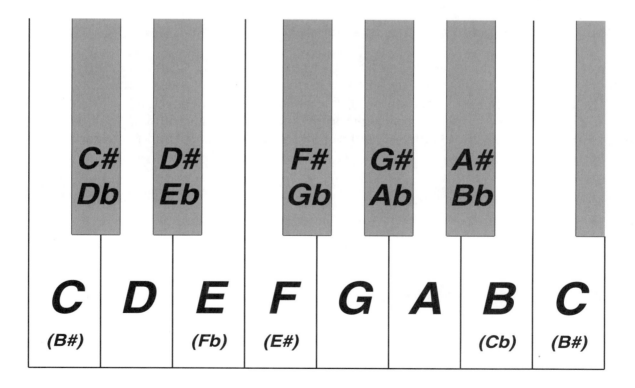

Note-naming conventions and the music alphabet (contd)

The following new enharmonic relationships have now been presented:-

-   The note **C** may also be known as **B#**, as it is one half-step higher than the note **B**.
-   The note **B** may also be known as **Cb**, as it is one half-step lower than the note **C**.
-   The note **F** may also be known as **E#**, as it is one half-step higher than the note **E**.
-   The note **E** may also be known as **Fb**, as it is one half-step lower than the note **F**.

At this point you may be wondering why we have different names (enharmonic equivalents) for the same pitch. Well, the choice of which enharmonic to use for a given note is generally based upon the key or scale 'in force' at the time, as we will see later on.

We can also now begin to use the unit of the halfstep interval as an entry-level tool to measure the distance between any two notes on our 'keyboard diagram'. Let's say we were trying to measure the distance (i.e. how many halfsteps) between the notes **C** and **G**. Moving from left to right on our diagram we observe that, starting on the note C on the left:-

-   Moving from the starting note **C** up to the note **C#** (or **Db**) is *1* halfstep.
-   Moving from the note **C#** (or **Db**) up to the note **D** is a further halfstep - *2* halfsteps total.
-   Moving from the note **D** up to the note **D#** (or **Eb**) is a further halfstep - *3* halfsteps total.
-   Moving from the note **D#** (or **Eb**) up to the note **E** is a further halfstep - *4* halfsteps total.
-   Moving from the note **E** up to the note **F** is a further halfstep - *5* halfsteps total.
-   Moving from the note **F** up to the note **F#** (or **Gb**) is a further halfstep - *6* halfsteps total.
-   Moving from the note **F#** (or **Gb**) up to the note **G** is a further halfstep - *7* halfsteps total.

So we see that there are seven halfsteps between the note **C** and the note **G**. This rather basic method of interval measurement (i.e. counting the halfsteps between two notes) will be superseded by the more scale-oriented interval methods described in *Chapter 2*. However, if you are new to the 'keyboard diagram' and note-naming conventions, working out intervals in this way initially will help you in the familiarization and learning process.

Music notation - why do we need it?

We will now begin to look at music notation - the language used for the reading and writing of music. This book is not intended as a complete notation reference, but serves as an introduction to the notation of notes and rests in the treble and bass clefs. First of all let me try to dispel some myths about the relevance of notation to the contemporary pop and jazz musician! As a teacher I sometimes hear these kinds of comments from pop and jazz students:-

"What do I need to read notes for - I'm never going to be playing classical music!"
"I don't need to bother with notation - I just want to play by ear..."
"All that reading stuff just gets in the way of my creativity..."

If you've found yourself being sympathetic to these or similar views - well, now's the time for a **REALITY CHECK!!** My own teaching experience is entirely in the pop and jazz field - I don't teach classical music - people use my books and classes to develop a total approach to understanding and performing in contemporary styles. A vital part of this 'big picture' is the ability to communicate music concepts to other musicians, and to absorb music ideas from a wide variety of different sources. Until someone invents a more efficient technique (and don't hold your breath..!), the best way to achieve this is to attain familiarity with music notation! You should think of music notation as a **communication channel**, via which you communicate with other musicians and absorb other ideas and influences. Don't make the all-too-common mistake of thinking that reading and writing music is somehow mutually exclusive with playing spontaneously or 'by ear' - any professional musician will tell you that these abilities need to be combined at a moment's notice in a working situation, for example when using a typical pop or jazz 'chart'. To summarize - familiarity with music notation is an enhancement to - **NOT** a detraction from - your abilities as a pop or jazz musician!

Music notation - location of notes on the treble and bass clefs

You'll recall that our previous 'keyboard diagram' started and ended on the note C. Our first notation example shows us where several C's are located, using a combination of **treble** and **bass** clefs called a **grand staff**:-

Figure 1.4. Grand staff showing C notes (two octaves either side of Middle C)

Note the **treble clef** symbol on the left of the top music staff. The lowest note written in this staff (using the single '**ledger line**' below) represents the note **Middle C**.

Note the **bass clef** symbol on the left of the bottom music staff. The highest note written in this staff (using the single '**ledger line**' above) **also** represents the note **Middle C**.

Music notation - location of notes on the treble and bass clefs (contd)

The term **Middle C** is used here as a central reference point and represents the **C in the middle of the piano keyboard**. Piano or keyboard notation typically uses a combination of these treble and bass clefs (together called a 'grand staff'), with the right hand playing the treble clef part and the left hand playing the bass clef part. Guitar players will read parts written using the treble clef, while bass players will read parts written using the bass clef. *(Arranging note - when guitar and bass players read these parts, the sound produced is actually one octave lower than written - as opposed to keyboard players whose parts sound exactly as written).*

I often encounter students who are only familiar with notation in one clef i.e. keyboard and guitar players who know the treble clef but not the bass clef. Please remember that, **regardless of which instrument you primarily play**, you should become equally familiar with both treble and bass clef notation!

You can see from the previous **Fig. 1.4.** that the C notes 'move outward' in a symmetrical manner from the **Middle C** which is on both treble and bass clef staffs. For example, the C's which are **one octave** from Middle C are in the second 'space' from the top of the treble clef, and the second 'space' from the bottom of the bass clef, respectively. Similarly, the C's which are **two octaves** from Middle C are on the second 'ledger line' above the treble clef, and the second 'ledger line' below the bass clef, respectively. Establishing these 'guideposts' in your mind is a good way to begin learning your notes on the staff! Now we'll add all the G notes within this range on the grand staff, as follows:-

Figure 1.5. Grand staff showing C & G notes (two octaves either side of Middle C)

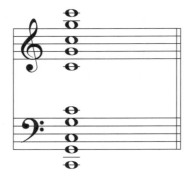

Note that the **G** immediately above Middle C is on the second 'line' from the bottom of the treble clef, while the **G** in the next octave above is right above the top 'line' of the treble clef.

Note that the **G** immediately below Middle C is in the top 'space' of the bass clef, while the **G** in the next octave below is on the bottom 'line' of the bass clef.

Again establishing these as 'guideposts' is I believe an aid to learning the remaining notes in the treble and bass clef staffs.

Now in the following example we will add in all the remaining notes in between the C's and G's studied so far:-

Music notation - location of notes on the treble and bass clefs (contd)

Figure 1.6. Grand staff showing all notes (two octaves either side of Middle C)

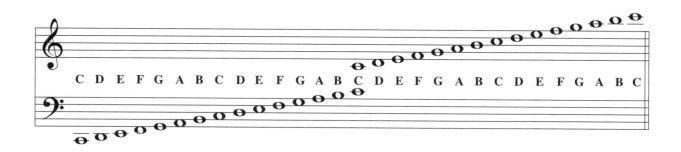

You should make it a **high priority** to learn and memorize the above treble and bass clef notes. Here are some observations I have on this learning process (for what they're worth!):-

- some entry-level and children's texts use mnemonics to help memorize the note names i.e. the treble clef 'line' notes in ascending order are **E**, **G**, **B**, **D** and **F**, which is sometimes represented by the mnemonic Every Good Boy Does Fine (!!) This may be of some value to the absolute beginner, but should be a strictly temporary phase in the learning process!

- another 'crutch' I have seen used is to work out the bass clef notation on a 'relative' basis from the treble clef. For example, the middle 'line' note on the treble clef is **B**, and the corresponding middle line on the bass clef is **D**, which is two letter names further on in the music alphabet (B, C, D). Again this may have some temporary value for the bass clef novice, but should be jettisoned as soon as possible!

- **there is really no substitute for developing an immediate recognition of each of the above notes individually**. The best way I have found for beginners to achieve this is to work regularly with **flashcards**, combined with graduated reading drills on your instrument. A set of flashcards contains a card for each note (in treble and bass clef), showing the notation on the front and the note name and keyboard location on the back. Go get a set from your local music store - it'll be the best five bucks you ever spent!

So far our work on notation has been concerned with the pitches and their location on the staff. Now we will consider how to notate and recognize **rhythmic values** i.e. how long the notes will last:-

Music notation - rhythmic values for notes

The 'rhythmic value' here refers to the **duration** or length of time for a particular note, defined as the number of **beats** (rhythmic units) that the note will last. We have already seen that the note occupying the second space from the top of the treble clef is the note **C** (above Middle C). We will now look at this note with a variety of rhythmic values or durations as follows:-

Figure 1.7. Whole note

An 'empty' notehead without a stem is referred to as a **whole note**, and lasts for **four** beats.

Figure 1.8. Half note

An 'empty' notehead with a stem is referred to as a **half note**, and lasts for **two** beats.

Figure 1.9. Dotted half note

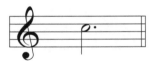

A dotted 'empty' notehead with a stem is referred to as a **dotted half note**, and lasts for **three** beats. (Note - a dot after a note adds **half as much again** to the original rhythmic duration - in this case the original two beats now becoming three beats).

Figure 1.10. Quarter note

A 'filled in' notehead with a separate stem (i.e. not joined to another note) is referred to as a **quarter note**, and lasts for **one** beat.

Music notation - rhythmic values for notes (contd)

Figure 1.11. Dotted quarter note

A dotted 'filled in' notehead with a separate stem is referred to as a **dotted quarter note**, and lasts for **one and a half** beats.

Figure 1.12. Eighth note

A 'filled in' notehead EITHER with a separate stem and single tail OR joined to another note via a single beam, is referred to as an **eighth note**, and lasts for **half a beat**.

Figure 1.13. Dotted eighth note

A dotted 'filled in' notehead EITHER with a separate stem and single tail OR joined to another note via a single beam, is referred to as a **dotted eighth note**, and lasts for **three-quarters of a beat**.

Figure 1.14. Sixteenth note

A 'filled in' notehead EITHER with a separate stem and double tail OR joined to another note via a double beam, is referred to as a **sixteenth note**, and lasts for a **quarter of a beat**.

The above is not a complete list of all the possible note durations - however it does include all those commonly found in contemporary applications.

Now we will review all of the 'rest' symbols corresponding to the above rhythmic durations. The use of a rest indicates silence or no sound during the rhythmic value being used, as in the following examples:-

Music notation - rhythmic values for rests

Figure 1.15. Whole note rest

This rest lasts for **four beats**.
(The rest symbol 'hangs' from the second line from
 the top of the staff).

Figure 1.16. Half note rest

This rest lasts for **two beats**.
(The rest symbol 'sits' on the middle line of the staff).

Figure 1.17. Dotted half note rest

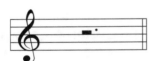

This rest lasts for **three beats**.
(The rest symbol 'sits' on the middle line of the staff).

Figure 1.18. Quarter note rest

This rest lasts for **one beat**.

Figure 1.19. Dotted quarter note rest

This rest lasts for **one and a half beats**.

Music notation - rhythmic values for rests (contd)

Figure 1.20. Eighth note rest

This rest lasts for **half a beat**.

Figure 1.21. Dotted eighth note rest

This rest lasts for **three quarters of a beat**.

Figure 1.22. Sixteenth note rest

This rest lasts for a **quarter of a beat**.

Music notation - time signatures

The time signature in music consists of two numbers on the staff (one above the other):-

- The **top** number indicates how many 'pulses' occur in each measure.
- The **bottom** number indicates what type of note 'gets the pulse' i.e. on what rhythmic unit the pulse is 'felt' - typically either half, quarter or eighth notes.

You'll recall that we have just defined a series of note and rest durations in terms of **number of beats**. If the bottom number of the time signature is set to **4**, implying that the **'pulse'** is felt on the quarter note (which has been defined as lasting for **one beat** - see **Fig. 1.10.**), then our concepts of 'pulse' and 'beat' here effectively mean the same thing - in other words the number of **'pulses'** in the measure (as defined by the top number of the time signature) is equivalent to the number of **beats** or rhythmic units in the measure. Be aware however, that this will not be the case for time signatures with a **bottom number other than 4** (i.e. if the 'pulse' is felt on half or eighth notes). We will now look at the following frequently-used time signatures:-

Music notation - time signatures (contd)

Figure 1.23. - 4/4 time

The most frequently used time signature. Again note that:-
- the **top** number of the time signature indicates how many 'pulses' in the measure (in this case **four**).
- the **bottom** number of the time signature indicates which rhythmic unit 'gets the pulse' (in this case the number **four** means that the pulse is felt on the **quarter note**).

4/4 time is also known as **common** time:-

Figure 1.24. - Common time

Musicians will use either **4/4** or **common** time signature according to personal preference - they both mean the same thing (i.e. four quarter note 'pulses' per measure).

Here are some other frequently used time signatures (again don't forget that the **top** number indicates how many 'pulses' in the measure, and the **bottom** number indicates which rhythmic unit 'gets the pulse'):-

Figure 1.25. - 2/2 time

This signifies **two pulses** per measure, each of which lasts for a **half note**.

Figure 1.26. - 'Cut' time

This is equivalent to **2/2** time, i.e. it also signifies **two pulses** per measure, each of which lasts for a **half note**.

Figure 1.27. - 3/4 time

This signifies **three pulses** per measure, each of which lasts for a **quarter note**.

Music notation - time signatures (contd)

Figure 1.28. - 6/8 time

This signifies **six pulses** per measure, each of which lasts for an **eighth note**.

Figure 1.29. - 9/8 time

This signifies **nine pulses** per measure, each of which lasts for an **eighth note**.

Figure 1.30. - 12/8 time

This signifies **twelve pulses** per measure, each of which lasts for an **eighth note**.

The above examples are of course not a complete list of all possible time signatures, however they do represent those most frequently encountered in contemporary applications.

Now we will look at some examples of combining notes and rests together within a measure. **The rhythmic sum of all notes and rests within a measure must add up to the time signature.** Here are some correct and incorrect examples of this principle:-

Figure 1.31. Notes and rests within a 4/4 measure - example 1

We can analyze this example as follows:-

Music notation - time signatures (contd)

- The first **dotted quarter note** (see **Fig. 1.11.**) lasts for **one and a half beats**.
- The following **eighth note rest** (see **Fig. 1.20.**) lasts for **half a beat**.
- The following **quarter note** (see **Fig. 1.10.**) lasts for **one beat**.
- The following two **eighth notes** (see **Fig. 1.12.**) last for **half a beat** each.

These rhythmic durations add up to **four beats**, which is required by the **4/4** time signature being used - this is therefore a **correct** example.

Figure 1.32. Notes and rests within a 4/4 measure - example 2

We can analyze this example as follows:-

- The first **dotted eighth note** (see **Fig. 1.13.**) lasts for **three quarters of a beat**.
- The following **sixteenth note** (see **Fig. 1.14.**) lasts for **one quarter of a beat**.
- The following **eighth note rest** (see **Fig. 1.20.**) lasts for **half a beat**.
- The following **eighth note** (see **Fig. 1.12.**) lasts for **half a beat**.
- The following **quarter note** (see **Fig. 1.10.**) lasts for **one beat**.
- The following **sixteenth note rest** (see **Fig. 1.22.**) lasts for **one quarter of a beat**.
- The following **sixteenth note** (see **Fig. 1.14.**) lasts for **one quarter of a beat**.
- The following **sixteenth note rest** (see **Fig. 1.22.**) lasts for **one quarter of a beat**.
- The following **sixteenth note** (see **Fig. 1.14.**) lasts for **one quarter of a beat**.

These rhythmic durations again add up to **four beats**, which is required by the **4/4** time signature being used - this is therefore another **correct** example.

Figure 1.33. Notes and rests within a 4/4 measure - example 3

We can analyze this example as follows:-

Music notation - time signatures (contd)

-   The first four **eighth notes** (see **Fig. 1.12.**) last for **half a beat** each.
-   The following **dotted quarter note** (see **Fig. 1.11.**) lasts for **one and a half beats**.
-   The following two **eighth notes** (see **Fig. 1.12.**) last for **half a beat** each.

These rhythmic durations add up to **four and a half beats** - however the **4/4** time signature requires **four beats** in the measure - this is therefore an **incorrect** example.

Figure 1.34. Notes and rests within a 4/4 measure - example 4

We can analyze this example as follows:-

-   The first **sixteenth note** (see **Fig. 1.14.**) lasts for **one quarter of a beat**.
-   The following **dotted eighth note** (see **Fig. 1.13.**) lasts for **three quarters of a beat**.
-   The following **dotted eighth note rest** (see **Fig. 1.21.**) lasts for **three quarters of a beat**.
-   The following **sixteenth note** (see **Fig. 1.14.**) lasts for **one quarter of a beat**.
-   The following **quarter note** (see **Fig. 1.10.**) lasts for **one beat**.
-   The following two **sixteenth notes** (see **Fig. 1.14.**) lasts for **one quarter of a beat** each.

These rhythmic durations add up to **three and a half beats** - however the **4/4** time signature again requires **four beats** in the measure - this is therefore another **incorrect** example.

Work through these examples to make sure you understand them - and when you are writing music, again make sure that the rhythmic sum (i.e. total number of 'beats') of all the notes and rests in each measure, is equal to the number of beats required by the time signature!

Constructing major tetrachords

We will now begin the process of constructing a '**major tetrachord**'. This will be used as a building block to create the **major scale** (the most important and fundamental scale in Western music), and to later derive a relationship known as the 'circle-of-fifths'.

A tetrachord is the name given to a group of four notes arranged in a 'scalewise' sequence. In order to build the major tetrachord, we need to define another music interval term - the **whole-step**. You'll recall that on pages **2-3** we defined a **half-step** interval as being the smallest unit of interval measurement - if we moved from any note on the 'keyboard diagram' to the nearest note on the right or the left, this created a half-step interval. The **whole-step** is now defined as **double the half-step** interval, i.e. if we moved from any note on the 'keyboard diagram' to the right or left by **two notes** (including black as well as white keys) then a whole-step interval will result. Let's see how this works using the keyboard diagram:-

Figure 1.35. Keyboard diagram (showing all note names and enharmonics)

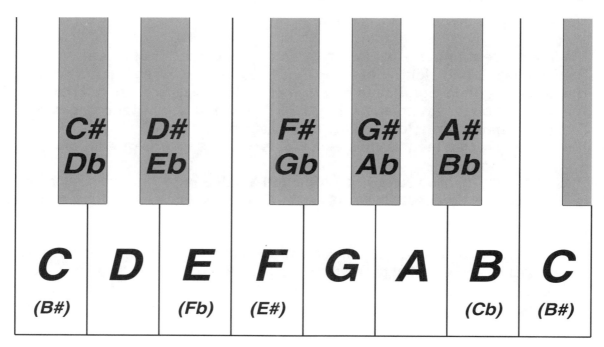

If we need to find the note which is a whole-step higher than **E** for example, we need to move two notes to the right of **E** - the first note would be **F (or E#)** which is a half-step higher than **E**, and the next note would be **F# (or Gb)** which is a **whole-step higher than E**. Similarly, if we needed to find the note which is a whole-step lower than **Bb (or A#)**, we need to move two notes to the left of this note - the first note would be **A** which is a half-step lower, and the next note would be **G# (or Ab)** which is a **whole-step lower than Bb (or A#)**.

Constructing major tetrachords (contd)

Note that in the previous examples we did not express a preference about which enharmonic name to use for notes with more than one possible name i.e. **F#** or **Gb**. However, when we build tetrachords and scales, it is important that the correct enharmonics are used - the good news is that if you follow the rules that I am about to give you, **this will always be taken care of!!**

We will now learn how to build a major tetrachord from any starting note using these two rules:-

1)   We will always use **consecutive ascending** letternames in the music alphabet. You remember that this alphabet consists of the letters **A-G**. After we use the lettername **G**, we 'wrap around' again to the lettername **A**.

2)   From the starting note, we will construct the following ascending intervals - *WHOLE-STEP, WHOLE-STEP, HALF-STEP.*

Let's try deriving some major tetrachords using this method. First of all we'll create a major tetrachord starting on the **E above Middle C**. Because of rule #1 above, we know right away that the letternames of the notes that we need are going to be **E, F, G** and then wrapping around to **A,** as follows:-

Figure 1.36. E major tetrachord - note letter names required

What we now need to do is to **adjust the notes using accidentals** (sharps/flats) to achieve the intervals required in rule #2 above i.e. whole-step, whole-step and half-step:-

-       We need a **whole-step** interval to begin with - however the interval shown on the staff above (**E** up to **F**) is only a **half-step** (see **Fig. 1.35.** on previous page) - so we need to **sharp the F** (i.e. to **F#**) to get the necessary **whole-step** above the starting note of **E**.
-       Similarly, we need to **sharp the G** (to **G#**) to get the necessary **whole-step** above the previous note **F#**.
-       Finally we note that the last interval (from **G# to A**) is already a **half-step** as required by rule #2 above - so we do not need to alter the note **A**.

The **E major tetrachord** with accidentals as applied above, is now shown as follows:-

Constructing major tetrachords (contd)

Figure 1.37. E major tetrachord - showing correct accidentals and intervals

(<WS> indicates whole-step and <HS> indicates half-step).

Note that the rule of using ascending letternames in the music alphabet, prevented us from calling the second note in this tetrachord **Gb** - this would have entailed going straight from the lettername of **E** to the lettername of **G**, incorrectly missing out the lettername of **F**.

Now we'll try another example of constructing a major tetrachord - this time using a starting note of **Db**. Again because of rule **#1** on the previous page we know that the following letternames in the tetrachord (after the **Db**) are going to be **E**, **F** and **G**, as follows:-

Figure 1.38. Db major tetrachord - note letter names required

Again we now need to adjust the notes following the note **Db**, using accidentals as necessary:-

- We need a **whole-step** interval to begin with - however the interval shown on the staff above (**Db** up to **E**) is actually **three half-steps** (check on **Fig. 1.35.** as necessary) - so we need to **flat the E** (i.e. to **Eb**) to get the necessary **whole-step** above the starting note of **Db**.
- We note that the next interval created (from **Eb to F**) is already a **whole-step** as required by rule **#2** on page **17** - so we do not need to alter the note **F**.
- We need a **half-step** as the last interval of the tetrachord - however the last interval shown (**F** up to **G**) is actually a **whole-step** (again check on **Fig. 1.35.** as necessary) - so we need to **flat the G** (i.e. to **Gb**) to get the necessary **half-step** at the end of the tetrachord.

The **Db major tetrachord** with accidentals as applied above, is now shown as follows:-

Constructing major tetrachords (contd)

Figure 1.39. Db major tetrachord - showing correct accidentals and intervals

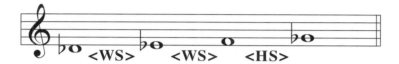

Constructing major scales

We are now in a position to construct a major scale. This we will first do by **combining two major tetrachords together, separated by a whole-step interval**. Let's derive a **C major scale** using this method - first we build a major tetrachord from **C** as follows:-

Figure 1.40. C major tetrachord

Note that the last note used in the above tetrachord was **F**. A whole-step interval above this note (and using the next letter in the music alphabet) results in the note **G**. We can then build another major tetrachord from the note **G** as follows:-

Figure 1.41. G major tetrachord

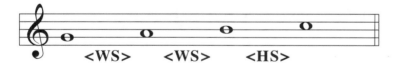

Finally we can now combine these two tetrachords to create a **C major scale**, as shown on the following page:-

Constructing major scales (contd)

Figure 1.42. C major scale (combining C major and G major tetrachords)

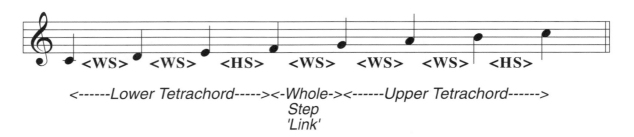

```
<------Lower Tetrachord----><-Whole-><------Upper Tetrachord------>
                            Step
                            'Link'
```

Note again that we have two major tetrachords (each with whole-step, whole-step, and half-step intervals), separated by a 'link' of a whole-step interval in between.

You will recall the method we used on page **17** to construct major tetrachords - namely, using consecutive letters in the music alphabet, and then using a specific interval pattern (i.e. whole-step, whole-step, and half-step). We can now adapt this method to **directly produce a major scale from any starting note**, using the following steps:-

1)	Beginning from the starting note, we will again use **consecutive ascending** letters in the music alphabet, again 'wrapping around' to the lettername **A** after the lettername **G**.

2)	From the starting note, we will construct the following ascending intervals:-
	WHOLE-STEP, WHOLE-STEP, HALF-STEP, WHOLE-STEP, WHOLE-STEP, WHOLE-STEP, HALF-STEP.
	(This of course is equivalent to two major tetrachords, separated by whole-step).

Let's try deriving a major scale using this method, beginning on the note **Eb**. Again because of rule **#1** above, we know right away that we'll be using the letternames **E**, **F**, and **G**, and then 'wrapping around' to the letternames **A**, **B**, **C**, **D** & **E** again, as follows:-

Figure 1.43. Eb major scale - note letternames required

What we now need to do is to adjust the notes using accidentals (sharps/flats) to achieve the intervals required in rule **#2** above:-

Constructing major scales (contd)

- We need a **whole-step** interval to begin with - we note that the first interval (**Eb** up to **F**) is already a **whole-step** - so we do not need to alter the note **F**.
- The next interval we need is also a **whole-step** - again we note that the second interval (**F** up to **G**) is already a **whole-step** - so we do not need to alter the note **G**.
- The next interval we need is a **half-step** - however the interval on the staff (**G** up to **A**) is a **whole-step** - so we need to flat the **A** (to **Ab**) to get the necessary **half-step** interval.
- The next interval we need is a **whole-step** - however from the previous **Ab** up to the note **B** is actually **three half-steps** - so we need to flat the **B** (to **Bb**) to get the necessary **whole-step** interval.
- The next interval we need is also a **whole-step** - we note that from the previous **Bb** up to the note **C** is already a **whole-step**, so we do not need to alter the note **C**.
- Again the next interval we need is also a **whole-step** - the interval **C** up to **D** is already a **whole-step**, so we do not need to alter the note **D**.
- The final interval we need is a **half-step** - however the interval on the staff (**D** up to **E**) is a **whole-step** - so we need to flat the **E** (to **Eb**) to get the necessary **half-step** interval (and also of course to get back to the same starting note of **Eb**).

The **Eb major scale** with accidentals as applied above, is now shown as follows:-

Figure 1.44. Eb major scale - showing correct accidentals and intervals

Now we'll try another example of constructing a major scale using this method - this time using a starting note of **B**. Again because of rule **#1** on the previous page, we know right away that we'll be using the letternames **B**, **C**, **D**, **E**, **F**, **G**, and then 'wrapping around' to the letternames **A** and **B** again, as follows:-

Figure 1.45. B major scale - note letternames required

Again what we need to do is to adjust the notes using accidentals, as follows:-

Constructing major scales (contd)

- We need a **whole-step** interval to begin with - however the interval on the staff (**B** up to **C**) is a **half-step** - so we need to sharp the **C** (to **C#**) to get the necessary **whole-step** interval.
- The next interval we need is also a **whole-step** - however from the previous **C#** up to the note **D** is a **half-step** - so we need to sharp the **D** (to **D#**) to get the necessary **whole-step** interval.
- The next interval we need is a **half-step** - we note that from the previous **D#** up to the note **E** is already a **half-step**, so we do not need to alter the note **E**.
- The next interval we need is a **whole-step** - however from the previous **E** up to the note **F** is a **half-step** - so we need to sharp the **F** (to **F#**) to get the necessary **whole-step** interval.
- The next interval we need is also a **whole-step** - however from the previous **F#** up to the note **G** is a **half-step** - so we need to sharp the **G** (to **G#**) to get the necessary **whole-step** interval.
- Again the next interval we need is also a **whole-step** - however from the previous **G#** up to the note **A** is a **half-step** - so we need to sharp the **A** (to **A#**) to get the necessary **whole-step** interval.
- The final interval we need is a **half-step** - we note that from the previous **A#** up to the note **B** is already a **half-step**, so we do not need to alter the note **B**.

The **B major scale** with accidentals as applied above, is now shown as follows:-

Figure 1.46. B major scale - showing correct accidentals and intervals

You will notice that I have given you this foolproof method of deriving any major scale, **ahead of any discussion about key signatures** (which however are fully explained later in this chapter). Many students I encounter (particularly those with a classical background!) want to use key signatures to derive their scales - this I feel is a serious case of putting the "cart before the horse" as we might say in England! My constant goal when defining and explaining theory concepts for the contemporary musician, is relate as closely as possible to **how the ear understands** harmonic relationships. ***YOUR EAR DOESN'T CARE HOW MANY SHARPS THERE ARE IN B MAJOR*** (to take the above example) - it is simply relating to a familiar pattern of intervals being used. Of course you need to know your key signatures for reading and writing reasons (more of this later), but **not for playing or application purposes** - this interval method is the most 'organic' and ear-oriented way to learn and understand your major scales!

Constructing the 'circle-of-fifths' and 'circle-of-fourths'

We will now use these concepts of **tetrachords** and **major scales** to derive the musical relationships known as the **'circle-of-fifths'** and **'circle-of-fourths'**. Everyone seems to have their own ideas about what these terms mean, and they are certainly subject to widely different interpretations depending upon which books or methods you have been exposed to! Therefore it is quite possible that the explanation I am about to give you here may be a new 'perspective' for you on this subject. I hope to persuade you that this method makes sense, is 'foolproof' and is consistent with the 'ear-oriented' contemporary approach we are establishing!

Earlier in this chapter we saw that a major scale can be constructed with two major tetrachords (each of which consist of whole-step, whole-step and half-step intervals), separated by a whole-step interval - see **C major scale** example in **Fig. 1.42.** Because these two tetrachords have the same interval construction, we can conclude that the upper tetrachord of this C major scale could also be the **lower tetrachord of some other major scale**, and that the lower tetrachord of this C major scale could also be the **upper tetrachord of some other major scale**. This concept can be re-stated in the following general principle:-

- **each major tetrachord must be present in TWO different major scales.**

Let's specifically work through some examples to make sure we understand this. We know that a C major tetrachord:-

Figure. 1.47. C major tetrachord

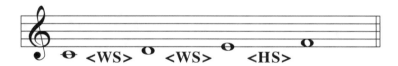

is the lower tetrachord of a C major scale:-

Figure. 1.48. C major scale

<-----C Major Tetrachord----->

But it must also be the upper tetrachord of another major scale. As the top note of a C major tetrachord is the note **F**, this tetrachord must also be present in an **F major scale**:-

Constructing the 'circle-of-fifths' and 'circle-of-fourths' (contd)

Figure. 1.49. F major scale

<-----C Major Tetrachord----->

Similarly, we know that a G major tetrachord:-

Figure 1.50. G major tetrachord

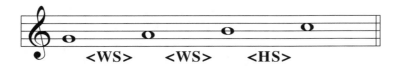

is not only the upper tetrachord of a C major scale:-

Figure 1.51. C major scale

<-----G Major Tetrachord----->

but is also the lower tetrachord of a G major scale, as it begins on the note **G**:-

Figure 1.52. G major scale

<-----G Major Tetrachord----->

Constructing the 'circle-of-fifths' and 'circle-of-fourths' (contd)

So we have established that the **F** and **G** major scales have **tetrachords in common** with the **C** major scale. This could be shown diagrammatically as follows:-

Figure 1.53. Partial 'circle' diagram showing C, F, and G major scales

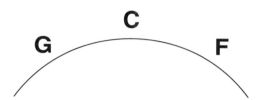

This diagram simply shows a **C** major scale (designated by the symbol 'C'), with the two scales either side that have tetrachords in common - **F** and **G** major.

Now we'll extend these relationships a little further, by looking at these **F** and **G** major scales, and establishing what other major scales they in turn have tetrachords in common with. Looking at the **F** major scale again, we notice that the lower tetrachord is an **F** major tetrachord:-

Figure 1.54. F major scale

Which is also the upper tetrachord of a **Bb** major scale:-

Figure 1.55. Bb major scale

Constructing the 'circle-of-fifths' and 'circle-of-fourths' (contd)

Now looking at the **G** major scale again, we notice that the upper tetrachord is a **D** major tetrachord:-

Figure 1.56. G major scale

<-----D Major Tetrachord----->

Which is also the lower tetrachord of a D major scale:-

Figure 1.57. D major scale

<-----D Major Tetrachord----->

So we have now established that the **F** major scale has a **tetrachord in common** with the **Bb** major scale, and that the **G** major scale has a **tetrachord in common** with the **D** major scale. These new relationships can now be incorporated into our partial 'circle diagram':-

Figure 1.58. Partial 'circle' diagram showing C, F, G, Bb and D major scales

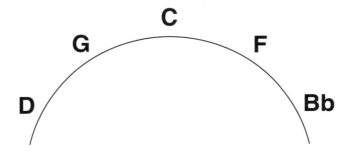

Again each symbol around the 'partial circle' represents a major scale. If we extend these tetrachord relationships to include all of the remaining major scales, we arrive at the 'completed' circle diagram on the following page:-

Constructing the 'circle-of-fifths' and 'circle-of-fourths' (contd)

Figure 1.59. 'Circle' diagram showing all major scale/tetrachord relationships

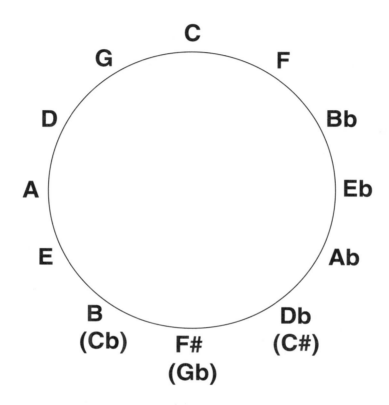

Note that in the above diagram each major scale (represented by a symbol around the circle) **shares a tetrachord in common with its two most immediate neighbours**. Note also that in three cases at the bottom of the circle, **enharmonic names** have been indicated (i.e. **B** or **Cb**, **F#** or **Gb**, **Db** or **C#**). This is because major scales can be constructed (using the principles covered earlier) and major keys exist (as we will see shortly in a discussion on key signatures) from **each** of these alternate note names or enharmonics.

Now that we have constructed the 'circle', we need to arrive at a definition of what the terms **'circle-of-fifths'** and **'circle-of-fourths'** mean. These terms will be defined as **different movement directions** around this same circle. A number of textbooks seem to adopt what I find is a rather superficial 'interval-based' method for creating and labelling these 'circles' - this logic might go something like - "well, **C** to **F** is a **fourth** interval, and so this clockwise direction around the circle must be circle-of-fourths, right?"

Well of course **C to F** is indeed a fourth interval if you go **up** from C to F (see example on next page):-

Constructing the 'circle-of-fifths' and 'circle-of-fourths' (contd)

Figure 1.60. C up to F (fourth interval)

(Don't worry if you're not sure just yet what is meant by the term 'fourth interval' - all interval concepts will be explained in **Chapter 2**).

...but what if we go **down** from C to F? In that case we create a **fifth** interval:-

Figure 1.61. C down to F (fifth interval)

(Note that for notation convenience we have used bass clef this time).

So it seems that this is a rather unreliable method for 'labelling' the directions around the circle, due to these different interval interpretations! A rather more foolproof method can be based upon our original concept of the 'circle' - namely, as a series of **interlocking major scales.**

When we move from one point to another on the circle, **we can consider each 'landing point' to represent a new major scale or key**. (This is totally consistent with how the ear hears movement around the circle, as you will know if you have worked through my *Contemporary Eartraining Level Two* course)! We'll now use this approach to analyze a movement from **G** to **C** on the circle as follows:-

Figure 1.62. Movement from G to C on the circle

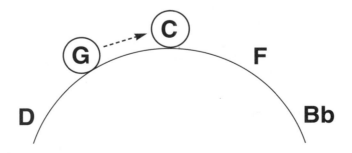

Constructing the 'circle-of-fifths' and 'circle-of-fourths' (contd)

We can now relate this **G to C** movement to the **C major scale** corresponding to where we have 'landed' on the circle, as follows:-

Figure 1.63. C major scale showing G to C ('Five to One') movement

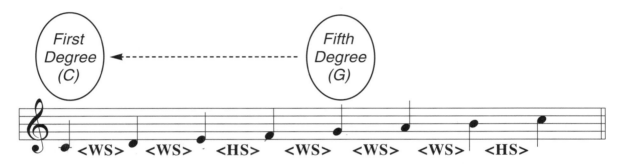

What we are saying here is that the movement from **G to C** is considered a **FIVE-TO-ONE relationship**, based on a C major scale which corresponds to where we have 'landed' on the circle. This concept neatly sidesteps the previously-mentioned interval problems i.e. the **G to C** movement can **always** be considered as a five-to-one relationship in the scale of C major, irrespective of any interval direction between **G** and **C**.

For this reason, the movement from **G to C** on the circle (and **clockwise movements** in general around the circle) with be defined as moving in a **CIRCLE-OF-FIFTHS** manner. Now we will use a similar approach to analyze a movement from **F** to **C** on the circle:-

Figure 1.64. Movement from F to C on the circle

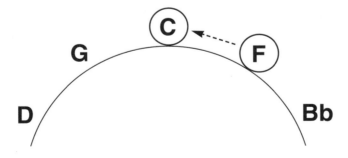

Again we will relate this **F to C** movement to the C major scale corresponding to where we have 'landed' on the circle (see following page):-

Constructing the 'circle-of-fifths' and 'circle-of-fourths' (contd)

Figure 1.65. C major scale showing F to C ('Four to One') movement

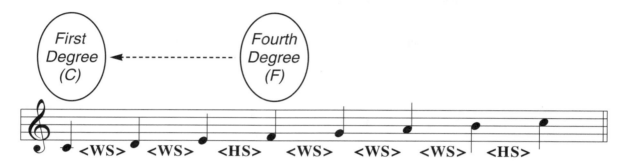

This movement from **F to C** can now be considered a **FOUR-TO-ONE relationship**, again based on a C major scale which corresponds to where we have 'landed' on the circle. For this reason, the movement from **F to C** on the circle (and **counter-clockwise movements** in general around the circle) with be defined as moving in a **CIRCLE-OF-FOURTHS** manner.

These definitions of **circle-of-fifths** and **circle-of-fourths** as **movement directions** around the same 'circle', can now be related to the original 'circle diagram' as follows:-

Figure 1.66. Circle diagram with circle-of-5ths and circle-of-4ths movement directions

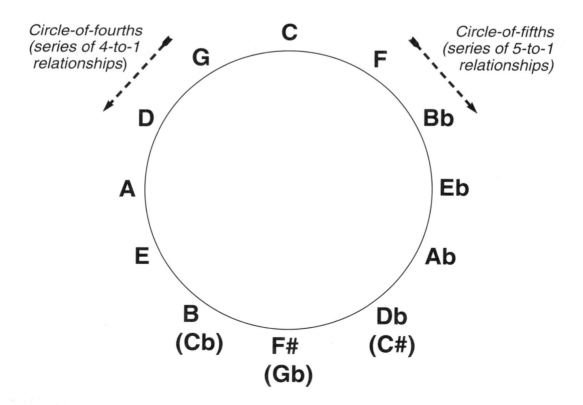

Constructing the 'circle-of-fifths' and 'circle-of-fourths' (contd)

So, to summarize - when figuring out whether you are moving around the circle in a **circle-of-fifths** or **circle-of-fourths** direction, all you need to ask yourself is - am I moving in a **5-to-1** or **4-to-1** manner? i.e. is where I have **just come from** (on the circle) the **5th** or **4th** degree of the **major scale** which I have **now landed on**? If you're not immediately sure, then build the necessary major scale (using our interval/tetrachord method as described earlier) to figure it out! Let's finally review the reasons why we define the 'circles' this way, which (as I mentioned earlier) may be different to other methods you have encountered:-

1)   It is consistent with our original concept of defining the circle as an **interlocking series of major scales**, with tetrachords in common.

2)   It neatly **sidesteps any problems** with defining the circle on an 'interval basis' i.e. between successive notes around the circle, as described on pages **27-28**.

3)   Perhaps most importantly, it **most accurately reflects how the ear works** to hear progressions and key changes around the circle (i.e. on a **5-to-1** or **4-to-1** basis) - you'll have to take my word for this unless you've worked through my Eartraining courses!

Major key signatures

We will now use the previous circle concepts, together with our knowledge of major scales and tetrachords, to derive all **major key signatures**. A key signature is a group of flats or sharps at the beginning of the staff which indicates which key we are in. (For the moment, we will restrict ourselves to major keys - more about minor keys later on).

I have to say at this point that I have met too many students over the years who are unable to 'logically derive' their key signatures - so if they lose that piece of paper they've had in their back pocket for the last 20 years that tells them there's **4 flats** in the key of **Ab**, then they're history! Worse still, they then use the key signature to figure out the notes in the major scale (which I counseled against earlier in this chapter)! Assuming you are now straightened out on how to build your major scales (I.e. by intervals and/or tetrachords as explained earlier), I am now going to give you a way to **logically derive all of your major key signatures**. Of course the more quickly you are able to recall your key signatures as needed for reading or writing purposes, the better off you will be - so I am **not** saying that you should not memorize your key signatures - what I **am** saying is that you should have a logical understanding of how they are derived, as a back up to the memorization process.

Major key signatures (contd)

When creating or recognizing key signatures, we need to be aware of the following:-

- the **number of flats** or **sharps** in the key signature
- **which** flats or sharps are in the key signature, in **which order or sequence**.

The first element (the number of flats or sharps in a key signature) is fairly easy to determine from our previous circle diagram, repeated here for convenience:-

Figure 1.67. Circle diagram, to be used for deriving key signatures

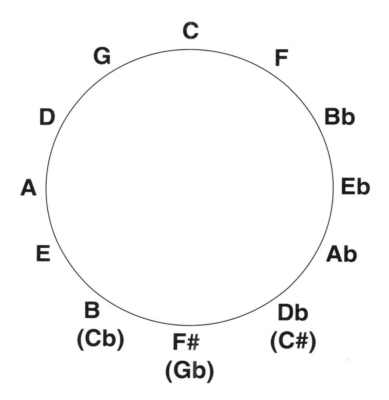

We recall that the C major scale required no sharps or flats:-

Figure 1.68. C major scale

Major key signatures (contd)

Moving one key to the right (in a circle-of-fifths direction) we arrive at the key of **F**. As we build the required whole-steps and half-steps in the **F** major scale, we recall that **one flat** was required:-

Figure 1.69. F major scale

And using the same process for the next key to the right, we find that the key of **Bb** requires **two flats** (the top note shown of **Bb** is of course a repeat of the starting note):-

Figure 1.70. Bb major scale

If we continue this process through all the **'flat'** keys (i.e. moving from the key of **C** in a **clockwise** or circle-of-fifths direction around the circle) we find that:-

The key of **Eb** has **three** flats.
The key of **Ab** has **four** flats.
The key of **Db** has **five** flats.
The key of **Gb** has **six** flats.
The key of **Cb** has **seven** flats.

This is as far as we can go in deriving 'flat' key signatures, as by the time we get to the key of **Cb** we have flatted all seven degrees of the original **C** major scale. (Go ahead and build a major scale from the starting note of **Cb** using our interval/tetrachord method, if you want to confirm this)!

Now moving one key to the left of **C** major (in a circle-of-fourths direction) we arrive at the key of **G**. As we build the required whole-steps and half-steps in the **G** major scale, we recall that **one sharp** was required, as shown on the following page:-

Major key signatures (contd)

Figure 1.71. G major scale

And again using the same process for the next key to the left on the circle, we find that the key of **D** requires **two sharps**:-

Figure 1.72. D major scale

If we continue this process through all the **'sharp'** keys (i.e. moving from the key of **C** in a **counter-clockwise** or circle-of-fourths direction around the circle) we find that:-

The key of **A** has **three** sharps.
The key of **E** has **four** sharps.
The key of **B** has **five** sharps.
The key of **F#** has **six** sharps.
The key of **C#** has **seven** sharps.

Again this is as far as we can go in deriving 'sharp' key signatures, as by the time we get to the key of **C#** we have sharped all seven degrees of the original **C** major scale.

So - to determine the **number of flats or sharps in a major key signature**, we simply have to count round the circle (starting from **C** at the top), until we get to the required **'flat'** key moving **clockwise** (in a circle-of-fifths direction), or to the required **'sharp'** key moving **counter-clockwise** (in a circle-of-fourths direction).

If all we had to do was to recognize key signatures, then memorizing these rules (along wirth the circle) would be sufficient! However we also need to know how to **write** them - which brings us to the second point at the top of page **32** - we need to know **which flats or sharps** occur in the key signature, and in **which sequence**.

Major key signatures (contd)

As we move clockwise around the circle from the starting point of **C**, we have seen that the key of **F** has **one flat**, the key of **Bb** has **two flats**, etc. You'll recall that the flat we needed for the **F** major scale (i.e. **Bb**) was also used in the following key (i.e. the key of **Bb**). Each time we 'add a flat' when moving clockwise through the 'flat keys', we do it on a **cumulative basis** - in other words **all flats in any given flat key signature** will be used in **all subsequent flat keys** after that point, moving clockwise around the circle (up until the last flat key of **Cb**). So given this rule, the only other thing we need to know is **which new flat to add to the key signature** at each stage (going through the flat keys around the circle). This rule for flat keys is:-

-       ***we add the fourth degree of each new scale*** (moving clockwise around the circle, through the flat keys) ***cumulatively to the key signature.***

Let's see how this works using some examples. Again we'll start with the **F** major scale:-

Figure 1.73. F major scale

(4th degree)

We already know that we need **one flat** in the key signature. Now using the above rule, we take the **fourth degree** of **F** major (i.e. **Bb**) as the flat we need for the key signature:-

Figure 1.74. F major key signature

Now we'll look again at the **Bb** major scale:-

Figure 1.75. Bb major scale

(4th degree)

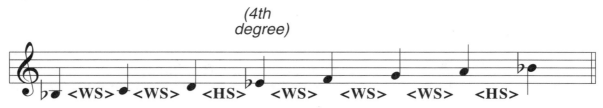

Major key signatures (contd)

We already know that we need **two flats** in the key signature of **Bb** major. Now again using the previous rule, we **add** the **fourth degree** of **Bb** major (i.e. **Eb**) to the previously-derived key signature for F major:-

Figure 1.76. Bb major key signature

*Here we have added the **fourth** degree of **Bb** major (**Eb**)*
*on to the end of the previous 'flat' key signature i.e. **F** major.*

Progressing through the remaining flat keys by moving clockwise around the circle, we therefore derive the remaining key signatures by **adding the 4th degree** of each scale as follows:-

Figure 1.77. Eb major key signature

*Here we have added the **fourth** degree of **Eb** major (**Ab**)*
*on to the end of the previous 'flat' key signature i.e. **Bb** major.*

Figure 1.78. Ab major key signature

*Here we have added the **fourth** degree of **Ab** major (**Db**)*
*on to the end of the previous 'flat' key signature i.e. **Eb** major.*

Figure 1.79. Db major key signature

*Here we have added the **fourth** degree of **Db** major (**Gb**)*
*on to the end of the previous 'flat' key signature i.e. **Ab** major.*

Figure 1.80. Gb major key signature

*Here we have added the **fourth** degree of **Gb** major (**Cb**)*
*on to the end of the previous 'flat' key signature i.e. **Db** major.*

Major key signatures (contd)

Figure 1.81. Cb major key signature

*Here we have added the **fourth** degree of **Cb** major (**Fb**) on to the end of the previous 'flat' key signature i.e. **Gb** major.*

Now we'll apply similar logic to derive all the **sharp key signatures**. As we move counter-clockwise around the circle from the starting point of **C**, we have seen that the key of **G** has **one sharp**, the key of **D** has **two sharps**, etc. You'll recall that the sharp we needed for the **G** major scale (i.e. **F#**) was also used in the following key (i.e. the key of **D**). Each time we 'add a sharp' when moving counter-clockwise through the 'sharp keys', we again do it on a **cumulative basis** - in other words **all sharps in any given sharp key signature** will be used in **all subsequent sharp keys** after that point, moving counter-clockwise around the circle (up until the last sharp key of **C#**). So given this rule, again the only other thing we need to know is **which new sharp to add to the key signature** at each stage (going through the sharp keys around the circle). This rule for sharp keys is:-

-       ***we add the seventh degree of each new scale*** (moving counter-clockwise around the circle, through the sharp keys) ***cumulatively to the key signature.***

Again we'll see how this works using some examples, beginning with the **G** major scale:-

Figure 1.82. G major scale

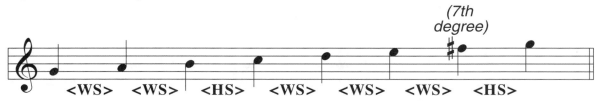

We already know that we need **one sharp** in the key signature. Now using the above rule, we take the **seventh degree** of **G** major (i.e. **F#**) as the sharp we need for the key signature:-

Figure 1.83. G major key signature

Major key signatures (contd)

Now we'll look again at the **D** major scale:-

Figure 1.84. D major scale

(7th degree)

<WS> <WS> <HS> <WS> <WS> <WS> <HS>

We already know that we need **two sharps** in the key signature of **D** major. Now again using the previous rule, we **add** the **seventh degree** of **D** major (i.e. **C#**) to the previously-derived key signature for G major:-

Figure 1.85. D major key signature

*Here we have added the **seventh** degree of **D** major (**C#**) on to the end of the previous 'sharp' key signature i.e. **G** major.*

Progressing through the remaining sharp keys by moving counter-clockwise around the circle, we derive the remaining key signatures by **adding the 7th degree** of each scale:-

Figure 1.86. A major key signature

*Here we have added the **seventh** degree of **A** major (**G#**) on to the end of the previous 'sharp' key signature i.e. **D** major.*

Figure 1.87. E major key signature

*Here we have added the **seventh** degree of **E** major (**D#**) on to the end of the previous 'sharp' key signature i.e. **A** major.*

Major key signatures (contd)

Figure 1.88. B major key signature

*Here we have added the **seventh** degree of **B** major (**A#**) on to the end of the previous 'sharp' key signature i.e. **E** major.*

Figure 1.89. F# major key signature

*Here we have added the **seventh** degree of **F#** major (**E#**) on to the end of the previous 'sharp' key signature i.e. **B** major.*

Figure 1.90. C# major key signature

*Here we have added the **seventh** degree of **C#** major (**B#**) on to the end of the previous 'sharp' key signature i.e. **F#** major.*

One final detail you will need to take into account when writing key signatures is the **location** within the staff of each flat or sharp required i.e. whether you write each accidental towards the top or bottom of the staff, where a choice exists. Check back on **Fig. 1.81.**, and you'll see that in the key signature of **Cb** major (which contains all other 'flat' key signatures), from the starting **Bb** in the middle of the staff, the 'shape' of the key signature moves *up-down-up-down-up-down*. However, in **Fig. 1.90.** above (**C#** major, containing all other 'sharp' key signatures), from the starting **F#** the 'shape' of the key signature moves *down-up-down-down-up-down*.

Don't forget that if you're not sure what the **fourth** degree (for a 'flat' key) or the **seventh** degree (for a 'sharp' key) is for a particular major scale - well, figure it out using the **interval and tetrachord method** described earlier in this chapter! - the more you do this, the more solid your grasp will be of major scales and therefore of everything that follows.

We mentioned before (on page **27**) that major keys exist for each of the enharmonic equivalents shown at the bottom of the circle (i.e. **B** & **Cb**, **F#** & **Gb**, and **Db** & **C#**), and we have now derived all these key signatures. These pairs of keys therefore are **alternate notation options** i.e. the keys of **B** & **Cb** will **sound the same**, but of course are **notated differently**.

*(All major scales, both with and without key signatures, are listed in the **Appendices** at the back of this book).*

Chapter One Workbook Questions

1. *Notation writing and recognition*

Write the letter names corresponding to the following treble and bass clef notes:-

1. _____   2. _____   3. _____   4. _____

5. _____   6. _____   7. _____   8. _____

9. _____   10. _____   11. _____   12. _____

13. _____   14. _____   15. _____   16. _____

*(N.B. Throughout the workbook sections in this book, always note **which clef** is being used for each question i.e. **treble** or **bass** clef).*

1. _Notation writing and recognition (contd)_

Write the notes (without using leger lines) corresponding to the letter names given:-

| 17. | _E_ | 18. | _A#_ | 19. | _F_ | 20. | _Db_ |

| 21. | _D#_ | 22. | _A_ | 23. | _Bb_ | 24. | _E_ |

| 25. | _C#_ | 26. | _B_ | 27. | _Gb_ | 28. | _D_ |

| 29. | _Ab_ | 30. | _B_ | 31. | _G#_ | 32. | _C_ |

Write the rhythmic note name (i.e. quarter note, eighth note etc.) and duration (i.e. one beat, half a beat etc.) for the following notes:-

33. _Name:-_ _____ 34. _Name:-_ _____ 35. _Name:-_ _____ 36. _Name:-_ _____
    Duration:- _____   _Duration:-_ _____   _Duration:-_ _____   _Duration:-_ _____

_1._   **_Notation writing and recognition (contd)_**

Write the **_G above Middle C_** on the treble clef staff using the rhythmic durations indicated:-

37. _Quarter note_   38. _Dotted half note_ 39. _Eighth note_   40. _Whole note_

Write the rhythmic rest name (i.e. quarter rest, eighth rest etc.) and duration (i.e. one beat, half a beat etc.) for the following rests:-

41. _Name:-_ _____ 42. _Name:-_ _____ 43. _Name:-_ _____ 44. _Name:-_ _____
    Duration:- _____   _Duration:-_ _____   _Duration:-_ _____   _Duration:-_ _____

Write the following rests on the staff:-

45. _Dotted eighth rest_ 46. _Dotted quarter rest_ 47. _Whole rest_   48. _Half rest_

For each note below, write the **_enharmonic equivalent_** next to it on the staff:-

49.   **_(EXAMPLE)_**   50.   51.   52.

(In the example question 49 above, we see that the **_enharmonic equivalent_** of the note **_Ab_** is the **_G#_** written to the right in the same measure).

1. ___Notation writing and recognition (contd)___

(Enharmonic equivalents contd)

53.   54.   55.   56.

2. ___Interval recognition (using halfsteps)___

Write the number of halfsteps between the following pairs of notes:-

57. _____   58. _____   59. _____   60. _____

61. _____   62. _____   63. _____   64. _____

3. ___Constructing major tetrachords___

Build major tetrachords from the following notes:-

65. *(EXAMPLE)*   66.   67.   68.

(In the example question 65 above, a **major tetrachord** has been built from the note C, using wholestep-wholestep-halfstep intervals and consecutive letter names from the music alphabet, resulting in the notes C, D, E & F).

3. Constructing major tetrachords (contd)

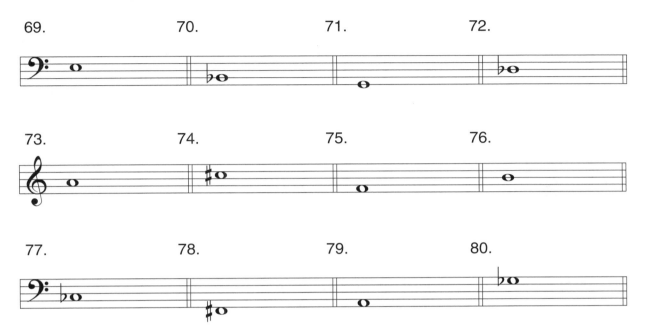

69. 70. 71. 72.

73. 74. 75. 76.

77. 78. 79. 80.

4. Constructing major scales

You are to build major scales from the following starting notes. No key signatures will be used - instead, write accidentals as necessary before each note. Remember that each letter name in the music alphabet will be used consecutively, and that the required intervals are wholestep-wholestep-halfstep-wholestep-wholestep-wholestep-halfstep (or two major tetrachords separated by a wholestep). See example question 81.

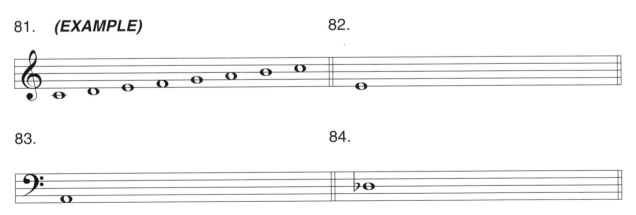

81. *(EXAMPLE)*   82.

83.   84.

4. _Constructing major scales (contd)_

85.   86.

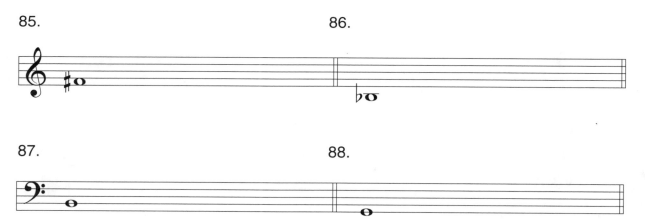

5. _Major key signature writing and recognition_

Write key signatures on the staff corresponding to the following major keys. Make sure that you consider:-

-       the **number** of flats or sharps in the key signature
-       the **order** in which the flats or sharps occur
-       the **location** within the staff of each flat or sharp required.

89. **Ab major**   90. **D major**   91. **Gb major**   92. **E major**

93. **Cb major**   94. **G major**   95. **Eb major**   96. **F# major**

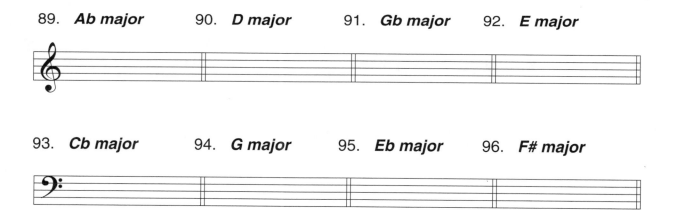

5. *Major key signature writing and recognition (contd)*

Write the major keys corresponding to the key signatures shown:-

97. *Key of* _____   98. *Key of* _____   99. *Key of* _____   100. *Key of* _____

101. *Key of* _____   102. *Key of* _____   103. *Key of* _____   104. *Key of* _____

Chapter One Workbook Answers

1. Notation writing and recognition - answers

1. **G**	2. **D#**	3. **Bb**	4. **E**
5. **C**	6. **Ab**	7. **G#**	8. **F**
9. **Eb**	10. **Db**	11. **F**	12. **A#**
13. **Eb**	14. **G**	15. **D#**	16. **A**

17.   18.   19.   20.

21.   22.   23.   24.

25.   26.   27.   28.

29.   30.   31.   32.

33.	Half note	-	Two beats
34.	Quarter note	-	One beat
35.	Sixteenth note	-	Quarter of a beat
36.	Dotted Eighth note	-	Three-quarters of a beat

1. *Notation writing and recognition - answers (contd)*

37.   38.   39.   40.

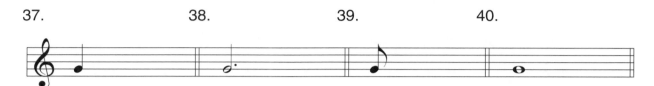

41.	Eighth note rest	-	Half a beat
42.	Dotted half note rest	-	Three beats
43.	Quarter note rest	-	One beat
44.	Sixteenth note rest	-	Quarter of a beat

45.   46.   47.   48.

49.   50.   51.   52.

53.   54.   55.   56.

2. *Interval recognition (using halfsteps) - answers*

57.	*5*	58.	*6*	59.	*3*	60.	*11*
61.	*7*	62.	*4*	63.	*6*	64.	*1*

3. *Constructing major tetrachords - answers*

65.   66.   67.   68.

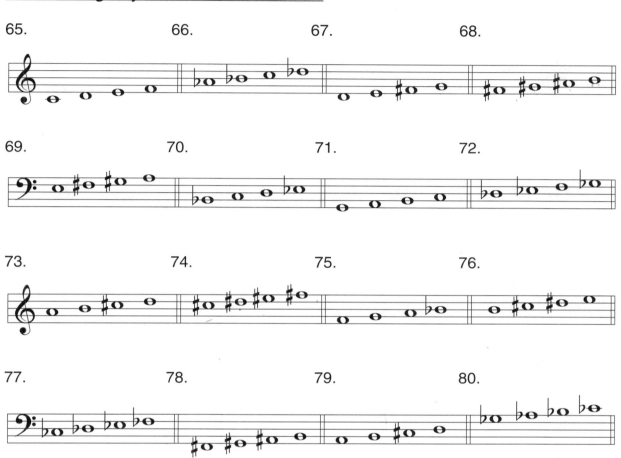

4. *Constructing major scales - answers*

81.   82.

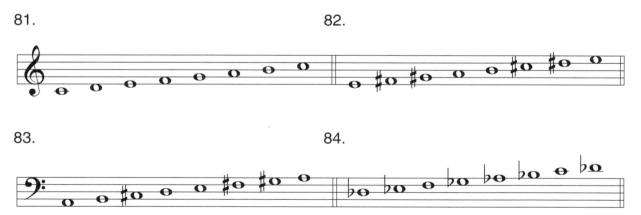

83.   84.

<u>4.</u> *<u>Constructing major scales - answers (contd)</u>*

85.   86.

87.   88.

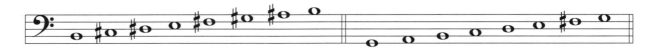

<u>5.</u> *<u>Major key signature writing and recognition - answers</u>*

89.   90.   91.   92.

93.   94.   95.   96.

97.	*Key of **Bb***	98.	*Key of **A***
99.	*Key of **F***	100.	*Key of **B***
101.	*Key of **Eb***	102.	*Key of **G***
103.	*Key of **Db***	104.	*Key of **A***

Diatonic and chromatic intervals

Introduction to intervals

An interval in music is defined as the **measurement of distance between any two notes**. We have already encountered one method of interval measurement in **Chapter 1** - namely, counting the half-steps between two notes (on the 'keyboard diagram'). Now we need to progress to a more 'scale-oriented' method of measuring intervals, as counting all intervals in half-steps is too cumbersome for practical applications.

In this new approach to labelling intervals, we will find that each **interval name** will always have **two components**:-

- a **description** (either major, perfect, minor, augmented or diminished).
- a **number** i.e. 2nd, 3rd, 4th etc.

As an aid to applying the correct **description** to an interval, we will consider all intervals as belonging to one of two overall categories - **diatonic** or **chromatic** - more about this in a moment!

Once you have learned how to measure intervals, you can then use this information to derive all the scales and chords you will ever need - because all scales and chords can always be defined by their internal intervals! Let's start by looking at the interval **number** mentioned above (i.e. 2nd, 3rd, 4th etc.) as it is the easiest of the two interval name components to start out with:-

Figure 2.1. Interval example #1 - C up to A

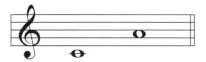

To determine the **interval number**, we count up from the bottom note (starting at **1**), and include all the successive line and space notes until we get to the top note, as follows:-

- The first note shown is **C** - this is **1**.
- The next note up (immediately below the bottom line of the staff) is **D** - this is **2**.
- The next note up (on the bottom line of the staff) is **E** - this is **3**.
- The next note up (in the bottom space of the staff) is **F** - this is **4**.
- The next note up (on the second line from the bottom of the staff) is **G** - this is **5**.
- The next note up (in the second space from the bottom of the staff) is **A** - this is **6**.

Introduction to intervals (contd)

So we see that the last number we got to was **6** - therefore the interval of **C** up to **A** is defined as a **sixth** interval. (Later we will decide what **type** of sixth interval it is)! Here's the next example, showing two intervals which we will see are related to each other:-

Figure 2.2. Interval example #2 - C up to E

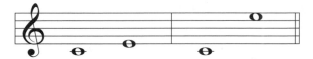

Again to determine the interval number here, we start at **1** and count upwards, including all line and space notes - and so on the left we have a **3rd** interval and on the right we have a **10th** interval. Note also that both of these intervals consist of **C** up to **E** - but the **E** on the right is **one octave higher** than the **E** on the left (in **Chapter 1** we saw that an octave was the interval distance between any note and the next-occurring note of the same name, either higher or lower). Therefore we can conclude that a **3rd** interval plus an **octave** is equal to a **10th** interval. Note that the difference between these two numbers (**3** and **10**) is **7**, which leads to the following rule:-

- ***Adding (or subtracting) the number 7 from an interval number, increases (or decreases) the size of the interval by ONE OCTAVE.***

Now we will consider the distinction between **diatonic** and **chromatic** intervals. (Again this is for the purpose of applying the correct description to the interval).

- A **diatonic** interval is created when the **upper** note of an interval **is contained within** the major scale built from the **lower** note.

- A **chromatic** interval is created when the **upper** note of an interval **is not contained within** the major scale built from the **lower** note.

Let's look at some examples of this process, starting with a **diatonic** interval as follows:-

Figure 2.3. Interval example #3 - C up to G (diatonic interval)

(C Major scale included for reference)

Introduction to intervals (contd)

Note that in the previous example, a **C major** scale has been included on the left, which is the **major scale built from the lowest note** of the interval i.e. in this case the note **C**. We can see that the **upper note** of the interval (in this case **G**) is also contained within the same major scale. This therefore means that the interval of **C** up to **G** is a **diatonic interval**. Now we will look at an example of a **chromatic** interval:-

Figure 2.4. Interval example #4 - C up to Gb (chromatic interval)

(C Major scale included for reference)

Again the **C** major scale built from the lowest note of the interval has been included for reference. We can see that the **upper note** of the interval (in this case **Gb**) is **not** contained within the same **C** major scale. This therefore means that the interval of **C** up to **Gb** is a **chromatic interval**. Now that we have defined what is meant by **diatonic** and **chromatic** intervals, we will look at each category more closely to determine which interval **descriptions** (i.e. major, perfect, minor, augmented or diminished) are used.

Diatonic intervals

The following diagram shows all of the diatonic intervals and descriptions, within a **C** major scale over a range of two octaves:-

Figure 2.5. Diatonic intervals within a C major scale

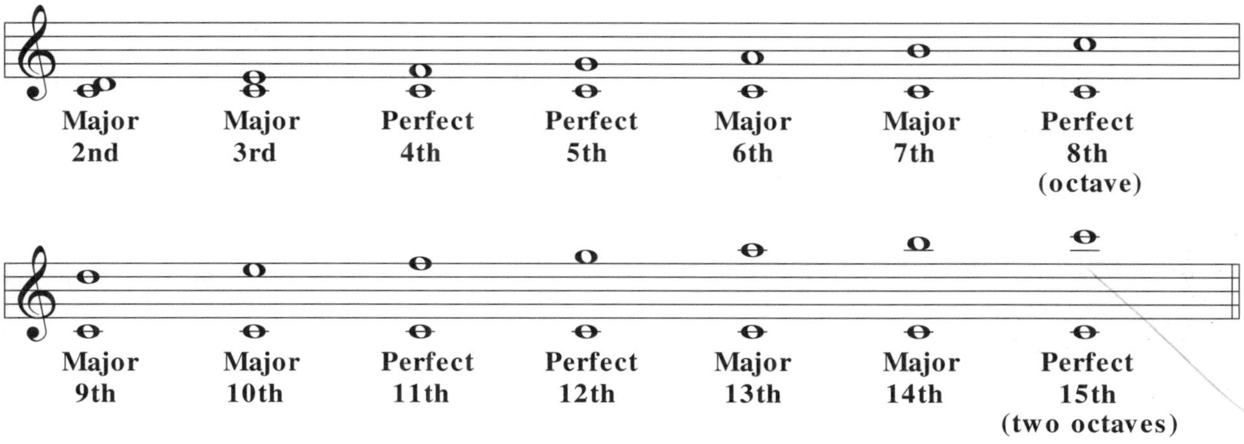

Major 2nd	Major 3rd	Perfect 4th	Perfect 5th	Major 6th	Major 7th	Perfect 8th (octave)

Major 9th	Major 10th	Perfect 11th	Perfect 12th	Major 13th	Major 14th	Perfect 15th (two octaves)

Diatonic intervals (contd)

Note the following rules regarding diatonic interval descriptions:-

- All diatonic intervals are either **MAJOR** or **PERFECT**.
- All **4ths**, **5ths**, **octaves (8ths)**, and octave displacements thereof (i.e. an octave plus a 4th which is an **11th**, an octave plus a 5th which is a **12th**, etc) are called **PERFECT**.
- All other diatonic intervals (i.e. **2nds**, **3rds**, **6ths**, **7ths** etc) are called **MAJOR**.

Why are the 4ths, 5ths and octaves called 'perfect'? - well, without getting too much into acoustic physics, a case could be made that these intervals occur 'in nature' as a result of the **overtone series** (a relationship of pitches which are produced in addition to the 'fundamental', when a note is played on an instrument). Other than that, this division of **diatonic** interval descriptions into **major** and **perfect** basically just needs to be memorized!

Chromatic intervals

Before we assign descriptions to the chromatic intervals, we need to deal with the concept of **double accidentals**, i.e. double flats and double sharps. For example, from our work in **Chapter 1** we know that if we flat (lower) the note **B** by a half-step, we get to **Bb**. It is now also possible to flat the **Bb** by a further half-step, creating **Bbb** (B double flat) as follows:-

Figure 2.6. Double flat example

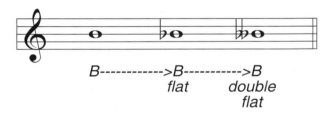

```
B------------>B------------>B
             flat        double
                          flat
```

Note that the pitch **Bbb** (B double flat) is actually equivalent to A - (review keyboard diagram in *Fig. 1.3.* as necessary).

Similarly we could sharp the note **A** to get **A#**, and then **Ax** (A double sharp) as follows:-

Figure 2.7. Double sharp example

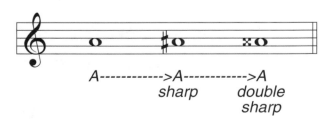

```
A------------>A------------>A
             sharp       double
                         sharp
```

Note that the pitch **Ax** (A double sharp) is actually equivalent to B.

Chromatic intervals (contd)

You may be wondering why we bother to have a note name of **Bbb** (B double flat) when it seems we could just use the note name **A**! Well, when we alter a **diatonic** interval to produce a **chromatic** interval, this may involve flatting a note which is already flatted, or sharping a note which is already sharped. However, the **interval number will not change** (just the interval description - to minor, augmented or diminished) and so therefore we need to preserve the **original note letternames** used in the interval, as we will see in the following examples.

The following **FIVE** interval description 'rules' apply for **chromatic** intervals:-

1)   *A __MAJOR__ interval reduced by a half-step becomes a __MINOR__ interval.*

   Figure 2.8. Minor interval example (major 7th becoming minor 7th)

<-Ma 7th->   <-Mi 7th->

In this example, C up to B on the left is a major 7th interval (see Fig. 2.5.) and therefore the C up to Bb on the right is a minor 7th interval.

2)   *A __MINOR__ interval reduced by a __further__ half-step becomes a __DIMINISHED__ interval.*

   Figure 2.9. Diminished interval example #1 (minor 7th becoming diminished 7th)

<-Mi 7th->   <-Dim 7th->

In this example, C up to Bb on the left is a minor 7th interval (see Fig. 2.8.) and therefore the C up to Bbb on the right is a diminished 7th interval.

3)   *A __MAJOR__ interval increased by a half-step becomes an __AUGMENTED__ interval.*

   Figure 2.10. Augmented interval example #1 (major 6th becoming augmented 6th)

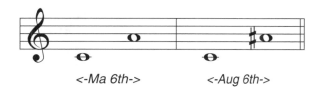

<-Ma 6th->   <-Aug 6th->

In this example, C up to A on the left is a major 6th interval (see Fig. 2.5.) and therefore the C up to A# on the right is an augmented 6th interval.

Chromatic intervals (contd)

4) A <u>*PERFECT*</u> *interval reduced by a half-step becomes a* <u>*DIMINISHED*</u> *interval.*

<u>Figure 2.11. Diminished interval example #2 (perfect 5th becoming diminished 5th)</u>

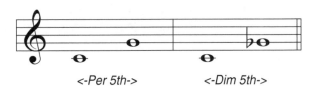

<-Per 5th->   <-Dim 5th->

*In this example, **C** up to **G** on the left is a **perfect 5th** interval (see **Fig. 2.5.**) and therefore the **C** up to **Gb** on the right is a **diminished 5th** interval.*

5) A <u>*PERFECT*</u> *interval increased by a half-step becomes an* <u>*AUGMENTED*</u> *interval.*

<u>Figure 2.12. Augmented interval example #2 (perfect 4th becoming augmented 4th)</u>

<-Per 4th->   <-Aug 4th->

*In this example, **C** up to **F** on the left is a **perfect 4th** interval (see **Fig. 2.5.**) and therefore the **C** up to **F#** on the right is an **augmented 4th** interval.*

Note that whereas **perfect** intervals reduced by one half-step become **diminished**, **major** intervals need to be reduced by **two** half-steps (equivalent to one whole-step) to become **diminished**. Also now we of course have alternate names for the 'whole-step' and 'half-step' interval terms first defined in **Chapter 1**. The **whole-step** can also be defined as a **major 2nd** interval (see **Fig. 2.5.**), and the **half-step** can also be defined as a **minor 2nd** interval as it can be derived by reducing the **major 2nd** interval by half-step (see **Fig. 2.8.** for an example of reducing a major interval by half-step to derive a minor interval).

Just as we saw that individual notes have enharmonic note names, the same (chromatic) interval span can also have more than one name, depending upon which diatonic interval was originally altered to create the chromatic interval. For example:-

- the **minor 7th** (in **Fig. 2.8.**) has the same span as the **augmented 6th** (see **Fig. 2.10.**).
- the **diminished 7th** (in **Fig. 2.9.**) has the same span as the **major 6th** (see **Fig. 2.5.**).
- the **diminished 5th** (in **Fig. 2.11.**) has the same span as the **augmented 4th** (see **Fig. 2.12.**) etc.

Now we will work through some examples of how to create and recognize various intervals, beginning on the following page:-

Examples of creating and recognizing intervals

First we will look at some examples of creating intervals - in other words, how to find the note which is a specified interval above a given note.

Interval creation example #1 - Find the note which is a MAJOR 3RD above the note B

(For the purposes of the example, we are considering the B immediately below the Middle C on the treble staff).

The **first thing** to always do in this situation is to **determine the letter name** of the note required. This is an easy process as it is simply a question of counting the successive line and space notes on the staff until the interval number (in this case a **3rd**) is reached, from the starting note (see text accompanying **Fig. 2.1.**), as follows:

Figure 2.13. Interval creation example #1 stage 1 - determine letter name required

*The letter name of the note required is **D**, as it is a third interval above the letter name **B**.*

The next thing to do is to build a major scale from the given note (i.e. **B** in this case):-

Figure 2.14. Interval creation example #1 stage 2 - build the B major scale

(If you haven't learned your major scales yet - well, figure out the notes using the interval/tetrachord method as presented in **Chapter 1**)!

If the interval we need is **diatonic** (i.e. either **major** or **perfect**), then we simply need to ensure that the upper note of the interval is **qualified** (i.e. has any necessary sharps/flats added) **in the same way as it appears in the major scale built from the given note.**

In this case we need a major 3rd interval above **B** - this is a diatonic interval, and therefore the required note will be **within the major scale built from B**. The third degree of this scale is the note **D#** - and so the lettername **D** that we first derived above (**Fig. 2.13.**) now needs to be qualified as follows:-

Examples of creating and recognizing intervals (contd)

Figure 2.15. Interval creation example #1 stage 3 - qualify upper note

The note **D#** is now a **major 3rd** interval above the note **B**.

Interval creation example #2 - Find the note which is a **MINOR 7TH** above the note **Eb**

(For the purposes of the example, we are considering the first Eb above Middle C on the treble staff).

Again the first thing to do is to determine the letter name of the note required, as follows:-

Figure 2.16. Interval creation example #2 stage 1 - determine letter name required

The letter name of the note required is **D**, as it is a seventh interval above the letter name **E**.

The next thing to do is to build a major scale from the given note (i.e. **Eb** in this case):-

Figure 2.17. Interval creation example #1 stage 2 - build the Eb major scale

If the interval we need is **chromatic** (i.e. either **minor, augmented** or **diminished**), then the letter name of the required upper note will **no longer be qualified** in the same way as it appears in the **major scale built from the given note** - in other words it will be **altered.**

In this case we need a **minor 7th** interval above **Eb** - this is a **chromatic** interval. We look in the **Eb** major scale for the 7th degree, and note that it is **D** - the interval **Eb** up to **D** is therefore a **major 7th** interval. We then recall from the chromatic interval 'rules' on **p57-58** that reducing a **major** interval by half-step produces a **minor** interval - so to get the required **minor 7th** interval above **Eb**, we need to finally qualify the note **D** as follows:-

Examples of creating and recognizing intervals (contd)

Figure 2.18. Interval creation example #2 stage 3 - qualify upper note

*The note **Db** is now a **minor 7th** interval above the note **Eb**.*

We can summarize this interval creation process as follows:-

- first of all, figure out the **letter name** of the note required (i.e. above the given note)
- build a **major scale from the given note**, for reference purposes
- if creating a **diatonic** (major or perfect) interval:-
    - 'qualify' the new note (i.e. add accidentals as necessary) according to how the note appears in the major scale
- if creating a **chromatic** (minor, augmented or diminished) interval:-
    - find the scale degree within the major scale built from the given note, corresponding to the interval number required
    - alter this note (i.e. add accidentals as necessary) to alter the diatonic interval to the required chromatic interval (review alteration rules on **p57-58** as needed).

Now we will look at some examples of recognizing intervals - this is where we already have two notes on the staff, and we need to determine the interval between them.

Interval recognition example #1 - *Determine the interval between the notes **F** & **Bb***

Figure 2.19. Interval recognition example #1 stage 1

*(We will now try to determine the correct interval number and description for this interval of **F up to Bb**).*

Again the interval number is straightforward - counting up from F on the staff, we can see that this is some kind of **4th interval**. Now to derive the description, we again build a major scale from the lowest note - this time an **F** major scale:-

Figure 2.20. Interval recognition example #1 stage 2 - build the F major scale

Examples of creating and recognizing intervals (contd)

If the upper note of the interval appears within the major scale built from the lowest note, then we have a **diatonic** interval (i.e. major or perfect). We notice that the upper note of the interval (**Bb**) is present in the **F** major scale. The interval description we need is therefore major or perfect - we have already determined the interval to be a **4th**, which we recall is perfect (see diatonic intervals in **Fig. 2.5.**). This interval of **F** up to **Bb** is therefore a **perfect 4th**. Now we will look at a final interval recognition example:-

*Interval recognition example #2 - Determine the interval between the notes **D** & **Ab***

Figure 2.21. Interval recognition example #2 stage 1

*(We will now try to determine the correct interval number and description for this interval of **D** up to **Ab**).*

Counting up from D on the staff, we can see that this is some kind of **5th interval**. Now we again build a major scale from the lowest note - this time a **D** major scale:-

Figure 2.22. Interval recognition example #2 stage 2 - build the D major scale

<WS> <WS> <HS> <WS> <WS> <WS> <HS>

If the upper note of the interval is **not** within the major scale built from the lowest note, then we have a **chromatic** interval (i.e. minor, augmented or diminished). We notice that the upper note of the interval (**Ab**) is **not** present in the **D** major scale. When this occurs, we look for the note within this major scale which **shares the same letter name** with the upper note of our interval (i.e. in this case the note **A**). We then determine the interval from our starting note (i.e. **D**) up to this new note, which of course will then be a diatonic interval:-

Figure 2.23. Interval recognition example #2 stage 3
- determine diatonic interval using same upper letter name

*(This 5th interval is contained within the **D** major scale - therefore it is a **perfect 5th** interval).*

Examples of creating and recognizing intervals (contd)

We then need to determine how this **diatonic** interval (in this case the **perfect 5th** interval of **D** up to **A**) would have been **altered** to create the interval of **D** up to **Ab** that we originally started with. We conclude that the '**D to A**' interval would need to be reduced by a **half-step** to create the '**D to Ab**' interval, and we recall from the chromatic interval description 'rules' (see **p57-58**) that any **perfect** interval **reduced by a half-step** becomes a **diminished** interval. Therefore the interval of **D** up to **Ab** is a **diminished 5th** interval.

Note that in this example, it was important to determine the description (i.e. **major** or **perfect**) of the diatonic interval sharing the same letter names as the original (chromatic) interval in question, as this influences the final description of the chromatic interval - reducing a **perfect** interval by half-step creates a **diminished** interval, whereas reducing a **major** interval by half-step creates a **minor** interval. (However, both **major** and **perfect** intervals when increased by half-step become **augmented** intervals). Again review chromatic interval 'rules' on pages **57-58** as required.

We can summarize this interval recognition process as follows:-

- first of all, figure out the **interval number** (i.e. 2nd, 3rd etc) by starting at the number **1** and 'counting up' from the bottom note on the staff to the top note
- build a **major scale** from the bottom note, for reference purposes
- if the top note of the interval is **within the major scale** built from the bottom note:-
    - then we have a **diatonic** interval - description will be **major** or **perfect** depending upon interval number (see **Fig. 2.5.** and accompanying text)
- if the top note of the interval is **not within the major scale** built from the bottom note (i.e. the note letter name is 'qualified' differently):-
    - then we have a **chromatic** interval - description will be **minor**, **augmented** or **diminished**. To determine the correct description, we figure out how the top note letter name **would have been qualified** in order for the interval to be diatonic (i.e. for the top note to be within the major scale built from the bottom note), and then we establish how this interval has been **altered** (i.e. reduced or increased by half-step) to create the actual chromatic interval that we have, using the chromatic interval 'rules' as presented on pages **57-58**.

The following workbook section also includes a further example of (chromatic) interval recognition - see page **67**.

Chapter Two Workbook Questions

1. Diatonic interval recognition

You are to write the interval description for the following diatonic intervals. Remember that the interval description consists of two parts:- an adjective (i.e. major, perfect etc.) and a number (3rd, 4th etc.). As all these intervals are diatonic (i.e. the upper note is within the major scale built from the lower note) they will either be major or perfect.

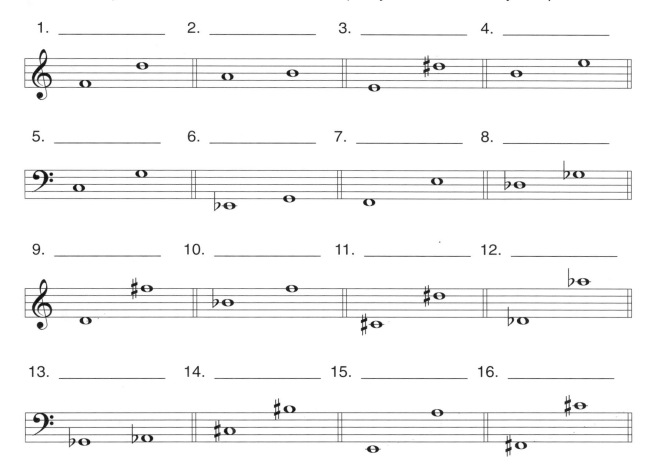

1. _____ 2. _____ 3. _____ 4. _____

5. _____ 6. _____ 7. _____ 8. _____

9. _____ 10. _____ 11. _____ 12. _____

13. _____ 14. _____ 15. _____ 16. _____

2. *Diatonic interval creation*

You are to write the remaining note for each question that will create the specified diatonic interval above the lower note provided. Again remember that all diatonic intervals (i.e. major and perfect) are contained within the major scale built from the lowest note. When creating these intervals, you should first write the note on the staff corresponding to the interval number (i.e. 2nd, 3rd etc.) that you need, and then qualify the note (if necessary) using accidentals, to achieve the desired interval description.

17. *Major 3rd*   18. *Major 6th*   19. *Perfect 4th*   20. *Major 2nd*

21. *Perfect 5th*   22. *Perfect 8th*   23. *Major 3rd*   24. *Perfect 4th*

25. *Major 10th*   26. *Perfect 5th*   27. *Major 9th*   28. *Perfect 11th*

29. *Perfect 4th*   30. *Major 13th*   31. *Major 7th*   32. *Perfect 12th*

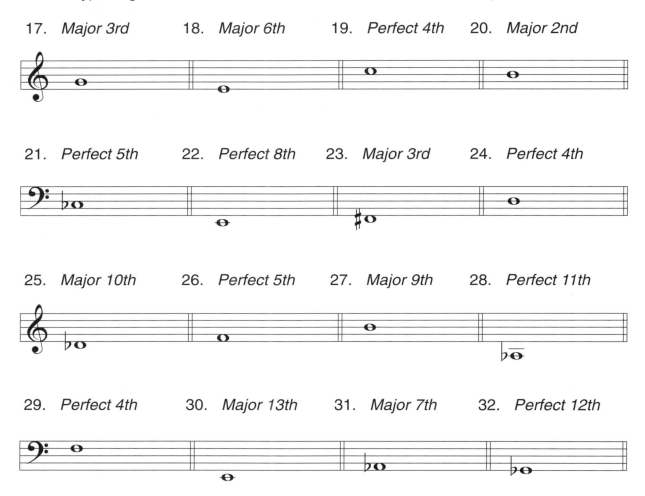

N.B. Some of these intervals are of course larger than an octave - don't forget that adding (or subtracting) the number **7** from an interval number, increases (or decreases) the size of the interval by an octave - see **p54** in Textbook.

3.   *Chromatic interval recognition*

You are to write the interval description for the following chromatic intervals. Again remember that the interval description consists of two parts:- an adjective (i.e. major, minor, perfect, augmented or diminished) and a number (3rd, 4th etc.). The upper note is now no longer within the major scale built from the lower note. When recognizing these intervals, you should go through the following process:-

-   recognize the **interval number** (3rd, 4th etc.) by measuring the visual distance (i.e. staff lines and spaces) between the two notes.
-   build a major scale from the lower note as necessary, to find out how the upper note **would have been** 'qualified' (i.e. if it would have been a sharp, flat or natural) to make the interval diatonic (i.e. perfect or major).
-   figure out how that diatonic interval has been **altered** (i.e. increased or reduced) to create the chromatic interval that you see.

Let's do question #33 as an example using this method. First assessing the **interval number**, we note that the lettername F up to the lettername D creates some kind of **sixth** interval. We then build a major scale from the lowest note F (using wholestep & halfstep intervals and/or tetrachords - NOT key signatures!) and we find that the 6th degree of the F major scale is D natural. Therefore in the interval shown in the question, the note D would have needed to be a natural (instead of a flat) for the interval to be diatonic - in this case a **major sixth**. We have therefore taken the major sixth interval of F up to D and **reduced** it by a halfstep, creating the interval F up to Db. According to the rules explained in the Chapter 2 text, when we reduce any **major** interval by a halfstep, it becomes **minor**. Therefore the answer to question #33 is a **minor sixth**.

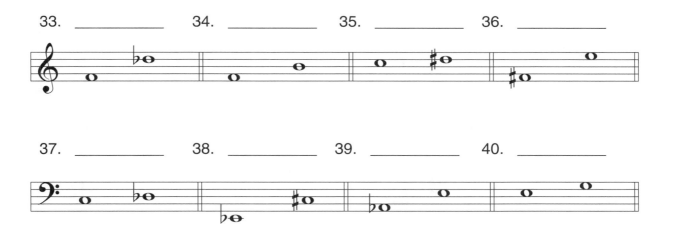

3. *Chromatic interval recognition (contd)*

41. _____   42. _____   43. _____   44. _____

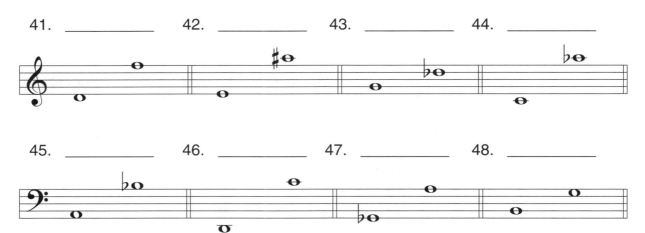

45. _____   46. _____   47. _____   48. _____

4. *Chromatic interval creation*

You are to write the remaining note for each question that will create the specified chromatic interval above the lower note provided. Again remember that for chromatic intervals, the upper note will **not** be within the major scale built from the lower note, but instead will represent an **alteration** of a diatonic interval according to the rules outlined in the Chapter 2 text. When creating these intervals, you should first write the note on the staff corresponding to the interval number (i.e. 2nd, 3rd etc.) that you need, and then qualify the note as necessary using accidentals, to achieve the desired interval description.

49. *Minor 3rd*   50. *Minor 6th*   51. *Augmented 4th* 52. *Augmented 5th*

53. *Augmented 5th* 54. *Diminished 5th* 55. *Augmented 2nd* 56. *Minor 7th*

4. *Chromatic interval creation (contd)*

57. *Minor 10th*   58. *Augmented 6th*   59. *Minor 13th*   60. *Augmented 9th*

61. *Minor 9th*   62. *Augmented 11th* 63. *Minor 2nd*   64. *Diminished 12th*

Chapter Two Workbook Answers

1.   Diatonic interval recognition - answers

1.	*Major 6th*	2.	*Major 2nd*
3.	*Major 7th*	4.	*Perfect 4th*
5.	*Perfect 5th*	6.	*Major 3rd*
7.	*Major 7th*	8.	*Perfect 4th*
9.	*Major 10th*	10.	*Perfect 5th*
11.	*Major 9th*	12.	*Perfect 12th*
13.	*Major 2nd*	14.	*Major 7th*
15.	*Perfect 11th*	16.	*Perfect 12th*

2.   Diatonic interval creation - answers

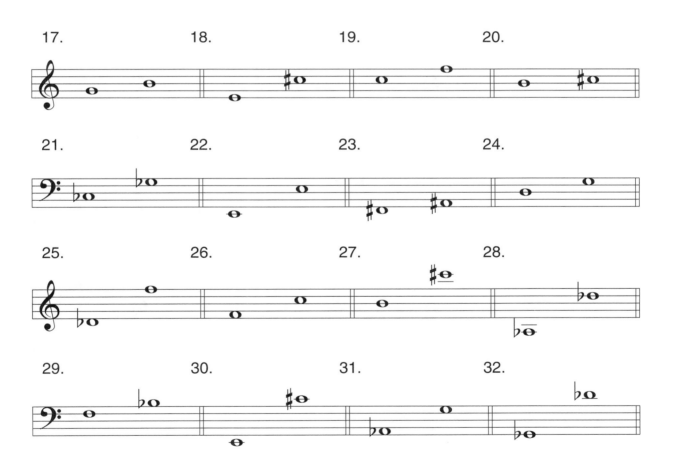

3. *Chromatic interval recognition - answers*

33.	*Minor 6th*	34.	*Augmented 4th*
35.	*Augmented 2nd*	36.	*Minor 7th*
37.	*Minor 2nd*	38.	*Augmented 6th*
39.	*Augmented 5th*	40.	*Minor 3rd*
41.	*Minor 10th*	42.	*Augmented 11th*
43.	*Diminished 5th*	44.	*Minor 13th*
45.	*Minor 9th*	46.	*Minor 14th*
47.	*Augmented 9th*	48.	*Minor 6th*

4. *Chromatic interval creation - answers*

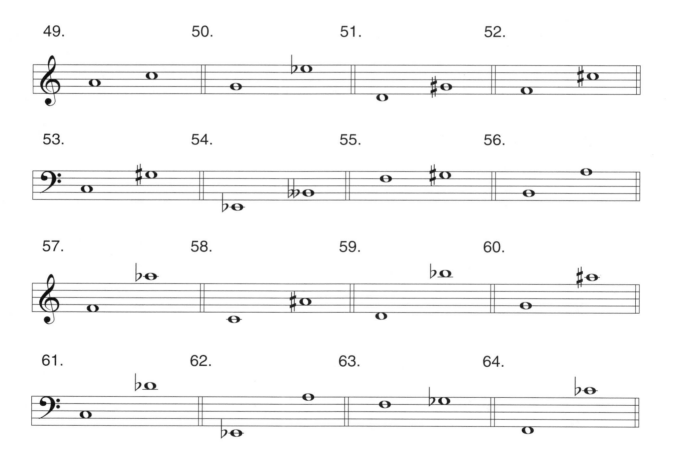

Triads and inversions

Introduction to triads

The first type of chord we will consider is called a **triad**. A triad is a chord consisting of three notes, which are commonly referred to as a **root**, **3rd** and **5th**. All chords (including triads) can be analyzed to determine the **intervals present** in the chord - and from our recent work in **Chapter 2**, we are now in a position to correctly derive any required interval. We will also look at the major scale (first derived in **Chapter 1**) to see if it can be used as a 'scale source' for the triads under consideration.

There are four basic types of triad to be derived - known as **major**, **minor**, **augmented** and **diminished**. You will recall that these words have already been used in **Chapter 2** as **interval descriptions** - now we will use them as **chord** (triad) **descriptions**. It's important that you understand the distinction between an interval description and a chord description, as the same adjectives can be used in each case - keeping these two different 'usages' clear in your mind will be helpful, especially later on when we get to larger (i.e. 4- and 5-part) chords.

The major triad

The first and most important triad to be studied is the **major** triad. It is derived by placing **major 3rd** and **perfect 5th** intervals above the root, as follows:-

Figure 3.1. C major triad - interval construction

```
<---Major 3rd---->
<---------------Perfect 5th------------->
```

Note that we have measured the intervals (major 3rd and perfect 5th) up from the root of the triad in each case. We recall from **Chapter 2** that major and perfect intervals were diatonic i.e. they occurred within a major scale built from the lowest note - this triad could therefore also be considered as the first, third and fifth degrees of a **C major scale** (review **Figs. 1.42.** and **2.5.** as necessary).

The major triad (contd)

Note also the letter 'C' which appears above the triad in the example on the previous page. This is our first example of a **chord symbol**. The chord symbol tells you which chord is contained in the measure. A chord symbol which simply consists of a note name with no additional 'suffix' or description, indicates a **major triad** built from the note indicated - so the chord symbol of 'C' means a **C major triad**.

Although using the chord symbol as described above (i.e. a note name with no suffix) is the correct way to write a major triad chord symbol, you may sometimes encounter suffixes used for the major triad chord symbol, as follows:-

- 'Ma', 'Maj', 'ma', 'maj', i.e. as in the chord symbols **CMa, CMaj, Cma** and **Cmaj**. All of these suffixes are unnecessary, as using just the note name in the chord symbol without a suffix (i.e. **C**) already explicitly tells you a major triad is required.
- 'M' i.e. as in the chord symbol **CM**. Same comments as above, and additionally the single upper-case 'M' can be confused with 'm' (lower-case) which is sometimes used to signify **minor** (see following page).
- 'Δ' i.e. as in the chord symbol **CΔ**. This 'triangle symbol' is sometimes used in older charts and fake books to indicate a major quality - however, it is not always clear whether a triad or larger (i.e. 4-part) form of the chord is needed. (Later on I will give you explicit rules for labelling all of your 4-part chords)!

So - when writing your major triad chord symbols, use the note name with no suffix (i.e. 'C' for a C major triad) - but **be prepared to recognize** the alternatives listed above. We will now look at the three other types of triad - **minor, augmented** and **diminished**. These triads can also be analyzed to determine the intervals present within them. We can also see how a major triad might be altered to create these other triads, as follows:-

The minor triad

The next triad to be studied is the **minor** triad. It is derived by placing **minor 3rd** and **perfect 5th** intervals above the root, as follows:-

Figure 3.2. C minor triad - interval construction

<---Minor 3rd---->
<---------------Perfect 5th------------->

The minor triad (contd)

When comparing this to the major triad in **Fig. 3.1.**, notice that the third interval (i.e. the interval between the root and the 3rd of the chord) is now a **minor 3rd** instead of a **major 3rd**. We recall from our work on intervals in **Chapter 2** that when a major interval is reduced by half-step, a minor interval is produced. Therefore, one way this **C minor** triad can be derived is by taking the previous **C major triad** and **lowering the third by a half-step** (in this case the note **E** becoming an **Eb**).

Also note the chord symbol above the staff which is '**Cmi**'. There are two components to this chord symbol - the chord root (in this case '**C**') and the chord 'suffix' or description (in this case '**mi**'). The suffix '**mi**' indicates a **minor triad** built from the chord root i.e. in this case a **C minor triad**. Although using the suffix '**mi**' is the preferred way to write this chord symbol, you will sometimes encounter other suffixes for the minor triad, as follows:-

- '**min**' i.e. as in the chord symbol **Cmin**. Unnecessary as the suffix '**mi**' already explicitly defines minor.
- '**m**' i.e. as in the chord symbol **Cm**. If just a single (lower-case) '**m**' is used, this can be confused with an upper-case '**M**' which is sometimes used to indicate a major quality - see explanation on previous page. Use '**mi**' to be explicit.
- '**-**' i.e. as in the chord symbol **C-**. The use of the '**-**' suffix to signify minor, is often encountered in older charts and in the 'illegal' fake books used in jazz circles! I personally find the '**mi**' suffix to be clearer and less error-prone - a view echoed by some of the better 'legal' fake books coming on to the market in recent years.

So - when writing your minor triad chord symbols, use the '**mi**' suffix - but again **be prepared to recognize** the alternatives listed above!

The augmented triad

The next triad to be studied is the **augmented** triad. It is derived by placing **major 3rd** and **augmented 5th** intervals above the root, as follows:-

Figure 3.3. C augmented triad - interval construction

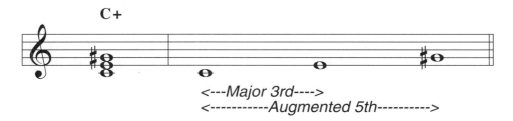

<---Major 3rd---->
<-----------Augmented 5th---------->

The augmented triad (contd)

When comparing the augmented triad to the major triad in **Fig. 3.1.**, notice that the fifth interval (i.e. the interval between the root and the 5th of the chord) is now an **augmented 5th** instead of a **perfect 5th**. We recall from our work on intervals in **Chapter 2** that when a perfect interval is increased by half-step, an augmented interval is produced. Therefore, one way this **C augmented** triad can be derived is by taking the **C major triad** and **raising the fifth by a half-step** (in this case the note **G** becoming a **G#**).

Note the chord symbol above the staff which is '**C+**'. Again there are two components to this chord symbol - the chord root (in this case '**C**') and the chord 'suffix' or description (in this case '**+**'). The suffix '**+**' used in a chord symbol actually indicates that the **5th is to by raised by a half-step** on the chord in question - so in this case the symbol '**C+**' means "raise the 5th of a C major triad by half-step" i.e. creating a **C augmented** triad. Another common and perfectly correct way to write this chord is to use the suffix '**aug**' i.e. as in the chord symbol **Caug**.

The diminished triad

The final triad to be studied is the **diminished** triad. It is derived by placing **minor 3rd** and **diminished 5th** intervals above the root, as follows:-

Figure 3.4. C diminished triad - interval construction

<---Minor 3rd---->
<-----------Diminished 5th----------->

When comparing the diminished triad to the major triad in **Fig. 3.1.**, notice that the third interval (i.e. the interval between the root and the 3rd of the chord) is now a **minor 3rd** instead of a **major 3rd**, and that the fifth interval (i.e. the interval between the root and the 5th of the chord) is now a **diminished 5th** instead of a **perfect 5th**. We recall from our work on intervals in **Chapter 2** that reducing a major interval by half-step produces a minor interval, and reducing a perfect interval by half-step produces a diminished interval. Therefore, one way this **C diminished** triad can be derived is by taking the **C major triad** and **lowering the third and fifth by a half-step** (in this case the note **E** becoming an **Eb**, and **G** becoming a **Gb**).

The diminished triad (contd)

Note the chord symbol above the staff which is '**C°**'. Again there are two components to this chord symbol - the chord root (in this case '**C**') and the chord 'suffix' or description (in this case '**°**' - a small circle appended to the top right of the chord symbol note name, similar to a degree sign). The suffix '**°**' indicates a diminished triad built from the root of the chord i.e. in this case a **C diminished** triad. Another common and perfectly correct way to write this chord is to use the suffix '**dim**' i.e. as in the chord symbol **Cdim**.

More examples of altering the major triad to produce the other triads

We have already seen that the preceding **C minor**, **C augmented** and **C diminished** triads can be viewed from the standpoint of how the major triad can be **altered** to produce the other types of triad. You'll recall that in each case the note letter names stayed the same, but were **qualified differently** (i.e. requiring a sharp or flat) depending upon the chromatic intervals needed in each triad. If we apply this procedure when altering different major triads (i.e. other than the **C major** triad) to produce the other types of triad, we will sometimes need to use **double accidentals** i.e. to **lower** a pitch which is **already flatted** will require a **double-flat**, and to **raise** a pitch which is **already sharped** will require a **double-sharp**. (We were first introduced to double accidentals in **Chapter 2** - review **Figs. 2.6.** and **2.7.** as necessary). We will now see this process at work, first of all taking an **F# major triad** (consisting of the notes **F#**, **A#** and **C#**) and altering it to produce the other types of triad, **while still using the note letternames of F, A and C throughout**, as follows:-

Figure 3.5. Altering an F# major triad to produce the other types of triad

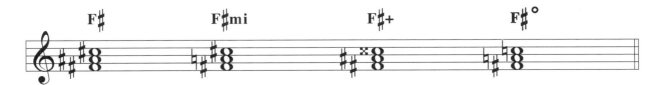

In this example:-

- The first **F# major** triad consists of the note **F#**, **A#** and **C#**. The note **A#** is a **major 3rd** interval above **F#**, and the note **C#** is a **perfect 5th** interval above **F#**. (These three notes are also the **1st**, **3rd** and **5th** degrees of an **F# major scale**).
- The second **F# minor** triad is derived by lowering the **3rd** of the **F# major** triad by a half-step - in this case the **A sharp** becoming an **A natural** (as evidenced by the 'natural' sign before the note, which is 'cancelling out' the previous sharp sign).

More examples of altering the major triad to produce the other triads (contd)

(*Figure 3.5. explanation contd*)

- The third **F# augmented** triad is derived by raising the **5th** of the **F# major** triad by a half-step - in this case the **C sharp** becoming a **C double-sharp**.
- The fourth **F# diminished** triad is derived by lowering the **3rd** and **5th** of the **F# major** triad by a half-step - in this case the **A sharp** becoming an **A natural**, and the **C sharp** becoming a **C natural**.

Now we will take a **Gb major triad** (consisting of the notes **Gb**, **Bb** and **Db**) and alter it to produce the other types of triad, **while still using the note letternames of G, B and D throughout**, as follows:-

Figure 3.6. Altering a Gb major triad to produce the other types of triad

In this example:-

- The first **Gb major** triad consists of the note **Gb**, **Bb** and **Db**. The note **Bb** is a **major 3rd** interval above **Gb**, and the note **Db** is a **perfect 5th** interval above **Gb**. (These three notes are also the **1st**, **3rd** and **5th** degrees of a **Gb major scale**). This **Gb major** triad is of course the **enharmonic equivalent** of the **F# major** triad in the previous example.
- The second **Gb minor** triad is derived by lowering the **3rd** of the **Gb major** triad by a half-step - in this case the **B flat** becoming a **B double-flat**.
- The third **Gb augmented** triad is derived by raising the **5th** of the **Gb major** triad by a half-step - in this case the **D flat** becoming a **D natural**.
- The fourth **Gb diminished** triad is derived by lowering the **3rd** and **5th** of the **Gb major** triad by a half-step - in this case the **B flat** becoming a **B double-flat**, and the **D flat** becoming a **D double-flat**.

Figures **3.5.** and **3.6.** are essentially two different ways of notating the same group of triads - work through these examples to familiarize yourself with the **enharmonic naming** conventions used in each case!

Locating the different triads within the major scale

We will now look within the major scale (first derived in **Fig. 1.42.**) to see if these triad relationships are found within the scale. We have already mentioned that a **major** triad can be derived from the **1st**, **3rd** and **5th** degrees of a major scale, and this can be reviewed as follows:-

Figure 3.7. Deriving the C major triad from a C major scale

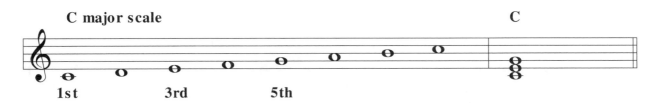

There will also be other places within the major scale (i.e. not just from the **1st** degree) from which major triads can be built - more about this in **Chapter 4**.

So far we have viewed the **minor** triad from the standpoint of **altering the major** triad to get the required minor triad - however we will now see that the minor triad **already** 'lives within' the major scale, if we **build the triad from the second degree of the scale**:-

Figure 3.8. Deriving the D minor triad from a C major scale

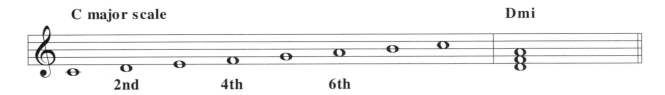

This is an important principle that we need to understand - if we build a triad from the **2nd** degree (i.e. take the **2nd**, **4th** and **6th** degrees) of a major scale, a **minor triad naturally occurs** - we didn't have to 'lower the 3rd' of anything to derive this D minor triad! (However of course were we to take a **D major** triad - consisting of the notes **D**, **F#** and **A** - and lower the 3rd by half-step, the same **D minor** triad would result).

There will also be other places within the major scale (i.e. not just from the **2nd** degree) from which minor triads can be built - more about this in **Chapter 4**.

So far we have viewed the **diminished** triad from the standpoint of **altering the major** triad to get the required diminished triad - however we will now see that (as with the minor triad) the diminished triad **already** 'lives within' the major scale, if we **build the triad from the seventh degree of the scale** as in the example on the following page:-

Locating the different triads within the major scale (contd)

Figure 3.9. Deriving the B diminished triad from a C major scale

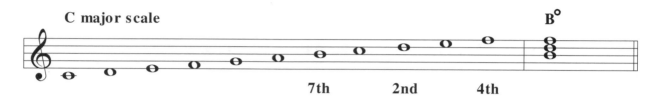

Here we see that if a triad is built from the **7th** degree (i.e. using the **7th** and then 'wrapping around' to use the **2nd** and **4th** degrees) of a major scale, a **diminished triad naturally occurs** - again we didn't have to 'lower the 3rd and 5th' of anything to derive this B diminished triad. (However of course were we to take a **B major** triad - consisting of the notes **B, D#** and **F#** - and lower both the 3rd and 5th by half-step, the same **B diminished** triad would result).

So we have seen that the **minor** and **diminished** triads, as well as the **major** triad, are found 'naturally' within the major scale. However, the other triad we have been studying (i.e. the **augmented** triad) is not found within any major scale. From an eartraining standpoint, I think this accounts for the somewhat 'restless' quality associated with the augmented triad - our Western-music-influenced ears tend to 'live within' the major scale (or at least use it as our main reference point), and the augmented triad is not contained within this familiar framework!

Inversions of triads

We will now look at a manipulation of a triad known as an **inversion**. First of all we should say that all of the triads studied so far have been built in '**root position**', meaning that the root of each chord has always been the lowest note, and we have then 'built up' from the root to add the 3rd and 5th of each triad. We can however **change the order** in which the notes of a triad occur (from bottom to top on the staff), so that the root of the triad is now no longer the lowest note on the staff, as in the following example of a **C major** triad:-

Figure 3.10. C major triad and inversions

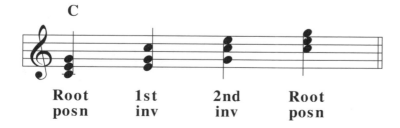

Inversions of triads

We can analyze the inversions in the previous example as follows:-

- The first and last **C major** triads are in **root position**. The root of the triad (**C**) is the **lowest note**. The sequence of notes from lowest to highest is:- **C**, **E**, and **G**.
- The second **C major** triad is in **first inversion**. The root of the triad (**C**) is the **highest note**. The sequence of notes from lowest to highest is:- **E**, **G**, and **C**.
- The third **C major** triad is in **second inversion**. The root of the triad (**C**) is the **middle note**. The sequence of notes from lowest to highest is:- **G**, **C**, and **E**.

As we move from left to right through this example, each successive triad form can be derived by taking the lowest note in each case and **moving it up by one octave** (i.e. to the next highest occurence of the same note on the staff) as follows:-

- Starting with the first **root position** triad, if we take the lowest note (**C**) and move it up by an octave, we derive the following **first inversion** triad.
- Similarly, if we then take the lowest note of the **first inversion** triad (**E**) and move that up by an octave, we derive the following **second inversion** triad.
- Finally if we take the lowest note of the **second inversion** triad (**G**) and move that up by an octave, we get back to the final root position triad, which overall is an **octave higher** than the starting **root position** triad.

Note also that inverting the triad has created a different **internal interval structure** - whereas root position triads always consist of successive **third intervals** on the staff (i.e. between the root and 3rd, and then between the 3rd and 5th, of the triad), now we have a **fourth interval** on top of a **third interval** within a **first inversion** triad, and a **third interval** on top of a **fourth interval** within a **second inversion** triad. In each case the fourth interval occurs between the **5th** and **root** of the triad. In the case of the **C major** triad, this interval occurs between the notes **G** and **C**, which is a **perfect fourth interval** (review interval descriptions in **Chapter 2** as needed).

Now we will look at the inversions of the other types of triad, starting with the **minor triad**:-

Figure 3.11. C minor triad and inversions

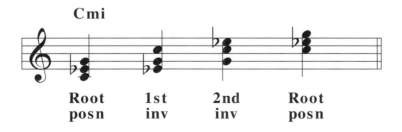

Inversions of triads

Exactly the same inversion concepts and terminology as before, now apply to the minor triad in the previous example. Again a **perfect 4th** interval is created between the 5th and root of the triad, in both first and second inversions.

Figure 3.12. C augmented triad and inversions

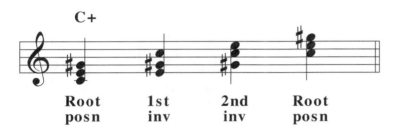

Again the same inversion concepts and terminology apply - but now we have a **diminished 4th** interval between the 5th and root of the triad, in both first and second inversions. As this is enharmonically equivalent to the **major 3rd** intervals within the triad in root position (even though the intervals appear to be different on the staff), the **internal intervals in this triad effectively do not change when the triad is inverted**. The augmented triad is the only one of the four triads which exhibits this characteristic.

Figure 3.13. C diminished triad and inversions

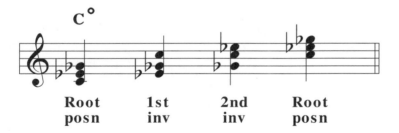

Again the same inversion concepts and terminology apply - but now we have an **augmented 4th** interval between the 5th and root of the triad, in both first and second inversions. (The **augmented 4th** interval is enharmonically equivalent to the **diminished 5th** interval, which is the interval between the root and 5th of this triad when in root position).

Triad recognition method and examples

We will now establish some rules for recognizing triads written on the staff, which will enable us to determine the correct chord symbol (and inversion) for a given triad, as in the following examples:-

Figure 3.14. Triad recognition example #1

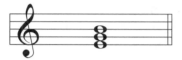

First we will figure out if the triad is in root position, first inversion or second inversion. (This will also tell us what the **root** of the triad is, which in turn will enable us to identify the triad). Looking at the triad in example **#1** above, we notice that it consists of consecutive 'line' notes on the staff i.e. it is two **third** intervals stacked on top of one another, which tells us that the triad is in **root position** (as opposed to an **inverted** triad, which would contain an internal **fourth** interval - see **Figs. 3.10. - 3.13.**). The **lowest** note (**E**) is therefore the **root** of this triad.

Then the next stage is to build a **major** triad from the root. If the notes in this triad are the same as in the example, then of course we have detected a major triad - otherwise we figure out how this major triad has been altered to create the triad in the example (which would then be either **minor**, **augmented** or **diminished**).

We recall that a **major** triad is built by adding **major 3rd** and **perfect 5th** intervals above the root, which is the same as adding the **3rd** and **5th** degrees of the **major scale** built from the root. The **E major** triad built in this case, therefore consists of the notes **E**, **G#** and **B**, which is not quite the same as the triad in example **#1** above (which consists of the notes **E**, **G** and **B**). In comparing the **E major** triad to the triad in example **#1** above, we find that the **3rd** of the **E major** triad (**G#**) has been **lowered by half-step** to obtain the **3rd** of the triad in example **#1** (i.e. the note **G**). We recall from the text accompanying **Fig. 3.2.** that **lowering the 3rd of a major triad by half-step creates a minor triad**. Therefore the triad in example **#1** is an **E minor triad** (in root position).

Figure 3.15. Triad recognition example #2

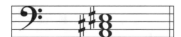

(Note that we have used bass clef in this example).

Triad recognition method and examples (contd)

Looking at the triad in example **#2** on the previous page, we notice that it consists of consecutive 'space' notes on the staff i.e. it is two **third** intervals stacked on top of one another, which again tells us that the triad is in **root position**. The **lowest** note (**A**) is therefore the **root** of this triad.

Again we then build a major triad from the root, and see how this compares to the triad in the example. The **A major** triad built in this case, consists of the notes **A**, **C#** and **E**, which is not quite the same as the triad in example **#2** (which consists of the notes **A**, **C#** and **E#**). In comparing the **A major** triad to the triad in example **#2**, we find that the **5th** of the **A major** triad (**E**) has been **raised by half-step** to obtain the **5th** of the triad in example **#2** (i.e. the note **E#**). We recall from the text accompanying **Fig. 3.3.** that **raising the 5th of a major triad by half-step creates an augmented triad**. Therefore the triad in example **#2** is an **A augmented triad** (in root position).

Figure 3.16. Triad recognition example #3

The internal intervals in this triad look different to the previous examples - now we have a **third** interval on top of a **fourth** interval. This is an indication of a **second inversion triad** (see text accompanying **Fig. 3.10.**). We also recall that the **root** of a second inversion triad is the **middle note** of the triad (which is also the higher note of the fourth interval present). The middle note of this second inversion triad is **C#**, which is therefore the **root** of this triad.

Again we then build a major triad from the root, and see how this compares to the triad in the example. The **C# major** triad built in this case, consists of the notes **C#**, **E#** and **G#**, which is not quite the same as the triad in example **#3** above (which consists of the notes **C#**, **E** and **G** if we consider the notes in the sequence of root, 3rd and then 5th). In comparing the **C# major** triad to the triad in example **#3**, we find that the **3rd** of the **C# major** triad (**E#**) has been **lowered by half-step** to obtain the **3rd** of the triad in example **#3** (i.e. the note **E**, which is the top note of this second inversion triad), and the **5th** of the **C# major** triad (**G#**) has also been **lowered by half-step** to obtain the **5th** of the triad in example **#3** (i.e. the note **G**, which is the bottom note of this second inversion triad). We recall from the text accompanying **Fig. 3.4.** that **lowering the 3rd and 5th of a major triad by half-step creates a diminished triad**. Therefore the triad in example **#3** is a **C# diminished triad** (in second inversion).

Triad recognition method and examples (contd)

Figure 3.17. Triad recognition example #4

(Again note that bass clef has been used here).

The internal intervals in this triad again look different to the previous examples - now we have a **fourth** interval on top of a **third** interval. This is an indication of a **first inversion triad** (see text accompanying **Fig. 3.10.**). We also recall that the **root** of a first inversion triad is the **top note** of the triad (which again is also the higher note of the fourth interval present). The top note of this first inversion triad is **Bb**, which is therefore the **root** of this triad.

Again we then build a major triad from the root, and see how this compares to the triad in the example. The **Bb major** triad built in this case, consists of the notes **Bb**, **D** and **F**, which is the same as the triad in example #4 above (which also consists of the notes **Bb**, **D** and **F** if we consider the notes in the sequence of root, 3rd and then 5th). Therefore the triad in example **#4** is a **Bb major triad** (in first inversion).

We can summarize the triad recognition process as follows:-

- first of all, figure out if the triad is in **root position**, **first inversion** or **second inversion**
  - the triad is in **root position** if the notes on the staff are all consecutive 'line' or 'space' notes (indicating two consecutive **third** intervals)
  - the triad is in **first inversion** if the triad consists of a **fourth** interval on top of a **third** interval
  - the triad is in **second inversion** if the triad consists of a **third** interval on top of a **fourth** interval
- then determine the **root** of the triad, which is
  - the **bottom** note of a **root position** triad
  - the **top** note of a **first inversion** triad
  - the **middle** note of a **second inversion** triad
- then build a **major triad** from this root, and compare it to the triad being recognized
  - if the triads are same, then of course the triad being recognized is **major**
  - if the triad being recognized has a **third lowered by half-step** in comparison to the major triad, then this triad is **minor**
  - if the triad being recognized has a **fifth raised by half-step** in comparison to the major triad, then this triad is **augmented**
  - if the triad being recognized has a **third and fifth lowered by half-step** in comparison to the major triad, then this triad is **diminished**.

Chapter Three Workbook Questions

1. *Root position triad spelling*

Write the notes on the staff corresponding to the following major triad chord symbols:-

1.
2.
3.
4.

C
A♭
E
F

5.
6.
7.
8.

G
E♭
A
G♭

Write the notes on the staff corresponding to the following minor triad chord symbols:-

9.
10.
11.
12.

Emi
C♯mi
Bmi
Fmi

13.
14.
15.
16.

G♭mi
Ami
D♯mi
Gmi

1. _Root position triad spelling (contd)_

Write the notes on the staff corresponding to the following augmented triad chord symbols:-

17.   18.   19.   20.

21.   22.   23.   24.

Write the notes on the staff corresponding to the following diminished triad chord symbols:-

25.   26.   27.   28.

29.   30.   31.   32.

2. *Root position triad recognition*

This section contains a mixture of (root-position) major, minor, augmented and diminished triads. Write the chord symbol above the staff for each question:-

33.   34.   35.   36.

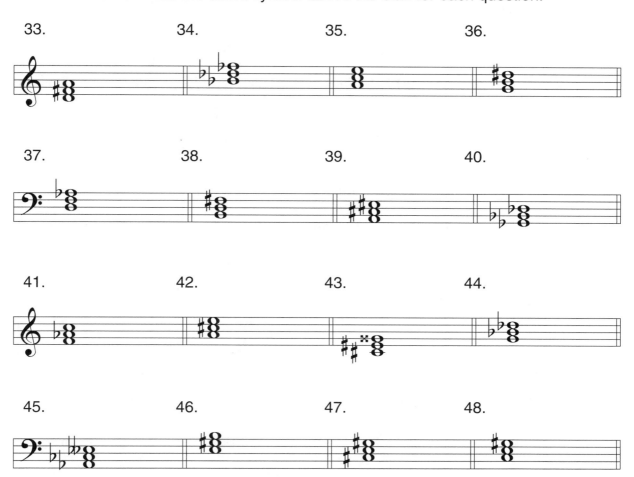

3. *Inverted triad spelling*

Write the notes on the staff corresponding to the following triad chord symbols and requested inversions. (For example, for question #49 you need to spell a second inversion D minor triad).

Questions 49 - 56 consist of major and minor triads only.

49. *2nd inversion*	50. *1st inversion*	51. *2nd inversion*	52. *1st inversion*
Dmi	F♯	B♭mi	C

53. *1st inversion*	54. *2nd inversion*	55. *1st inversion*	56. *1st inversion*
E♭	D♭mi	B	C♯mi

Questions 57 - 64 now include major, minor, augmented and diminished triads.

57. *2nd inversion*	58. *2nd inversion*	59. *2nd inversion*	60. *1st inversion*
A°	B♭	D♭+	G♯mi

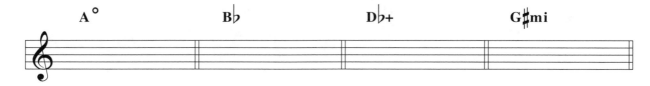

61. *2nd inversion*	62. *1st inversion*	63. *2nd inversion*	64. *1st inversion*
D	C♯°	Bmi	G♭+

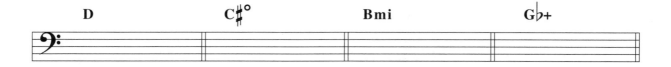

4.   *Inverted triad recognition*

This section contains a mixture of major, minor, augmented and diminished triads. Each triad may be in root position, 1st inversion or 2nd inversion. You are to write the chord symbol above the staff for each question.

Remember that a **root position** triad will look like a **3rd** interval on top of another **3rd** interval, a **1st inversion** triad will look like a **4th** interval on top of a **3rd** interval, and a **2nd inversion** triad will look like a **3rd** interval on top of a **4th** interval. For inverted triads, the highest note in the **4th** interval is the actual root of the triad (and is therefore the note name used in the chord symbol).

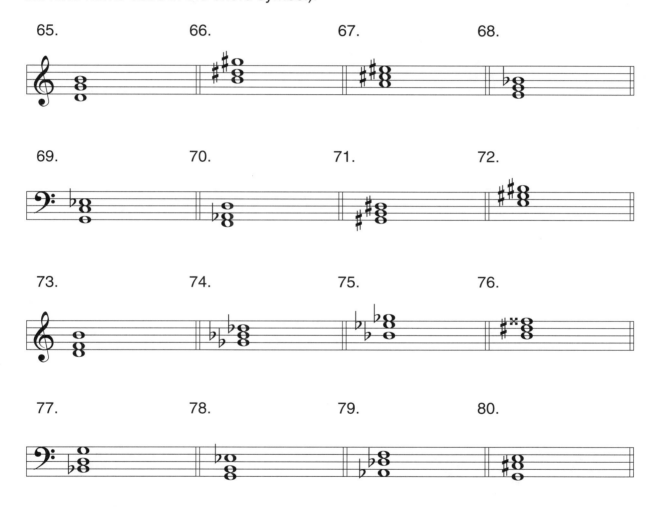

Chapter Three Workbook Answers

1. *Root position triad spelling - answers*

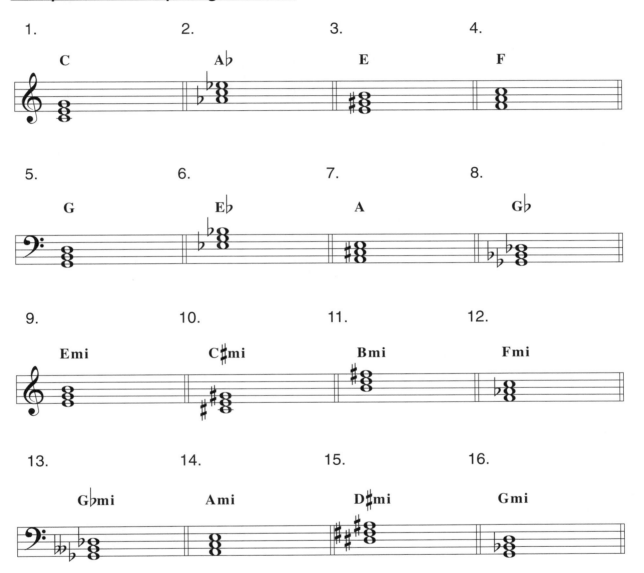

1. *Root position triad spelling - answers (contd)*

2. *Root position triad recognition - answers*

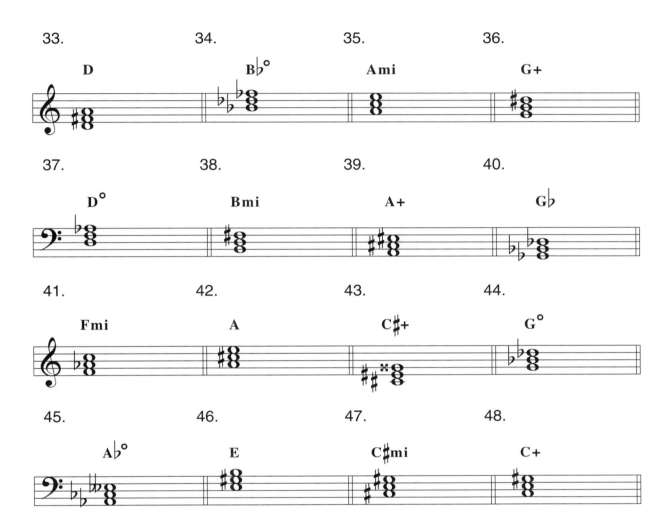

3. *Inverted triad spelling - answers*

49. *2nd inversion*   50. *1st inversion*   51. *2nd inversion*   52. *1st inversion*

53. *1st inversion*   54. *2nd inversion*   55. *1st inversion*   56. *1st inversion*

57. *2nd inversion*   58. *2nd inversion*   59. *2nd inversion*   60. *1st inversion*

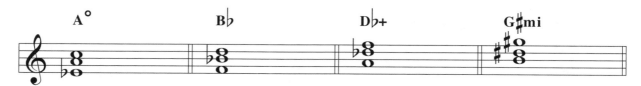

61. *2nd inversion*   62. *1st inversion*   63. *2nd inversion*   64. *1st inversion*

4. *Inverted triad recognition - answers*

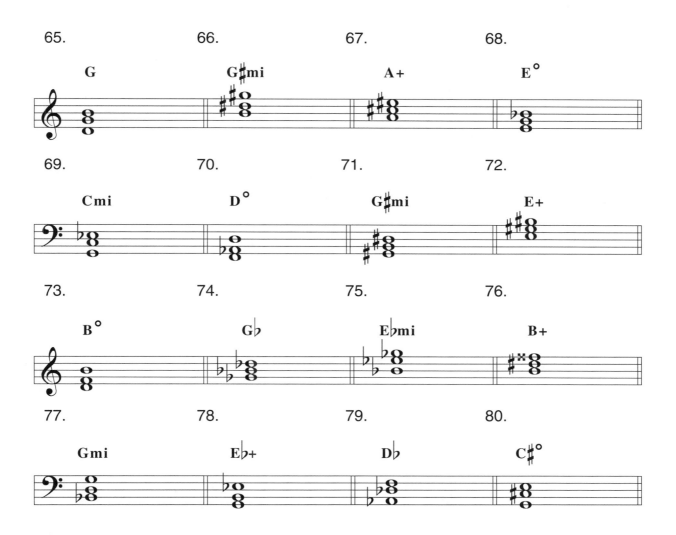

Diatonic triads

Introduction

We have already used the term **diatonic** to apply to notes and/or intervals which are **contained within the major scale**, during our analysis of intervals in **Chapter 2**. When deriving triads in **Chapter 3**, we further realized that three types of triad (major, minor and diminished) could also be found within the major scale. Triads which are wholly contained within a major scale (i.e. can be 'built from' some degree of a major scale) are termed **diatonic triads**.

Building diatonic triads from each degree of a major scale

We will now go through a **C major scale** and build triads from each degree of the scale (while staying within the major scale restriction) to see which triad qualities (i.e. major, minor etc) are produced in each case:-

Figure 4.1. Triad built from the 1st degree of the C major scale (C major)

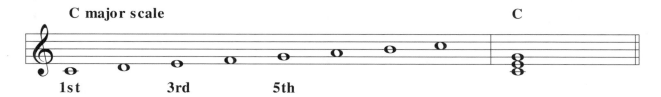

We have already seen in **Fig. 3.7.** that a **major** triad is built from the **1st** degree of the major scale (i.e. when we take the 1st, 3rd and 5th degrees of the scale). Relating back to the derivation of the major triad by **intervals** in **Fig. 3.1.**, we note that the interval between **C** and **E** (the **root** and **3rd** of the triad) is a **major 3rd**, and that the interval between **C** and **G** (the **root** and **5th** of the triad) is a **perfect 5th**.

Figure 4.2. Triad built from the 2nd degree of the C major scale (D minor)

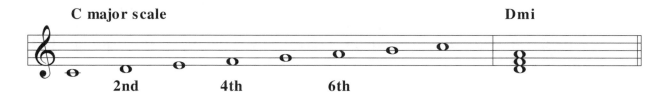

Building diatonic triads from each degree of a major scale (contd)

Regarding **Fig. 4.2.** on the previous page, we have already seen in **Fig. 3.8.** that a **minor** triad is built from the **2nd** degree of the major scale (i.e. when we take the 2nd, 4th and 6th degrees of the scale). Relating back to the derivation of the minor triad by **intervals** in **Fig. 3.2.**, we note that the interval between **D** and **F** (the **root** and **3rd** of the triad) is a **minor 3rd**, and that the interval between **D** and **A** (the **root** and **5th** of the triad) is a **perfect 5th**.

Figure 4.3. Triad built from the 3rd degree of the C major scale (E minor)

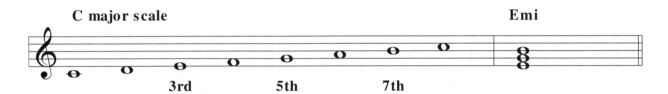

In the above example we see that a **minor** triad is now also built from the **3rd** degree of the major scale (i.e. when we take the 3rd, 5th and 7th degrees of the scale). Again considering the minor triad **intervals** in **Fig. 3.2.**, we note that the interval between **E** and **G** (the **root** and **3rd** of the triad) is a **minor 3rd**, and that the interval between **E** and **B** (the **root** and **5th** of the triad) is a **perfect 5th**.

Figure 4.4. Triad built from the 4th degree of the C major scale (F major)

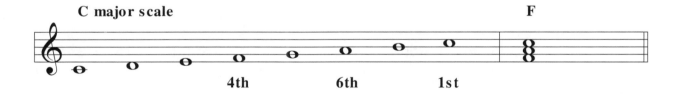

In the above example we see that a **major** triad is now also built from the **4th** degree of the major scale (i.e. when we take the 4th, 6th and 1st degrees of the scale). Again considering the major triad **intervals** in **Fig. 3.1.**, we note that the interval between **F** and **A** (the **root** and **3rd** of the triad) is a **major 3rd**, and that the interval between **F** and **C** (the **root** and **5th** of the triad) is a **perfect 5th**.

Building diatonic triads from each degree of a major scale (contd)

Figure 4.5. Triad built from the 5th degree of the C major scale (G major)

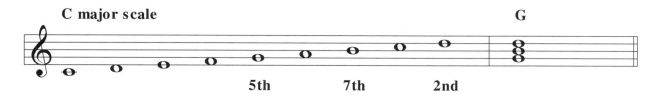

In the above example we see that a **major** triad is now also built from the **5th** degree of the major scale (i.e. when we take the 5th, 7th and 2nd degrees of the scale). Again considering the major triad **intervals** in **Fig. 3.1.**, we note that the interval between **G** and **B** (the **root** and **3rd** of the triad) is a **major 3rd**, and that the interval between **G** and **D** (the **root** and **5th** of the triad) is a **perfect 5th**.

Figure 4.6. Triad built from the 6th degree of the C major scale (A minor)

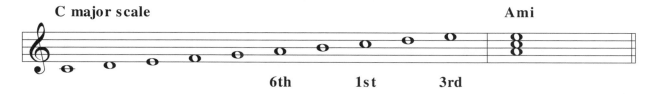

In the above example we see that a **minor** triad is now also built from the **6th** degree of the major scale (i.e. when we take the 6th, 1st and 3rd degrees of the scale). Again considering the minor triad **intervals** in **Fig. 3.2.**, we note that the interval between **A** and **C** (the **root** and **3rd** of the triad) is a **minor 3rd**, and that the interval between **A** and **E** (the **root** and **5th** of the triad) is a **perfect 5th**.

Figure 4.7. Triad built from the 7th degree of the C major scale (B diminished)

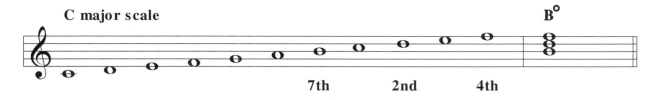

We have already seen in **Fig. 3.9.** that a **diminished** triad is built from the **7th** degree of the major scale (i.e. when we take the 7th, 2nd and 4th degrees of the scale). Relating back to the derivation of the diminished triad by **intervals** in **Fig. 3.4.**, we note that the interval between **B** and **D** (the **root** and **3rd** of the triad) is a **minor 3rd**, and that the interval between **B** and **F** (the **root** and **5th** of the triad) is a **diminished 5th**.

Building diatonic triads from each degree of a major scale (contd)

We can summarize these **diatonic triad qualities** as follows:-

- The triad built from the *1st* degree of a major scale is always *major*.
- The triad built from the *2nd* degree of a major scale is always *minor*.
- The triad built from the *3rd* degree of a major scale is always *minor*.
- The triad built from the *4th* degree of a major scale is always *major*.
- The triad built from the *5th* degree of a major scale is always *major*.
- The triad built from the *6th* degree of a major scale is always *minor*.
- The triad built from the *7th* degree of a major scale is always *diminished*.

Of course all of the previous triad examples were contained within a **C major** scale. It is important to realize that **all of these diatonic triad qualities are simply the result of the intervals already present in the major scale** (first derived in **Fig. 1.42.**) - in other words we build the triads within the major scale restriction, and only afterwards do we then **analyze the triad qualities that the scale has 'given back to us'**. This is consistent with an important principle, namely that it is the **scale that came first** and that the triads are simply **incomplete representations of the scale**.

*(Diatonic triads in all keys are listed in **Appendix Three** at the back of this book).*

Triad plurality

In this context plurality is defined as a chord occurring in **more than one major scale**. If the same **triad quality** can be built from **more than one place** in the major scale, then it follows that a **particular triad of that quality** will occur in more than one major scale. This is perhaps best seen by working through some examples! We see that the **major** triad in the above table, can be built from the **1st**, **4th** and **5th** degrees of a major scale. Therefore a particular major triad (let's say a **C major** triad) must occur from:-

- the **1st** degree of a major scale,
- the **4th** degree of another major scale, and
- the **5th** degree of yet another major scale.

To establish the major scales containing the **C major** triad, you would therefore need to figure out the major scales which contained the note **C** as their **1st**, **4th** and **5th** degrees i.e.:-

- which major scale do I know that contains the note **C** as its **1st** degree?
- which major scale do I know that contains the note **C** as its **4th** degree?
- which major scale do I know that contains the note **C** as its **5th** degree?

Triad plurality (contd)

To answer these questions, we need to use our knowledge of the **intervals present within the major scale** as learned in **Chapter 1**. (Being able to determine the major scale which contains a certain note as its 2nd, 3rd, 4th, 5th, 6th or 7th degree, is an important skill - not only do we need it here to figure out triad 'plurality', but we will also need it in **Chapter 5** when establishing the 'relative major scale' of a mode - more about this later)!

Make sure you **don't fall into the trap of just counting up or down the music alphabet** from the given note, to obtain the tonic of the required major scale - this just gives you a note lettername - you will frequently need to further qualify this (i.e. with a sharp or flat) to get the required major scale tonic. **There is no substitute for figuring this out by intervals** (i.e. whole-steps and half-steps), while remembering that all major scales use consecutive letternames in the music alphabet.

We'll now answer the questions at the bottom of the previous page using this process. (The major scale which contains **C** as its **1st** degree is of course **C major**)! Now we'll figure out which major scale contains **C** as its **4th** degree:-

Figure 4.8. Finding out which major scale contains C as its 4th degree - stage 1

We recall that our first derivations of the major scale by interval (**Figs. 1.42., 1.44., 1.46.** etc) all **contained the above interval sequence** (i.e. whole-step, whole-step, half-step, whole-step, whole-step, whole-step and half-step) and that each scale was constructed **beginning and ending on the tonic** or 1st degree. After placing the given note (in this case **C**) within the above interval sequence (in this case between the first half-step and the following whole-step, as we have been given the 4th degree of the scale), we then either **work up or down** (towards the tonic at either end of the scale) using the **correct intervals** and **consecutive letternames in the music alphabet**.

The above placement of the note **C** is a little nearer the left-hand end of the scale (as it is the **4th** degree), so in this case we'll work **downwards** (i.e. to the left) to derive the tonic or **1st** degree of the scale. The note immediately to the left of **C** will use the lettername of **B**, and needs to be a **half-step** lower than **C**. As the note **B** is already a **half-step** lower than **C**, this note needs no further qualification (see **Stage 2** on following page):-

103

Triad plurality (contd)

Figure 4.9. Finding out which major scale contains C as its 4th degree - stage 2

Now the note immediately to the left of **B** will use the lettername of **A**, and needs to be a **whole-step** lower than **B**. As the note **A** is already a **whole-step** lower than **B**, this note again needs no further qualification, as follows:-

Figure 4.10. Finding out which major scale contains C as its 4th degree - stage 3

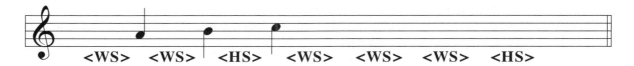

Now the note immediately to the left of **A** is the **tonic of the major scale** that we need. This note will use the lettername of **G**, and needs to be a **whole-step** lower than **A**. As the note **G** is already a **whole-step** lower than **A**, this note again needs no further qualification, as follows:-

Figure 4.11. Finding out which major scale contains C as its 4th degree - stage 4

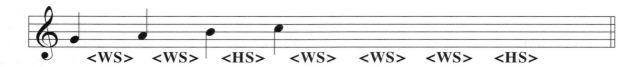

So we conclude that the **G major scale contains the note C as its 4th degree.**

Now looking at the bottom question on **p102**, we will find the major scale which contains **C** as its **5th** degree. First we will again place the note **C** within the **major scale interval pattern**:-

Figure 4.12. Finding out which major scale contains C as its 5th degree - stage 1

Triad plurality (contd)

The above placement of the note **C** in the example at the bottom of the previous page, is a little nearer the right-hand end of the scale (as it is the **5th** degree), so in this case we'll work **upwards** (i.e. to the right) to derive the tonic or **1st** degree of the scale. The note immediately to the right of **C** will use the lettername of **D**, and needs to be a **whole-step** higher than **C**. As the note **D** is already a **whole-step** higher than **C**, this note needs no further qualification:-

Figure 4.13. Finding out which major scale contains C as its 5th degree - stage 2

Now the note immediately to the right of **D** will use the lettername of **E**, and needs to be a **whole-step** higher than **D**. As the note **E** is already a **whole-step** higher than **D**, this note again needs no further qualification, as follows:-

Figure 4.14. Finding out which major scale contains C as its 5th degree - stage 3

Now the note immediately to the right of **E** is the **tonic of the major scale** that we need. This note will use the lettername of **F**, and needs to be a **half-step** higher than **E**. As the note **F** is already a **half-step** higher than **E**, this note again needs no further qualification, as follows:-

Figure 4.15. Finding out which major scale contains C as its 5th degree - stage 4

So we conclude that the **F major scale contains the note C as its 5th degree**.

Triad plurality (contd)

Looking back at our initial comments on the plurality of the **C major** triad at the bottom of **p102**, and now factoring in the analysis of the required major scales containing the note **C**, we can now summarize that a **C major** triad occurs from:-

- the **1st** degree of a major scale - this is the **C major** scale.
- the **4th** degree of a major scale - this is the **G major** scale.
- the **5th** degree of a major scale - this is the **F major** scale.

Now we'll look at these three occurrences of the **C major** triad, within the diatonic triads built from the **C major**, **G major** and **F major** scales:-

Figure 4.16. C major triad - built from the 1st degree of a C major scale

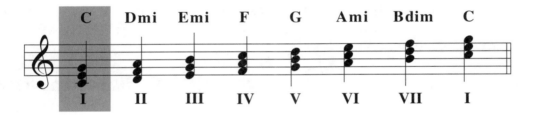

Figure 4.17. C major triad - built from the 4th degree of a G major scale

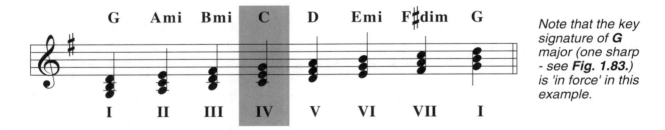

*Note that the key signature of **G** major (one sharp - see **Fig. 1.83.**) is 'in force' in this example.*

Figure 4.18. C major triad - built from the 5th degree of an F major scale

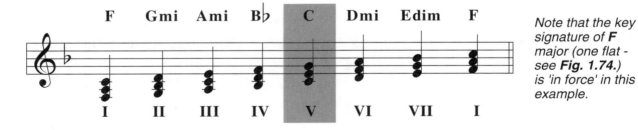

*Note that the key signature of **F** major (one flat - see **Fig. 1.74.**) is 'in force' in this example.*

Triad plurality (contd)

Now we'll look at a plurality example involving minor triads. We have seen that the **minor** triad can be built from the **2nd**, **3rd** and **6th** degrees of a major scale (review summary at the top of **p102** as necessary). Therefore a particular minor triad (let's say a **D minor** triad) must occur from:-

- the **2nd** degree of a major scale,
- the **3rd** degree of another major scale, and
- the **6th** degree of yet another major scale.

To establish the major scales containing the **D minor** triad, you would therefore need to figure out the major scales which contained the note **D** as their **2nd**, **3rd** and **6th** degrees i.e.:-

- which major scale do I know that contains the note **D** as its **2nd** degree?
- which major scale do I know that contains the note **D** as its **3rd** degree?
- which major scale do I know that contains the note **D** as its **6th** degree?

Again we'll use our '**major scale interval**' method to answer these questions, starting with the major scale containing the note **D** as its **2nd** degree - first we again place the note **D** within the **major scale interval pattern**:-

Figure 4.19. Finding out which major scale contains D as its 2nd degree - stage 1

The above placement of the note **D** is nearer the left-hand end of the scale (as it is the **2nd** degree), so in this case we'll work **downwards** (i.e. to the left) to derive the tonic or **1st** degree of the scale. The note immediately to the left of **D** is the **tonic of the major scale** that we need. This note will use the lettername of **C**, and needs to be a **whole-step** lower than **D**. As the note **C** is already a **whole-step** lower than **D**, this note needs no further qualification:-

Figure 4.20. Finding out which major scale contains D as its 2nd degree - stage 2

So we conclude that the **C major scale contains the note D as its 2nd degree**.

Triad plurality (contd)

Now we will establish which major scale contains the note **D** as its **3rd** degree:-

Figure 4.21. Finding out which major scale contains D as its 3rd degree - stage 1

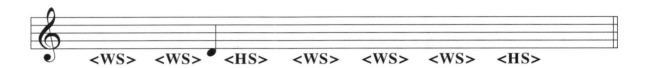

The above placement of the note **D** is again nearer the left-hand end of the scale (as it is the **3rd** degree), so in this case we'll again work **downwards** (i.e. to the left) to derive the tonic or **1st** degree of the scale. The note immediately to the left of **D** will use the lettername of **C**, and needs to be a **whole-step** lower than **D**. As the note **C** is already a **whole-step** lower than **D**, this note needs no further qualification, as follows:-

Figure 4.22. Finding out which major scale contains D as its 3rd degree - stage 2

Now the note immediately to the left of **C** is the **tonic of the major scale** that we need. This note will use the lettername of **B**, and needs to be a **whole-step** lower than **C**. However, **the note B is only a half-step lower than C**, and so we need to **flat the B** (to **Bb**) to obtain the tonic of the major scale, as follows:-

Figure 4.23. Finding out which major scale contains D as its 3rd degree - stage 3

So we conclude that the **Bb major scale contains the note D as its 3rd degree**.

Triad plurality (contd)

Finally we will establish which major scale contains the note **D** as its **6th** degree:-

Figure 4.24. Finding out which major scale contains D as its 6th degree - stage 1

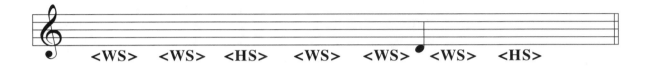

The above placement of the note **D** is now nearer the right-hand end of the scale (as it is the **6th** degree), so in this case we'll work **upwards** (i.e. to the right) to derive the tonic or **1st** degree of the scale. The note immediately to the right of **D** will use the lettername of **E**, and needs to be a **whole-step** higher than **D**. As the note **E** is already a **whole-step** higher than **D**, this note needs no further qualification, as follows:-

Figure 4.25. Finding out which major scale contains D as its 6th degree - stage 2

Now the note immediately to the right of **E** is the **tonic of the major scale** that we need. This note will use the lettername of **F**, and needs to be a **half-step** higher than **E**. As the note **F** is already a **half-step** higher than **E**, this note again needs no further qualification, as follows:-

Figure 4.26. Finding out which major scale contains D as its 6th degree - stage 3

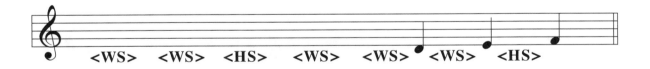

So we conclude that the **F major scale contains the note D as its 6th degree**.

Triad plurality (contd)

Looking back at our initial comments on the plurality of the **D minor** triad at the top of **p107**, and now factoring in the analysis of the required major scales containing the note **D**, we can now summarize that a **D minor** triad occurs from:-

- the **2nd** degree of a major scale - this is the **C major** scale.
- the **3rd** degree of a major scale - this is the **Bb major** scale.
- the **6th** degree of a major scale - this is the **F major** scale.

Now we'll look at these three occurrences of the **D minor** triad, within the diatonic triads built from the **C major**, **Bb major** and **F major** scales:-

Figure 4.27. D minor triad - built from the 2nd degree of a C major scale

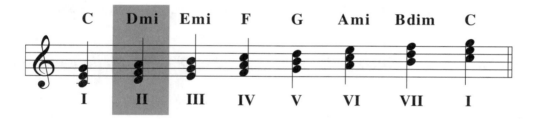

Figure 4.28. D minor triad - built from the 3rd degree of a Bb major scale

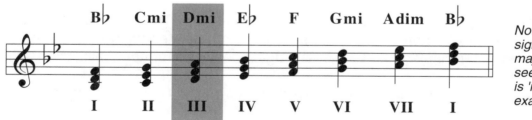

Note that the key signature of **Bb** major (two flats - see **Fig. 1.76.**) is 'in force' in this example.

Figure 4.29. D minor triad - built from the 6th degree of an F major scale

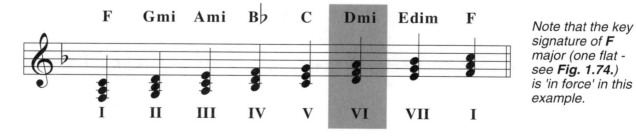

Note that the key signature of **F** major (one flat - see **Fig. 1.74.**) is 'in force' in this example.

Triad plurality (contd)

Note that we have not included an example of the **diminished** triad in these plurality examples. That is because the diminished triad only occurs from the 7th degree of the major scale, and will therefore never be found within (i.e. diatonic to) more than one major scale.

We can finally summarize these triad plurality relationships as follows:-

- Any **major** triad can be built from the **1st**, **4th** and **5th** degrees of three different major scales respectively.
- Any **minor** triad can be built from the **2nd**, **3rd** and **6th** degrees of three different major scales respectively.
- Any **diminished** triad can only be built from the **7th** degree of one major scale.

Diatonic triad progressions

We will now look at some diatonic triad progression examples. Of course it is important that you are able to derive diatonic chords and chord symbols from all the scale degrees (**I - VII**) in any key. As we have seen in the previous examples, all diatonic triad chord symbols consist of **two** components:-

- the **root** of the chord - this is the major scale degree from which the chord is built
- the chord **suffix** (the part of the chord symbol immediately following the root):-
    - no suffix at all for **major** triads (built from the **1st**, **4th** and **5th** degrees)
    - 'mi' suffix used for **minor** triads (built from the **2nd**, **3rd** and **6th** degrees)
    - '**o**' or '**dim**' suffix used for **diminished** triads (built from the **7th** degree).

Let's say we wanted to create the diatonic triads and chord symbols for a **I - IV - V** progression (i.e. triads built from the **1st**, **4th** and **5th** degrees) in **A major**. First we would spell the **A major** scale to determine that the 1st, 4th and 5th degrees were the notes **A**, **D** and **E** respectively. As **major triads** are built from these scale degrees, the chord symbols would consist of these note names only i.e. no chord suffixes are needed. We would then build triads on the staff from each of these scale degrees as follows:-

Figure 4.30. I - IV - V diatonic triad progression in A major

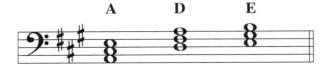

Note that the key signature of ***A*** *major (three sharps - see* ***Fig. 1.86.****) is 'in force' in this example, and that* ***bass clef*** *has been used.*

Diatonic triad progressions (contd)

The **I - IV - V** progression is an often used triad chord sequence, particularly in various forms of pop music - it is especially handy to have these triads **learned and memorized in every key!**

Now we will create the diatonic triads and chord symbols for a **II - V - I** progression (i.e. triads built from the **2nd**, **5th** and **1st** degrees) in **Eb major**. Again we would spell the **Eb major** scale to determine that the 2nd, 5th and 1st degrees were the notes **F**, **Bb** and **Eb** respectively. Again **major triads** are built from the 5th and 1st scale degrees, and so these chord symbols would consist of these note names only, without suffixes. However a **minor** triad is built from the **2nd** degree, and so we would use the suffix '**mi**' in this chord symbol. We would then build triads on the staff from each of these scale degrees as follows:-

Figure 4.31. II - V - I diatonic triad progression in Eb major

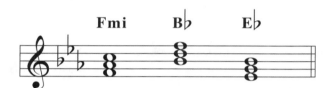

*Note that the key signature of **Eb** major (three flats - see **Fig. 1.77.**) is 'in force' in this example.*

(The **II - V - I** progression is another often-used sequence, particularly when using **four-part chords** - more about this in **Chapter 7** and in *Contemporary Music Theory Level 2*)!

Analyzing triad progressions to determine the major key being used

We will now look at some triad chord progressions to determine **which major key is being used** i.e. which major scale all of the triads are **found in**, or 'diatonic to'. To do this we need to apply the '**triad plurality**' rules as summarized at the top of **p111**. Initially we will look at each chord in the progression, to determine which keys the chord could belong to. At the end of this process, we will then determine if there is one key 'in common' among all of the possibilities. Again this is best demonstrated by working through some examples, as follows:-

Figure 4.32. Triad progression analysis example #1

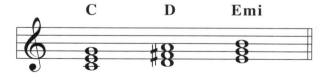

*Note that there is now **no key signature in force** - any necessary accidentals are supplied directly on the staff.*

Analyzing triad progressions to determine the major key being used (contd)

We will now analyze each triad to determine which keys it could belong to, as follows:-

- **C major** - We have already seen in **p103-106** (and specifically in **Figs. 4.16. - 4.18.**) that a **C major triad** can be built from:-
  - the **1st** degree of a **C major** scale
  - the **4th** degree of a **G major** scale
  - the **5th** degree of an **F major** scale.

- **D major** - Using the same process as above, but applied to a **D major triad**, we see that this triad can be built from:-
  - the **1st** degree of a **D major** scale
  - the **4th** degree of an **A major** scale
  - the **5th** degree of a **G major** scale.

- **E minor** - Using the same process as outlined for the **D minor** triad in **p107-110** (and **Figs. 4.27. - 4.29.**), but applied to an **E minor triad**, we see that this triad can be built from:-
  - the **2nd** degree of a **D major** scale
  - the **3rd** degree of a **C major** scale
  - the **6th** degree of a **G major** scale.

Now we look at these options to see if there is a key 'in common' between the triads:-

Figure 4.33. Triad progression analysis example #1 - with major key options

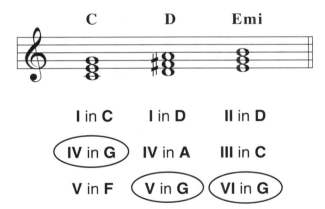

*Note that all of the diatonic options above have been listed under each triad - the one key in common throughout is the **key of G** - so we conclude that the progression constitutes a **IV - V - VI** sequence in **G major**.*

As you look at further triad progressions, you will learn to recognize certain diatonic relationships more quickly, as an alternative to the rather 'step-by-step' method outlined above. For example, reviewing the diatonic triad qualities at the top of **p102**, we see that the only place that two major triads occur with roots one scale-step apart, is from the **4th** and **5th** degrees of the major scale. We could conclude therefore that the above **C** and **D** major triads (with roots a scale-step apart i.e. using consecutive letternames) are a **IV** and **V** in **G major**.

Analyzing triad progressions to determine the major key being used (contd)

Figure 4.34. Triad progression analysis example #2

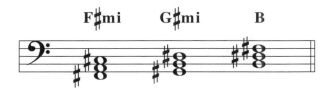

- **F# minor** - We see that this minor triad can be built from:-
    - the **2nd** degree of an **E major** scale
    - the **3rd** degree of a **D major** scale
    - the **6th** degree of an **A major** scale.
- **G# minor** - We see that this minor triad can be built from:-
    - the **2nd** degree of an **F# major** scale
    - the **3rd** degree of an **E major** scale
    - the **6th** degree of a **B major** scale.
- **B major** - We see that this major triad can be built from:-
    - the **1st** degree of a **B major** scale
    - the **4th** degree of an **F# major** scale
    - the **5th** degree of an **E major** scale.

Again we look at these options to see if there is a key 'in common' between the triads:-

Figure 4.35. Triad progression analysis example #2 - with major key options

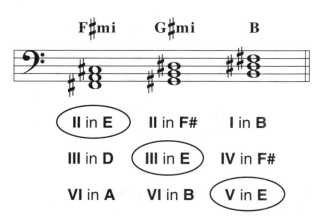

*Again all of the diatonic options above have been listed under each triad - the one key in common throughout is the **key of E** - so we conclude that the progression constitutes a* **II - III - V** *sequence in* **E major**.

Again in reviewing the diatonic triad qualities at the top of **p102**, we see that the only place that two minor triads occur with roots one scale-step apart, is from the **2nd** and **3rd** degrees of the major scale. We could conclude therefore that the above **F#mi** and **G#mi** triads (with roots a scale-step apart i.e. using consecutive letternames) are a **II** and **III** in **E major**.

Chapter Four Workbook Questions

1. *Writing diatonic triads for specified keys*

Write the key signatures, followed by all of the diatonic triads on the staff (in root position), and corresponding chord symbols above the staff, for the following major keys:-

1. *Key of G major*

2. *Key of Bb major*

3. *Key of F major*

4. *Key of D major*

5. *Key of B major*

1. **_Writing diatonic triads for specified keys (contd)_**

6. *Key of Ab major*

7. *Key of Eb major*

8. *Key of E major*

9. *Key of F# major*

10. *Key of Db major*

2. _Writing diatonic triads for specified progressions_

Write the key signatures, followed by the diatonic triads on the staff (in root position) and corresponding chord symbols above the staff, for the following diatonic triad progressions.

You are to write a **I - IV - V** diatonic triad progression in the keys requested, for questions 11 - 14. For example, in the key of **G** you would write the G major key signature followed by the notes and chord symbols for the diatonic triads **G major**, **C major** and **D major**.

11.   _Key of F Major_   12.   _Key of D Major_

13.   _Key of Ab Major_   14.   _Key of E Major_

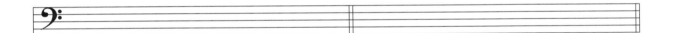

You are to write a **II - V - I** diatonic triad progression in the keys requested, for questions 15 - 18. For example, in the key of **B** you would write the B major key signature followed by the notes and chord symbols for the diatonic triads **C# minor**, **F# major** and **B major**.

15.   _Key of G Major_   16.   _Key of Bb Major_

17.   _Key of Db Major_   18.   _Key of A Major_

117

2.   *Writing diatonic triads for specified progressions (contd)*

You are to write a *I - II - III - IV* diatonic triad progression in the keys requested, for questions 19 - 22. For example, in the key of *F* you would write the F major key signature followed by the notes and chord symbols for the diatonic triads *F major*, *G minor*, *A minor* and *Bb major*.

19.   *Key of Eb Major*   20.   *Key of B Major*

21.   *Key of Gb Major*   22.   *Key of E Major*

3.   *Diatonic triad key analysis*

You are to write chord symbols above the staff, and then determine the major key, for each of the following diatonic triad progressions. Remember that:-
- the major triad can occur from the 1st, 4th, or 5th degrees of a major key
- the minor triad can occur from the 2nd, 3rd, or 6th degrees of a major key
- the diminished triad can only occur from the 7th degree of a major key.

23.   *Key of _____*   24.   *Key of _____*

3. *Diatonic triad key analysis (contd)*

25. *Key of* _____

26. *Key of* _____

27. *Key of* _____

28. *Key of* _____

29. *Key of* _____

30. *Key of* _____

Chapter Four Workbook Answers

1. Writing diatonic triads for specified keys - answers

1. *Key of G major*

2. *Key of Bb major*

3. *Key of F major*

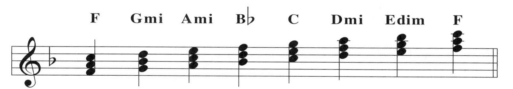

4. *Key of D major*

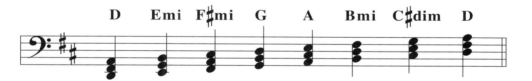

5. *Key of B major*

1. **_Writing diatonic triads for specified keys - answers (contd)_**

6.   _Key of Ab major_

7.   _Key of Eb major_

8.   _Key of E major_

9.   _Key of F# major_

10.   _Key of Db major_

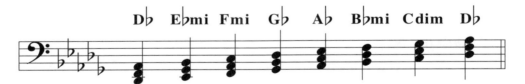

2. **_Writing diatonic triads for specified progressions - answers_**

(***I - IV - V*** diatonic triad progressions)

11.   *Key of F Major*   12.   *Key of D Major*

13.   *Key of Ab Major*   14.   *Key of E Major*

(***II - V - I*** diatonic triad progressions)

15.   *Key of G Major*   16.   *Key of Bb Major*

17.   *Key of Db Major*   18.   *Key of A Major*

2. **_Writing diatonic triads for specified progressions - answers (contd)_**

(**_I - II - III - IV_** diatonic triad progressions)

19. *Key of Eb Major*   20. *Key of B Major*

21. *Key of Gb Major*   22. *Key of E Major*

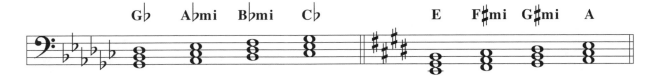

3. **_Diatonic triad key analysis - answers_**

23. *Key of E Major*   24. *Key of Eb Major*

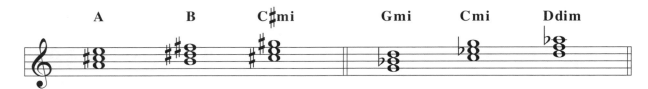

25. *Key of G Major*   26. *Key of C Major*

3. *Diatonic triad key analysis - answers (contd)*

27. *Key of Bb Major*   28. *Key of D Major*

29. *Key of E Major*   30. *Key of Ab Major*

Modal scales

Introduction

We will now begin our study of **modal scales** or '**modes**'. A modal scale can most conveniently be thought of as a **displaced version of an already existing scale**. The term 'displaced' here means that we are starting the scale from a point other than the normal tonic or starting scale degree. I believe that this is the central point to keep in mind when learning your 'modes' - unfortunately there are a number of music textbooks out there which list all the modal scales, without any attempt to indicate which scale has been displaced to create the mode in question - so the students often think that they have to learn a bunch of new scales! This of course is **not the case** at all - **modes are simply the result of taking an existing scale and starting it from a different note**.

There are a number of scales which can be displaced in this way, but by far the most commonly used scale is the **major scale** (first derived in **Chapter 1**). When the term 'mode' or 'modal scale' is used **without an indication of which scale is being displaced** to create the mode, then the assumption is that the **major scale** is being used. In particular the various modal 'descriptions' we will learn in this chapter (i.e. Dorian, Phrygian etc.) specifically relate to displaced versions of the major scale.

As we will see shortly the different modal scales have different **interval characteristics**, which will in turn facilitate their usage within different **musical styles**. Modal scales may also be considered as '**scale sources**' for the diatonic triads derived in **Chapter 3**.

Creating the modal scales by displacing the C major scale

We will now take a **C major** scale (first derived in **Fig. 1.42.**) and displace it to create the various modal scales. Any major scale starting from its **2nd** degree is referred to as a **Dorian mode**, and as the **2nd** degree of a **C major** scale is the note **D**, the following mode is therefore a **D Dorian** mode:-

Figure 5.1. D Dorian mode (C Major scale starting from its 2nd degree)

Creating the modal scales by displacing the C major scale (contd)

Note that the previous mode name of **D Dorian** has of course two components:-

- the **starting note** (in this case the note **D**)
- the **mode description** (in this case **Dorian** - i.e. major scale starting from its 2nd degree).

So - this mode name is telling us that we are using some major scale starting from its **2nd** degree, which is the note **D**. Relating back to our work on diatonic triads in **Chapter 4**, we saw that a **D minor** triad was also built from the 2nd degree of a C major scale (see **Fig. 4.2.**). We can therefore say that the **D Dorian** mode on the previous page, could be considered a **scale source** for this **D minor** diatonic triad, as the mode contains all of the notes needed in the triad, and both the mode and the triad share the same starting note (i.e. the note **D** in this case).

We have already mentioned that the different modal scales exhibit different **interval characteristics**. We recall from the original derivation of the major scale in **Fig. 1.42.** that the half-steps occurred between the **3rd** and **4th** degrees, and between the **7th** and **1st** (tonic) degrees (in a **C major** scale, between the notes **E** & **F**, and **B** & **C**). Of course these half-steps have now been displaced when creating the previous **D Dorian** mode - the half-step intervals in the scale are now between the **2nd** and **3rd** degrees (where the notes **E** & **F** are now located) and between the **6th** and **7th** degrees (where the notes **B** & **C** are now located).

The next mode to be discussed is **Phrygian**. Any major scale starting from its **3rd** degree is referred to as a **Phrygian mode**, and as the **3rd** degree of a **C major** scale is the note **E**, the following mode is therefore an **E Phrygian** mode:-

Figure 5.2. E Phrygian mode (C Major scale starting from its 3rd degree)

Again connecting this with our work on diatonic triads, we saw that an **E minor** triad was also built from the 3rd degree of a C major scale (see **Fig. 4.3.**). We can therefore say that the **E Phrygian** mode could be considered a **scale source** for this **E minor** diatonic triad, as the mode contains all of the notes needed in the triad, and both the mode and the triad share the same starting note (i.e. the note **E** in this case). The half-steps in the **Phrygian** mode are now located between the **1st** and **2nd** degrees, and between the **5th** and **6th** degrees.

Creating the modal scales by displacing the C major scale (contd)

The next mode to be discussed is **Lydian**. Any major scale starting from its **4th** degree is referred to as a **Lydian mode**, and as the **4th** degree of a **C major** scale is the note **F**, the following mode is therefore an **F Lydian** mode:-

Figure 5.3. F Lydian mode (C Major scale starting from its 4th degree)

Again connecting this with our work on diatonic triads, we saw that an **F major** triad was also built from the 4th degree of a C major scale (see **Fig. 4.4.**). We can therefore say that the **F Lydian** mode could be considered a **scale source** for this **F major** diatonic triad, as the mode contains all of the notes needed in the triad, and both the mode and the triad share the same starting note (i.e. the note **F** in this case). The half-steps in the **Lydian** mode are now located between the **4th** and **5th** degrees, and between the **7th** and **1st** degrees.

The next mode to be discussed is **Mixolydian**. Any major scale starting from its **5th** degree is referred to as a **Mixolydian mode**, and as the **5th** degree of a **C major** scale is the note **G**, the following mode is therefore a **G Mixolydian** mode:-

Figure 5.4. G Mixolydian mode (C Major scale starting from its 5th degree)

Again connecting this with our work on diatonic triads, we saw that a **G major** triad was also built from the 5th degree of a C major scale (see **Fig. 4.5.**). We can therefore say that the **G Mixolydian** mode could be considered a **scale source** for this **G major** diatonic triad, as the mode contains all of the notes needed in the triad, and both the mode and the triad share the same starting note (i.e. the note **G** in this case). The half-steps in the **Mixolydian** mode are now located between the **3rd** and **4th** degrees, and between the **6th** and **7th** degrees.

The next mode to be discussed is **Aeolian**. Any major scale starting from its **6th** degree is referred to as an **Aeolian mode**, and as the **6th** degree of a **C major** scale is the note **A**, the following mode is therefore an **A Aeolian** mode (on following page):-

Creating the modal scales by displacing the C major scale (contd)

Figure 5.5. A Aeolian mode (C Major scale starting from its 6th degree)

Again connecting this with our work on diatonic triads, we saw that an **A minor** triad was also built from the 6th degree of a C major scale (see **Fig. 4.6.**). We can therefore say that the **A Aeolian** mode could be considered a **scale source** for this **A minor** diatonic triad, as the mode contains all of the notes needed in the triad, and both the mode and the triad share the same starting note (i.e. the note **A** in this case). The half-steps in the **Aeolian** mode are now located between the **2nd** and **3rd** degrees, and between the **5th** and **6th** degrees. The **Aeolian** mode is also identical to a **natural minor** scale (more about this in **Chapter 8**).

The final mode derived by displacing a major scale is **Locrian**. Any major scale starting from its **7th** degree is referred to as a **Locrian mode**, and as the **7th** degree of a **C major** scale is the note **B**, the following mode is therefore a **B Locrian** mode:-

Figure 5.6. B Locrian mode (C Major scale starting from its 7th degree)

Again connecting this with our work on diatonic triads, we saw that a **B diminished** triad was also built from the 7th degree of a C major scale (see **Fig. 4.7.**). We can therefore say that the **B Locrian** mode could be considered a **scale source** for this **B diminished** diatonic triad, as the mode contains all of the notes needed in the triad, and both the mode and the triad share the same starting note (i.e. the note **B** in this case). The half-steps in the **Locrian** mode are now located between the **1st** and **2nd** degrees, and between the **4th** and **5th** degrees.

A final mode name we will be introduced to is **Ionian**. An Ionian mode is a major scale which has **not been displaced** i.e. the scale is starting from the normal tonic or 1st degree. For example, a **C major** scale beginning with the note **C** (as in **Fig. 1.42.**) could also be referred to as a **C Ionian** mode. Of course the half-step placements in this mode are the same as for the major scale, namely between the **3rd** and **4th** degrees, and between the **7th** and **1st** degrees, of the mode.

Relative major scale concept

We will now define a term known as '**relative major**'. The relative major scale of a mode, is the major scale which has been **displaced** to create the mode in question. I believe that it is especially important for players to be able to quickly determine the relative major scale of any mode. For example, jazz charts will sometimes indicate **modal scale** symbols instead of regular chord symbols - the most efficient way to approach this is to know which major scale is 'hiding in the mode' i.e. the **relative major** scale of the mode being used. (Contemporary pop styles also frequently make use of modal scale sources, and again the best approach is to know the relative major being used). As I mentioned in the introduction, this approach means that we don't have to learn and memorize all the modal scales in a separate and disconnected way - we just think of them in terms of their relationship to a **relative major** scale that we already know. Reviewing the previous examples in **Figs. 5.1. - 5.6.**, we can say that the **relative major** scale for all of these examples is the **C major** scale - because **this is the scale which has been displaced** to create all of these modes.

Creating the modal scales starting from the note C

We will now re-create each of the modal scales **starting from the note C** instead of **displacing** a **C major** scale. In other words instead of using different starting notes within the **C major** scale as in **Figs. 5.1. - 5.6.**, we will now **keep the starting note of C** and **derive the remaining scale degrees from the new relative major scale** in each case. We will also see that another way to look at this process is to **alter the major scale built from the starting note** (i.e. in this case **C major**) to create the mode required.

We will start out by deriving a **Dorian** mode, but instead of simply displacing a **C major** scale to start on the note **D** as in **Fig. 5.1.**, we will now create a **Dorian mode starting on the note C**. (i.e. **C Dorian**). First of all we need to figure out the relative major scale of **C Dorian**. We recall that '**Dorian**' means 'major scale starting from its **2nd** degree' - so if we can find the major scale which has the note **C** as its **2nd** degree, this would then be the required relative major. We recall that this type of problem was solved in **Chapter 4** by placing the given note (i.e. the note **C** as the **2nd** degree in this case) within the major scale interval pattern, as follows:-

Figure 5.7. Finding out which major scale contains C as its 2nd degree - stage 1

<WS> <WS> <HS> <WS> <WS> <WS> <HS>

As the above placement of the note **C** is nearer the left-hand end of the scale, we'll work **downwards** (i.e. to the left) to derive the tonic of the required **relative major scale**.

Creating the modal scales starting from the note C (contd)

The note immediately to the left of **C** in the example at the bottom of the previous page, is now the tonic of the **relative major** that we need. This note will use the lettername of **B**, and needs to be a **whole-step** lower than **C**. However, **the note B is only a half-step lower than C**, and so we need to **flat the B** (to **Bb**) to obtain the required tonic, as follows:-

Figure 5.8. Finding out which major scale contains C as its 2nd degree - stage 2

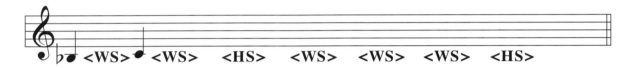

So we can see from this that the required relative major is **Bb major** - in other words this is the major scale that **C Dorian** is a displaced version of. Now we'll derive the rest of the notes in the **Bb major** scale, using of course the **interval method** first learned in **Chapter 1**:-

Figure 5.9. Bb major scale (required relative major of C Dorian)

Now finally we will displace the above **Bb major** scale to start on the note **C**, creating a **C Dorian** mode:-

Figure 5.10. C Dorian mode - created by displacing a Bb major scale

Now in comparing this mode to a **C major** scale, we note that **the 3rd and 7th degrees have been flatted to create a Dorian mode from the same starting note** (i.e. **C Dorian** in this case). This is therefore an alternative way to create a Dorian mode from a given starting note.

As the **C Dorian** mode is of course entirely diatonic to **Bb major**, this mode could be notated with the **Bb major** key signature (i.e. the **key signature of the relative major**) as in the example at the top of the following page:-

Creating the modal scales starting from the note C (contd)

Figure 5.11. C Dorian mode - notated with the Bb (relative) major key signature

The key signature for **Bb major** was first derived in **Chapter 1** (see **Fig. 1.76.**).

The steps taken to solve the above problem (i.e. **how to build a modal scale from a given starting note**) can now be summarized as follows:-

- find the **relative major scale** of the mode:-
    - using the given starting note as the scale degree implied by the mode name (i.e. **C Dorian** implies that **C** is the **2nd** degree), work either upwards or downwards within the '**major scale intervals**' (i.e. whole-steps and half-steps) to establish the tonic of the relative major - we first saw this technique used in **Chapter 4** (**Figs. 4.8. - 4.15.** and **4.19. - 4.26.**) and again in this chapter (**Figs. 5.7. - 5.8.**).
- derive the **complete relative major scale** (again using whole-step and half-step intervals), working from the scale **tonic** derived above
- **displace** the **relative major scale** to start on the original **starting note** given.

As we have seen, as an alternative method to the above, you can do the following:-

- build a **major scale** from the **given starting note**
- **alter** the various scale degrees (i.e. with sharps/flats/naturals) to create the required **modal scale** quality.

For example (as noted at the bottom of the previous page), we can create a **C Dorian** mode by taking a **C major** scale and **flatting the 3rd and 7th degrees**. As we derive the remaining modes starting on the note **C** in this section, we will also derive these 'alteration' rules (i.e. how to alter a major scale from the same starting note) for each of the modes. However, although you need to know this as it will be useful in certain playing/application situations, I think the most fundamental way to build a mode from a given starting note is as first explained here i.e. by finding the **relative major scale** and then **displacing it** as required.

We will now derive all of the remaining modes starting from the note **C**. The next mode to be derived is **C Phrygian**, and again the first stage is to find the relative major. We recall that **Phrygian** means 'major scale starting from its **3rd** degree', and so we will place the given note (i.e. the note **C** as the **3rd** degree in this case) within the major scale interval pattern, as shown on the following page:-

Creating the modal scales starting from the note C (contd)

Figure 5.12. Finding out which major scale contains C as its 3rd degree - stage 1

Again we'll work downwards (i.e. to the left) to derive the required tonic, as the given note is nearer the left-hand end of the scale. The note immediately to the left of **C** will use the lettername **B**, and needs to be a **whole-step** lower than **C**. As the note **B** is only a **half-step** lower than **C**, we need to **flat the B** (to **Bb**) as follows:-

Figure 5.13. Finding out which major scale contains C as its 3rd degree - stage 2

Now the note immediately to the left of **Bb** is the tonic of the relative major scale that we need. This note will use the lettername **A**, and needs to be a **whole-step** lower than **Bb**. As the note **A** is only a **half-step** lower than **Bb**, we need to **flat the A** (to **Ab**) to obtain the required tonic, as follows:-

Figure 5.14. Finding out which major scale contains C as its 3rd degree - stage 3

So we can see from this that the required relative major is **Ab major** - in other words this is the major scale that **C Phrygian** is a displaced version of. Now we'll derive the rest of the notes in the **Ab major** scale, again using the major scale **interval method** as shown on the following page:-

Creating the modal scales starting from the note C (contd)

Figure 5.15. Ab major scale (required relative major of C Phrygian)

Now finally we will displace the above **Ab major** scale to start on the note **C**, creating a **C Phrygian** mode:-

Figure 5.16. C Phrygian mode - created by displacing an Ab major scale

Now in comparing this mode to a **C major scale**, we note that **the 2nd, 3rd, 6th and 7th degrees have been flatted to create a Phrygian mode from the same starting note** (i.e. **C Phrygian** in this case). This is therefore an alternative way to create a Phrygian mode from a given starting note.

As the **C Phrygian** mode is of course entirely diatonic to **Ab major**, this mode could be notated with the **Ab major** key signature (i.e. the **key signature of the relative major**) as follows:-

Figure 5.17. C Phrygian mode - notated with the Ab (relative) major key signature

The key signature for **Ab major** was first derived in **Chapter 1** (see **Fig. 1.78.**).

The next mode to be derived is **C Lydian**, and again the first stage is to find the relative major. We recall that **Lydian** means 'major scale starting from its **4th** degree', and so we need to find the major scale that has **C** as its **4th** degree. We already solved this particular problem in **Chapter 4** - rather than reprint all of the stages again here, please refer to **Figs. 4.8. - 4.11.** as required. We concluded then that the **G major** scale has the note **C** as its **4th** degree - so again we'll derive the **G major** scale using the interval method, as shown on the next page:-

Creating the modal scales starting from the note C (contd)

Figure 5.18. G major scale (required relative major of C Lydian)

Now finally we will displace the above **G major** scale to start on the note **C**, creating a **C Lydian** mode:-

Figure 5.19. C Lydian mode - created by displacing a G major scale

Now in comparing this mode to a **C major scale**, we note that **the 4th degree has been sharped to create a Lydian mode from the same starting note** (i.e. **C Lydian** in this case). This is therefore an alternative way to create a Lydian mode from a given starting note.

As the **C Lydian** mode is of course entirely diatonic to **G major**, this mode could be notated with the **G major** key signature (i.e. the **key signature of the relative major**) as follows:-

Figure 5.20. C Lydian mode - notated with the G (relative) major key signature

The key signature for **G major** was first derived in **Chapter 1** (see **Fig. 1.83.**).

The next mode to be derived is **C Mixolydian**, and again the first stage is to find the relative major. We recall that **Mixolydian** means 'major scale starting from its **5th** degree', and so we need to find the major scale that has **C** as its **5th** degree. Again we already solved this particular problem in **Chapter 4** - rather than reprint all of the stages again here, please refer to **Figs. 4.12. - 4.15.** as required. We concluded then that the **F major** scale has the note **C** as its **5th** degree - so again we'll derive the **F major** scale using the interval method, as shown on the next page:-

Creating the modal scales starting from the note C (contd)

Figure 5.21. F major scale (required relative major of C Mixolydian)

Now finally we will displace the above **F major** scale to start on the note **C**, creating a **C Mixolydian** mode:-

Figure 5.22. C Mixolydian mode - created by displacing an F major scale

Now in comparing this mode to a **C major scale**, we note that **the 7th degree has been flatted to create a Mixolydian mode from the same starting note** (i.e. **C Mixolydian** in this case). This is therefore an alternative way to create a Mixolydian mode from a given starting note.

As the **C Mixolydian** mode is of course entirely diatonic to **F major**, this mode could be notated with the **F major** key signature (i.e. the **key signature of the relative major**) as follows:-

Figure 5.23. C Mixolydian mode - notated with the F (relative) major key signature

The key signature for **F major** was first derived in **Chapter 1** (see **Fig. 1.74.**).

The next mode to be derived is **C Aeolian**, and again the first stage is to find the relative major. We recall that **Aeolian** means 'major scale starting from its **6th** degree', and so we will place the given note (i.e. the note **C** as the **6th** degree in this case) within the major scale interval pattern, as shown on the following page:-

Creating the modal scales starting from the note C (contd)

Figure 5.24. Finding out which major scale contains C as its 6th degree - stage 1

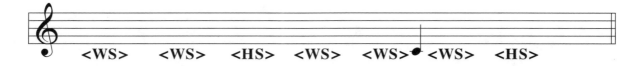

This time we'll work upwards (i.e. to the right) to derive the required tonic, as the given note is nearer the right-hand end of the scale. The note immediately to the right of **C** will use the lettername **D**, and needs to be a **whole-step** higher than **C**. As the note **D** is already a **whole-step** higher than **D**, this note needs no further qualification, as follows:-

Figure 5.25. Finding out which major scale contains C as its 6th degree - stage 2

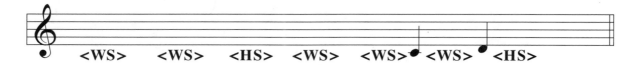

Now the note immediately to the right of **D** is the tonic of the relative major scale that we need. This note will use the lettername **E**, and needs to be a **half-step** higher than **D**. As the note **E** is however a **whole-step** higher than **D**, we need to **flat the E** (to **Eb**) to obtain the required tonic, as follows:-

Figure 5.26. Finding out which major scale contains C as its 6th degree - stage 3

So we can see from this that the required relative major is **Eb major** - in other words this is the major scale that **C Aeolian** is a displaced version of. Now we'll derive the rest of the notes in the **Eb major** scale, again using the major scale **interval method** as shown on the following page:-

Creating the modal scales starting from the note C (contd)

Figure 5.27. Eb major scale (required relative major of C Aeolian)

Now finally we will displace the above **Eb major** scale to start on the note **C**, creating a **C Aeolian** mode:-

Figure 5.28. C Aeolian mode - created by displacing an Eb major scale

Now in comparing this mode to a **C major scale**, we note that **the 3rd, 6th and 7th degrees have been flatted to create an Aeolian mode from the same starting note** (i.e. **C Aeolian** in this case). This is therefore an alternative way to create an Aeolian mode from a given starting note.

As the **C Aeolian** mode is of course entirely diatonic to **Eb major**, this mode could be notated with the **Eb major** key signature (i.e. the **key signature of the relative major**) as follows:-

Figure 5.29. C Aeolian mode - notated with the Eb (relative) major key signature

The key signature for **Eb major** was first derived in **Chapter 1** (see **Fig. 1.77.**).

The last mode to be derived is **C Locrian**, and again the first stage is to find the relative major. We recall that **Locrian** means 'major scale starting from its **7th** degree', and so we will place the given note (i.e. the note **C** as the **7th** degree in this case) within the major scale interval pattern, as shown on the following page:-

Creating the modal scales starting from the note C (contd)

Figure 5.30. Finding out which major scale contains C as its 7th degree - stage 1

Again we'll work upwards (i.e. to the right) to derive the required tonic, as the given note is nearer the right-hand end of the scale. The note immediately to the right of **C** is the tonic of the relative major scale that we need. This note will use the lettername **D**, and needs to be a **half-step** higher than **C**. As the note **D** is however a **whole-step** higher than **C**, we need to **flat the D** (to **Db**) to obtain the required tonic, as follows:-

Figure 5.31. Finding out which major scale contains C as its 7th degree - stage 2

So we can see from this that the required relative major is **Db major** - in other words this is the major scale that **C Locrian** is a displaced version of. Now we'll derive the rest of the notes in the **Db major** scale, again using the major scale **interval method** as follows:-

Figure 5.32. Db major scale (required relative major of C Locrian)

Now finally we will displace the above **Db major** scale to start on the note **C**, creating a **C Locrian** mode:-

Figure 5.33. C Locrian mode - created by displacing a Db major scale

140

Creating the modal scales starting from the note C (contd)

Now in comparing this mode to a **C major scale**, we note that **the 2nd, 3rd, 5th, 6th and 7th degrees have been flatted to create a Locrian mode from the same starting note** (i.e. **C Locrian** in this case). This is therefore an alternative way to create a Locrian mode from a given starting note.

As the **C Locrian** mode is of course entirely diatonic to **Db major**, this mode could be notated with the **Db major** key signature (i.e. the **key signature of the relative major**) as follows:-

Figure 5.34. C Locrian mode - notated with the Db (relative) major key signature

The key signature for **Db major** was first derived in **Chapter 1** (see **Fig. 1.79.**).

Examples of creating and recognizing modes

We will now look at some examples of creating and recognizing modes, both with and without key signatures. In each case an important part of the process will be to determine the **relative major** scale for each mode. First we will work through some examples of creating modes, as follows:-

Mode creation example #1
- Create an **F# Aeolian** mode (in the **treble** clef) **with** a key signature.

As **Aeolian** means 'major scale starting from its **6th** degree', we first of all find the relative major by placing the starting note of the mode (i.e. **F#**) within the major scale interval pattern:-

Figure 5.35. Mode creation example #1 stage 1 - determine relative major
(Finding out which major scale contains **F#** as its **6th** degree - stage 1)

Examples of creating and recognizing modes (contd)

This time we'll work upwards (i.e. to the right) to derive the required tonic, as the given note is nearer the right-hand end of the scale. The note immediately to the right of **F#** will use the lettername **G**, and needs to be a **whole-step** higher than **F#**. As the note **G** is only a **half-step** higher than **F#**, we need to **sharp the G** (to **G#**) as follows:-

Figure 5.36. Mode creation example #1 stage 1 - determine relative major
*(Finding out which major scale contains **F#** as its **6th** degree - stage 2)*

Now the note immediately to the right of **G#** is the tonic of the relative major scale that we need. This note will use the lettername **A**, and needs to be a **half-step** higher than **G#**. As the note **A** is already a **half-step** higher than **G#**, this note needs no further qualification, as follows:-

Figure 5.37. Mode creation example #1 stage 1 - determine relative major
*(Finding out which major scale contains **F#** as its **6th** degree - stage 3)*

So we can see from this that the required relative major is **A major** - in other words this is the major scale that **F# Aeolian** is a displaced version of. We have been asked to provide this mode with a key signature, and we recall from **Chapter 1** that the key signature for **A major** contained three sharps (see **Fig. 1.86.** and accompanying text). Therefore we simply need to notate the mode beginning and ending on F#, and **with the key signature of A major in force**, in order to create an **F# Aeolian** mode with a key signature:-

Figure 5.38. Mode creation example #1 stage 2 - notate mode on the staff
*(Beginning on requested starting note of **F#**, using **relative major** key signature)*

Examples of creating and recognizing modes (contd)

Mode creation example #2   - *Create an **A Locrian** mode (in the **bass** clef) **without** a key signature.*

As **Locrian** means 'major scale starting from its **7th** degree', we first of all find the relative major by placing the starting note of the mode (i.e. **A**) within the major scale interval pattern:-

Figure 5.39. Mode creation example #2 stage 1 - determine relative major
*(Finding out which major scale contains **A** as its **7th** degree - stage **1**)*

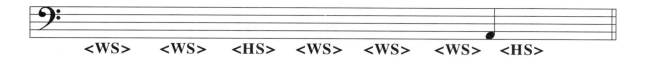

(Note that we are using bass clef this time, as requested). Again we'll work upwards (i.e. to the right) to derive the required tonic, as the given note is nearer the right-hand end of the scale. The note immediately to the right of **A** is the tonic of the relative major scale that we need. This note will use the lettername **B**, and needs to be a **half-step** higher than **A**. As the note **B** is however a **whole-step** higher than **A**, we need to **flat the B** (to **Bb**) to obtain the required tonic, as follows:-

Figure 5.40. Mode creation example #2 stage 1 - determine relative major
*(Finding out which major scale contains **A** as its **7th** degree - stage **2**)*

So we can see from this that the required relative major is **Bb major** - in other words this is the major scale that **A Locrian** is a displaced version of. We have been asked to provide this mode without a key signature, and so we will derive the **Bb major** scale (using the normal interval method) and then displace it to create the **A Locrian** mode. We build the **Bb major** scale as follows:-

Figure 5.41. Mode creation example #2 stage 2 - building relative major scale (Bb)

Examples of creating and recognizing modes (contd)

Now finally we will displace the **Bb major** scale (on the previous page) to start on the note **A**, to create an **A Locrian** mode without a key signature (i.e. retaining all necessary flats):-

Figure 5.42. Mode creation example #2 stage 3 - displacing relative major scale (Bb)

Now we will look at some mode recognition examples. The first example includes a key signature (with no additional accidentals):-

Figure 5.43. Mode recognition example #1 (original mode with key signature)

Again the first task is to find out the relative major, and as there is a key signature 'in force' we simply need to recall which major key uses this particular key signature (i.e. **six sharps**) - in **Chapter 1** we derived this as being the **F# major** key signature (see **Fig. 1.89.** and accompanying text). We therefore need to figure out where the note **B** (the starting note of the mode) occurs within an **F# major** scale, i.e. which scale degree of an **F# major** scale is the note **B**. As we can see by building an **F# major** scale (or by counting up from the note **F#** in the above example), the note **B** is the **4th** degree of an **F# major** scale. We recall that any major scale beginning on its **4th** degree is referred to as a **Lydian** mode, and therefore the correct name for the above example is a **B Lydian** mode.

Figure 5.44. Mode recognition example #2 (original mode without key signature)

The first thing to do is to determine the **intervals** being used. (I would suggest at this point that you resist any temptation to simply 'add up' the number of sharps of flats to get the relative major! Although that may technically work within the narrow parameters of these examples, I feel that analyzing this by interval will better prepare you for more 'real-world' situations). Here is the above example with the intervals analyzed (on following page):-

Examples of creating and recognizing modes (contd)

Figure 5.45. Mode recognition example #2 *(intervals analyzed)*

Working on the assumption that the example is a displaced version of some major scale, we would expect to see **two half-step** intervals and **five whole-step** intervals within the mode. We know that one of the half-steps must be between the **7th** and **1st** (tonic) degrees of the **relative major** scale. If we could establish **which** half-step this is (i.e. either **G#** up to **A**, or **D#** up to **E**, in the above example), then this would be an efficient way to determine the **relative major**, which of course would have the same name as the **1st** degree of the scale. You can determine **which** half-step is between the **7th** and **1st** degrees as follows:-

- if there are **two consecutive whole-steps** between the two half-step intervals, then the **lowest** of the two half-steps is between the **7th** and **1st** degrees of the **relative major**.
- if there are **three consecutive whole-steps** between the two half-step intervals, then the **highest** of the two half-steps is between the **7th** and **1st** degrees of the **relative major**.

Using this method on the above example, we see that there are **three** consecutive whole-steps between the two half-step intervals - therefore the **highest** of the two halfsteps (i.e. **D#** up to **E** in this case) is between the **7th** and **1st** degrees of the **relative major**, which is therefore **E major**. It remains to then determine where the starting note (in this case **G#**) occurs within an **E major** scale, i.e. which scale degree of an **E major** scale is the note **G#**. As we can see by building an **E major** scale (or by counting up from the note **E** in the above example), the note **G#** is the **3rd** degree of an **E major** scale. We recall that any major scale beginning on its **3rd** degree is referred to as a **Phrygian** mode, and therefore the correct name for the above example is a **G# Phrygian** mode.

Figure 5.46. Mode recognition example #3 *(original mode without key signature)*

First of all we again analyze the intervals (whole-steps and half-steps) present in the mode, as shown on the following page:-

Examples of creating and recognizing modes (contd)

Figure 5.47. Mode recognition example #3 *(intervals analyzed)*

<WS>   <WS>   <HS>   <WS>   <WS>   <HS>   <WS>

In this example we see that there are now **two** consecutive whole-steps between the two half-step intervals - therefore the **lowest** of the two halfsteps (i.e. **G** up to **Ab** in this case) is between the **7th** and **1st** degrees of the **relative major**, which is therefore **Ab major**. Again we then determine where the starting note (in this case **Eb**) occurs within an **Ab major** scale, i.e. which scale degree of an **Ab major** scale is the note **Eb**. As we can see by building an **Ab major** scale (or by counting up from the note **Ab** in the above example), the note **Eb** is the **5th** degree of an **Ab major** scale. We recall that any major scale beginning on its **5th** degree is referred to as a **Mixolydian** mode, and therefore the correct name for the above example is an **Eb Mixolydian** mode.

Summary list of mode names and definitions

Here for your reference are all of the mode names we have encountered, together with their descriptions:-

- An **Ionian** mode is a major scale starting from its **1st** degree (i.e. **not** displaced).
- A **Dorian** mode is a major scale starting from its **2nd** degree.
- A **Phrygian** mode is a major scale starting from its **3rd** degree.
- A **Lydian** mode is a major scale starting from its **4th** degree.
- A **Mixolydian** mode is a major scale starting from its **5th** degree.
- An **Aeolian** mode is a major scale starting from its **6th** degree.
- A **Locrian** mode is a major scale starting from its **7th** degree.

Chapter Five Workbook Questions

1.   Identifying relative major scale for specified modes

The relative major scale is the scale which has been 'displaced' (i.e. starting on a note other than the normal tonic) to create the mode in question. Identify the following relative major scales:-

1.   The relative major of **E Phrygian** is   _____
2.   The relative major of **B Dorian** is   _____
3.   The relative major of **C Mixolydian** is   _____
4.   The relative major of **Db Lydian** is   _____
5.   The relative major of **F# Locrian** is   _____
6.   The relative major of **C# Aeolian** is   _____
7.   The relative major of **A Mixolydian** is   _____
8.   The relative major of **E Dorian** is   _____
9.   The relative major of **Eb Phrygian** is   _____
10. The relative major of **F Aeolian** is   _____
11. The relative major of **G Lydian** is   _____
12. The relative major of **B Locrian** is   _____
13. The relative major of **G# Dorian** is   _____
14. The relative major of **D Phrygian** is   _____
15. The relative major of **E Aeolian** is   _____
16. The relative major of **Bb Mixolydian** is   _____
17. The relative major of **Gb Lydian** is   _____
18. The relative major of **A# Aeolian** is   _____
19. The relative major of **E Locrian** is   _____
20. The relative major of **D# Phrygian** is   _____

2.   Writing modal scales with key signatures

You are to write the the following modal scales by identifying the relative major, writing the necessary key signature, and then writing the notes in ascending sequence beginning with the tonic. No extra accidentals are required as the relative major key signature will be 'in force'.

21. **D Dorian**   22. **A Phrygian**

2.   *Writing modal scales with key signatures (contd)*

23. **E Mixolydian**   24. **F# Locrian**

25. **Ab Lydian**   26. **G# Aeolian**

27. **Ab Mixolydian**   28. **E Dorian**

3.   *Writing modal scales without key signatures*

You are to write the following modal scales by identifying the relative major, and then writing that scale **with any necessary accidentals** from the starting note specified. No key signatures are to be written or used - instead, build the required relative major scale using the interval method (wholesteps and halfsteps) and then **displace it** to begin on the starting note required by the mode.

29. **A Lydian**   30. **G Aeolian**

31. **Ab Dorian**   32. **F# Mixolydian**

3. Writing modal scales without key signatures (contd)

33. **B Locrian**

34. **C Phrygian**

35. **G Lydian**

36. **C Aeolian**

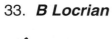

4. Identifying modal scales with key signatures

You are to identify the following modal scales. Use the key signature to find out the relative major, and then determine which degree of the relative major is being used as the 'tonic' or starting note of the mode. The mode name you provide will have two parts:-
- the note name of the starting note (i.e. C, C#, etc.)
- the modal adjective (i.e. Dorian, Phrygian etc.) corresponding to the relative major scale degree **used** as the starting note.

For example, if the key signature is indicating **Bb major** (two flats) and the mode starts on **D**, we would determine that D is the 3rd degree of Bb major, and that the mode is therefore a Phrygian mode. As D is the starting note, the full name of the mode would be **D Phrygian**.

37. _____ _____

38. _____ _____

39. _____ _____

40. _____ _____

149

4. *Identifying modal scales with key signatures (contd)*

41. ____ _____   42. ____ _____

43. ____ _____   44. ____ _____

5. *Identifying modal scales without key signatures*

You are to identify the following modal scales, which are presented without key signatures. First determine the relative major by analyzing the intervals used (whole-steps and halfsteps). Remember that;-
-     if the two halfsteps are separated by **three** consecutive wholesteps, the **highest** halfstep will be between the **7th** and **1st** degrees of the relative major scale
-     if the two halfsteps are separated by **two** consecutive wholesteps, the **lowest** halfstep will be between the **7th** and **1st** degrees of the relative major scale.

DO NOT 'add up' the sharps or flats to try to determine the relative major by key signature! - instead use the interval analysis as described above! Once the relative major is established, we again determine which degree of the relative major is used as the starting note, to arrive at the correct modal adjective (i.e. Dorian, Phrygian) needed.

45. ____ _____   46. ____ _____

47. ____ _____   48. ____ _____

5. Identifying modal scales without key signatures (contd)

49. _____ _____

50. _____ _____

51. _____ _____

52. _____ _____

Chapter Five Workbook Answers

1. _Identifying relative major scale for specified modes - answers_

1.	*C*	2.	*A*	3.	*F*	4.	*Ab*
5.	*G*	6.	*E*	7.	*D*	8.	*D*
9.	*Cb*	10.	*Ab*	11.	*D*	12.	*C*
13.	*F#*	14.	*Bb*	15.	*G*	16.	*Eb*
17.	*Db*	18.	*C#*	19.	*F*	20.	*B*

2. _Writing modal scales with key signatures - answers_

21. **D Dorian**   22. **A Phrygian**

23. **E Mixolydian**   24. **F# Locrian**

25. **Ab Lydian**   26. **G# Aeolian**

27. **Ab Mixolydian**   28. **E Dorian**

3. <u>*Writing modal scales without key signatures - answers*</u>

29. **A Lydian**　　　　　　　　　　　　30. **G Aeolian**

31. **Ab Dorian**　　　　　　　　　　　32. **F# Mixolydian**

33. **B Locrian**　　　　　　　　　　　34. **C Phrygian**

35. **G Lydian**　　　　　　　　　　　36. **C Aeolian**

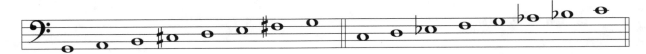

4. <u>*Identifying modal scales with key signatures - answers*</u>

37.	**G Mixolydian**	38.	**E Aeolian**	39.	**B Dorian**
40.	**Eb Lydian**	41.	**E Locrian**	42.	**D# Phrygian**
43.	**Ab Ionian**	44.	**B Mixolydian**		

5. <u>*Identifying modal scales without key signatures - answers*</u>

45.	**Bb Aeolian**	46.	**F Lydian**	47.	**A Dorian**
48.	**G Locrian**	49.	**Eb Phrygian**	50.	**D Mixolydian**
51.	**D# Aeolian**	52.	**Bb Lydian**		

Four-part chords and inversions

Introduction to four-part chords

The next type of chord we will consider (following on from our work on **triads** in **Chapter 3**) is the **four-part** chord. As the name suggests, this type of chord has **four** notes, as opposed to triads which only contain **three** notes. Again we will look at these chords and analyze them to determine the intervals present, and to see if the major scale can be used as a 'scale source' for each chord.

At this stage we will concern ourselves with **four** 'basic' types of four-part chord - known as **major 7th**, **major 6th**, **minor 7th** and **dominant 7th** chords respectively. We recall that some of these terms have previously been used to describe intervals - again (as discussed in **Chapter 3**) it is important that you understand whether these terms are being used to describe an **interval** or a **chord** (which in turn contains intervals)! As we will see in this chapter, these four basic four-part chords are all available within a major scale - later on we will deal with 'altered' versions of these chords, as well as other four-part chords derived from minor scales.

The major seventh chord

The first four-part chord to be studied is the **major 7th** chord. It is derived by placing **major 3rd**, **perfect 5th** and **major 7th** intervals above the root, as follows:-

Figure 6.1. C major seventh chord - interval construction

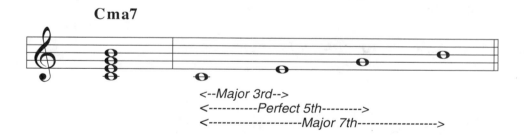

Note that we have measured the intervals (major 3rd, perfect 5th and major 7th) up from the root of the four-part chord in each case. We recall from **Chapter 2** that major and perfect intervals were diatonic i.e. they occurred within a major scale built from the lowest note - this four-part chord could therefore also be considered as the first, third, fifth and seventh degrees of a **C major scale** (again review **Figs. 1.42.** and **2.5.** if required). This chord can also be derived by taking the major triad (as in **Fig. 3.1.**) and adding the note which creates a **major 7th** interval from the root of the chord (i.e. the note **B** in the above example).

The major seventh chord (contd)

Note the chord symbol from the example on the previous page, which is '**Cma7**'. There are two components to this chord symbol - the chord root (in this case '**C**') and the chord 'suffix' or description (in this case '**ma7**'). The suffix '**ma7**' indicates a **major seventh chord** built from the root i.e. in this case a **C major seventh chord**. Although using the suffix '**ma7**' is the preferred way to write this chord symbol, you will sometimes encounter other suffixes for the major seventh chord, as follows:-

- '**Maj7**', '**maj7**', i.e. as in the chord symbols **CMaj7**, **Cmaj7**. Unnecessary as the suffix '**ma7**' already explicitly defines a major seventh chord.
- '**M7**' i.e. as in the chord symbol **CM7**. As we saw when discussing triads, the single upper-case '**M**' can be confused with '**m**' (lower-case) which is sometimes used to signify a **minor** quality.
- '**Δ7**' i.e. as in the chord symbol **CΔ7**. As previously discussed, the 'triangle symbol' is sometimes used in older charts and fake books to indicate a major quality - at least with the number **7** used afterwards, it is easier to see that a 4-part chord is intended - however, I personally find the '**ma7**' suffix to be clearer and less error-prone.

So - when writing your **major seventh** chord symbols, use the '**ma7**' suffix - but **be prepared to recognize** the alternative chord suffixes listed above.

The major sixth chord

The next four-part chord to be studied is the **major 6th** chord (which functionally can be considered as a variation of the major seventh chord). It is derived by placing **major 3rd**, **perfect 5th** and **major 6th** intervals above the root, as follows:-

Figure 6.2. C major sixth chord - interval construction

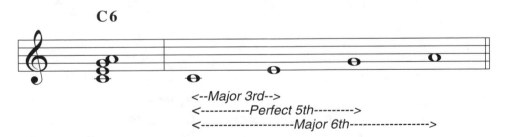

As all of these intervals (again measured from the root) are diatonic, this four-part chord could also be considered as the first, third, fifth and sixth degrees of a **C major scale**. This chord can also be derived by taking the major triad (as in **Fig. 3.1.**) and adding the note which creates a **major 6th** interval from the root of the chord (i.e. the note **A** in the above example).

The major sixth chord (contd)

Note the chord symbol used in the previous example ('**C6**'). The suffix '**6**' indicates a **major sixth chord** built from the root i.e. in this case a **C major sixth chord**. Another common and correct way to write this chord symbol is to use the suffix '**ma6**' (i.e. as in **Cma6**), although strictly speaking this is somewhat redundant, as the suffix '**6**' explicitly defines a **major sixth** chord.

Although using the suffix '**6**' (or '**ma6**') is the preferred way to write this chord symbol, you will sometimes encounter other suffixes for the major sixth chord, as follows:-

- '**Maj6**', '**maj6**', i.e. as in the chord symbols **CMaj6**, **Cmaj6**. Unnecessary as the suffix '**6**' (or '**ma6**') already explicitly defines a major sixth chord.
- '**M6**' i.e. as in the chord symbol **CM6**. See previous comments - can be confused with '**m**' (lower-case) implying minor.

So - when writing your **major sixth** chord symbols, use the '**6**' (or '**ma6**') suffix - but again **be prepared to recognize** the alternative chord suffixes listed above.

The minor seventh chord

The next four-part chord to be studied is the **minor 7th** chord. It is derived by placing **minor 3rd**, **perfect 5th** and **minor 7th** intervals above the root, as follows:-

Figure 6.3. C minor seventh chord - interval construction

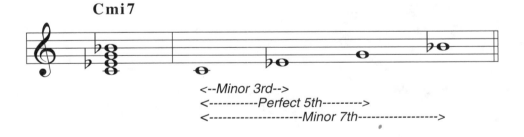

This chord can also be derived by taking the minor triad (as in **Fig. 3.2.**) and adding the note which creates a **minor 7th** interval from the root of the chord (i.e. the note **Bb** above).

Note the chord symbol used in the above example ('**Cmi7**'). The suffix '**mi7**' indicates a **minor seventh chord** built from the root i.e. in this case a **C minor seventh chord**. Although using the suffix '**mi7**' is the preferred way to write this chord symbol, you will sometimes encounter other suffixes for the minor seventh chord, as detailed on the following page:-

The minor seventh chord (contd)

- '**min7**' i.e. as in the chord symbol **Cmin7**. Unnecessary as the suffix '**mi7**' already explicitly defines a minor 7th chord.
- '**m7**' i.e. as in the chord symbol **Cm7**. As we saw when discussing triads in **Chapter 3**, if just a single (lower-case) '**m**' is used, this can be confused with an upper-case '**M**' which is sometimes used to indicate a major quality. Use '**mi7**' to be explicit.
- '**-7**' i.e. as in the chord symbol **C-7**. Again as discussed in **Chapter 3**, the '**-**' suffix is often used in older charts and 'illegal' fake books to signify a minor quality, and therefore you will sometimes encounter the '**-7**' suffix for a **minor seventh** chord. However, I personally find the '**mi7**' suffix to be clearer and less error-prone.

So - when writing your minor seventh chord symbols, use the '**mi7**' suffix - but again **be prepared to recognize** the alternatives listed above!

The dominant seventh chord

The last four-part chord to be studied in this chapter is the **dominant 7th** chord. It is derived by placing **major 3rd**, **perfect 5th** and **minor 7th** intervals above the root, as follows:-

Figure 6.4. C dominant seventh chord - interval construction

```
<--Major 3rd-->
<-----------Perfect 5th--------->
<--------------------Minor 7th----------------->
```

This chord can also be derived by taking the major triad (as in **Fig. 3.1.**) and adding the note which creates a **minor 7th** interval from the root of the chord (i.e. the note **Bb** above).

Note the chord symbol used in the above example ('**C7**'). The suffix '**7**' indicates a **dominant seventh chord** built from the root i.e. in this case a **C dominant seventh chord**. At first sight this chord symbol looks similar to the one used for a major sixth chord (i.e. the '**C6**' used in **Fig. 6.2.**), in that it simply consists of the root note name followed by a numeric suffix. We need to make sure therefore that we can distinguish between **major** and **dominant** chords using this type of chord symbol. The following rules will apply to chord symbols consisting solely of a root note name followed by a number, with no other qualification (see following page):-

The dominant seventh chord (contd)

- If the number in the chord symbol is **less than 7** (i.e. as in the chord symbol **C6**) the chord has a **major** quality or implication.
- If the number in the chord symbol is **7 or greater** (i.e. as in the chord symbol **C7**) the chord has a **dominant** quality or implication.

One convenient way to remember this distinction, is to realize that any **dominant** chord **must have a seventh** i.e. none of the triads discussed in **Chapter 3** had a **dominant** quality. *(Please refer to my Contemporary Music Theory Level 2 book for a more complete discussion on the function and harmonic implications of the dominant chord).*

Examples of other chord symbols in the **first** category above would include:-

- **'C5'** The suffix **'5'** is sometimes used on pop and rock charts to indicate a triad with the **3rd** omitted i.e. just using the **root** and **5th** of the chord. Although technically the chord is not explicitly major as there is no **3rd** present, generally a major implication can be assumed unless the context indicates otherwise.
- **'C2'** This is a rather unsatisfactory chord symbol which however still finds its way on to some pop and rock charts! The implication is that we have added the **2nd** degree (which more accurately should be referred to as the **9th** as it is really an upper extension) to a major triad - for example adding the note **D** to a **C** major triad. *(The correct way to write this chord symbol would be 'Cadd9' or 'C(add9)' - more on this in Contemporary Music Theory Level 2).* Another problem with this chord symbol is that it is not clear whether or not the **3rd** of the chord also needs to be included.

Examples of other chord symbols in the **second** category at the top of this page would include **C9**, **C11** etc. which are larger (i.e. five- or six-part) versions of dominant chords - again more on this in *Contemporary Music Theory Level 2*.

Summary of intervals present within these four-part chords

In reviewing the intervals contained within the **major seventh** (**Fig. 6.1.**), **major sixth** (**Fig. 6.2.**), **minor seventh** (**Fig. 6.3.**) and **dominant seventh** (**Fig 6.4.**) chords, we find that each chord contains a **perfect 5th** interval (measured from the root in each case). This interval therefore does **not** contribute towards our sense of **chord quality** i.e. it does not help us to distinguish between the 'sounds' of these different chords. The **5th** of each chord is therefore considered to be harmonically 'neutral' (unless it is subsequently 'altered' by half-step, as we shall see in **Chapter 9**).

159

Summary of intervals present within these four-part chords (contd)

However, the different types of **third** and **seventh** intervals (or in the case of the **major 6th chord**, the **third** and **sixth** intervals), **do** determine the particular chord quality of each chord. These interval relationships can be summarized as follows:-

Type of chord	Third interval contained in chord	Seventh (or sixth) interval contained in chord
Major 7th	Major 3rd	Major 7th
Major 6th	Major 3rd	Major 6th
Minor 7th	Minor 3rd	Minor 7th
Dominant 7th	Major 3rd	Minor 7th

Don't forget that the terms used in the **first** column are **chord descriptions**, while the terms used in the **second** and **third** columns are **interval descriptions**. (Note therefore that the term **dominant 7th** is a **chord** description and not an **interval** description - we have already derived all necessary interval descriptions in **Chapter 2** - however I still sometimes hear even experienced musicians make the mistake of referring to "dominant 7th intervals"! Don't forget that the **dominant 7th chord** contains a **minor 7th interval** within it, as shown above).

Locating the different four-part chords within the major scale

We will now look within the major scale (first derived in **Fig. 1.42.**) to see where these four-part chords are found within the scale. We have already mentioned that a **major seventh** chord can be derived from the **1st**, **3rd, 5th and 7th** degrees of a major scale, and this can be reviewed as follows:-

Figure 6.5. Deriving the C major seventh chord from a C major scale

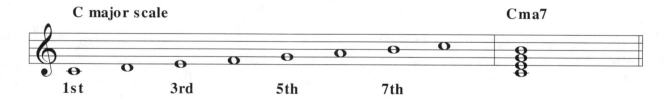

Locating the different four-part chords within the major scale (contd)

Also we have already seen that a **major sixth** chord can be derived from the **1st, 3rd, 5th and 6th** degrees of a major scale, and this can be reviewed as follows:-

**Figure 6.6. Deriving the C major sixth chord from a C major scale**

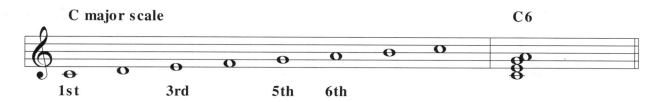

There will also be another place within the major scale (i.e. not just from the **1st** degree) from which **major seventh** (and **major sixth**) chords can be built - more about this in **Chapter 7**.

We first saw in **Chapter 3** that the minor triad already 'lives within' the major scale, if we build the triad from the second degree of the scale. In a similar manner, we can now derive the four-part **minor seventh** chord from the **2nd** degree of a major scale, as follows:-

**Figure 6.7. Deriving the D minor seventh chord from a C major scale**

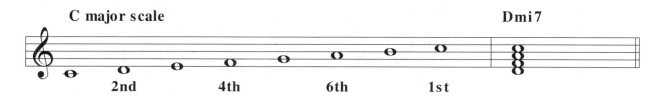

There will also be other places within the major scale (i.e. not just from the **2nd** degree) from which **minor seventh** chords can be built - more about this in **Chapter 7**.

We first saw in **Chapter 4** that the triad built from the **5th** degree of a major scale (as well as from the **1st** and **4th** degrees) is a **major** triad. Now if we build a four-part chord from the **5th** degree of a major scale, we get a **dominant seventh** chord, as follows:-

**Figure 6.8. Deriving the G dominant seventh chord from a C major scale**

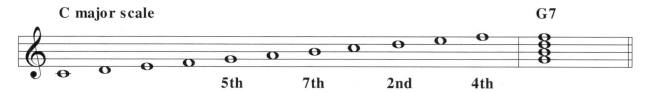

Inversions of four-part chords

In a similar manner to our work on triads, we will now look at **inversions** of these four-part chords. Again we should say that all of the four-part chords studied so far have been built in '**root position**', meaning that the root of each chord has always been the lowest note, and we have then 'built up' from the root to add the 3rd, 5th, and 7th (or 6th) of each chord. We can however **change the order** in which the notes of a four-part chord occur (from bottom to top on the staff), so that the root of the chord is now no longer the lowest note on the staff, as in the following example of a **C major seventh** chord:-

Figure 6.9. C major seventh chord and inversions

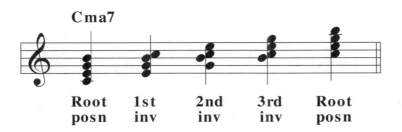

We can analyze the inversions in this example as follows:-

- The first and last **C major seventh** chords are in **root position**. The root of the chord (**C**) is the **lowest note**. The sequence of notes from lowest to highest is:- **C**, **E**, **G** and **B**.
- The second **C major seventh** chord is in **first inversion**. The root of the chord (**C**) is the **highest note**. The sequence of notes from lowest to highest is:- **E**, **G**, **B** and **C**.
- The third **C major seventh** chord is in **second inversion**. The root of the chord (**C**) is the **second note from the top**. The sequence of notes from lowest to highest is:- **G**, **B**, **C**, and **E**.
- The fourth **C major seventh** chord is in **third inversion**. The root of the chord (**C**) is the **second note from the bottom**. The sequence of notes from lowest to highest is:- **B**, **C**, **E** and **G**.

As we move from left to right through this example, each successive inversion can be derived by taking the lowest note in each case and **moving it up by one octave** (i.e. to the next highest occurence of the same note on the staff) as follows:-

- Starting with the first **root position** chord, if we take the lowest note (**C**) and move it up by an octave, we derive the following **first inversion** chord.
- Similarly, if we then take the lowest note of the **first inversion** chord (**E**) and move that up by an octave, we derive the following **second inversion** chord.
- Similarly, if we then take the lowest note of the **second inversion** chord (**G**) and move that up by an octave, we derive the following **third inversion** chord.

Inversions of four-part chords (contd)

- Finally if we take the lowest note of the **third inversion** chord (**B**) and move that up by an octave, we get back to the final root position chord, which overall is an **octave higher** than the starting **root position** chord.

Note also that inverting the chord on the previous page has created a different **internal interval structure** - whereas **root position seventh chords** consists of successive **third intervals** on the staff (i.e. between the root and 3rd, 3rd and 5th, and 5th & 7th of the chord), now we have a **second interval** on **top** of **two third intervals** within a **first inversion** chord, a **second interval between two third intervals** within a **second inversion** chord, and a **second interval** below two **third intervals** within a **third inversion** chord. In each case the **second** interval (which is actually a **minor second** interval in the case of an inverted **major seventh** chord) occurs between the **7th** and **root** of the chord (the notes **B** and **C** in this case).

Rather than separately analyze the inversions of the **major sixth** chord, we will see that this chord in itself can be seen as an **inversion of the minor seventh** chord, as follows:-

Figure 6.10. C minor seventh chord and inversions

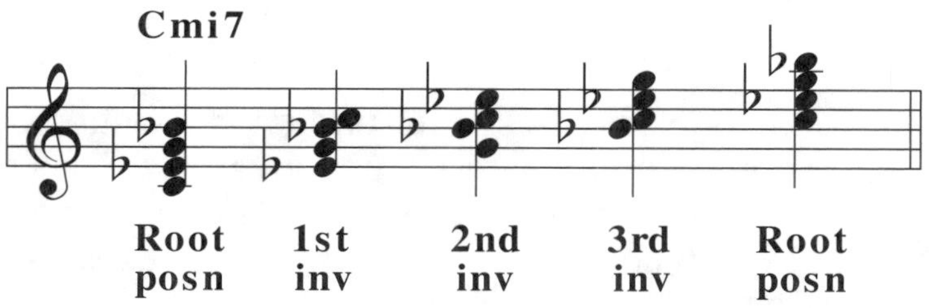

Exactly the same inversion concepts and terminology as before, now apply to the **minor seventh** chord in this example. Again a **second** interval (this time a **major second**, equivalent to a **whole-step**) is created between the 7th and root of the chord, in first, second and third inversions. Note that the first inversion **C minor 7th** shown above (i.e. the notes **Eb, G, Bb** and **C** from bottom to top) is equivalent to a **root position Eb major sixth** chord. (The remaining chords in the above example could also therefore be considered as inversions of an **Eb major sixth** chord). This leads to the following rule concerning these chords:-

- The **minor 7th chord** can be considered an inversion of the **major 6th chord**, and
- The **major 6th chord** can be considered an inversion of the **minor 7th chord**.

Next we will look at inversions of the **dominant seventh** chord (see example on the following page):-

Inversions of four-part chords (contd)

Figure 6.11. C dominant seventh chord and inversions

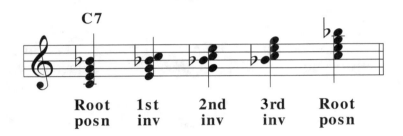

| Root posn | 1st inv | 2nd inv | 3rd inv | Root posn |

Again the same inversion concepts and terminology as before, also apply to the **dominant seventh** chord in this example. Again a **second** interval (this time a **major second**, equivalent to a **whole-step**) is created between the 7th and root of the chord, in first, second and third inversions.

Four-part chord recognition method and examples

We will now establish some rules for recognizing these four-part chords written on the staff, which will enable us to determine the correct chord symbol (and inversion) for a given chord. For the purpose of these examples, the chords may be in **root** position or **1st**, **2nd** or **3rd** inversion, and we will assume that **major 6th** chords are not being used (as we already know that the **major 6th** chord is an inversion of the **minor 7th** chord).

Figure 6.12. Four-part chord recognition example #1

First we will figure out if the chord is in root position, or first, second or third inversion. (This will also tell us what the **root** of the chord is, which in turn will enable us to identify the chord). Looking at the chord in example **#1** above, we notice that it consists of consecutive 'line' notes on the staff i.e. it is three **third** intervals stacked on top of one another, which tells us that the chord is in **root position** (as opposed to an **inverted** four-part chord, which would contain an internal **second** interval - see **Figs. 6.9. - 6.11.**). The **lowest** note (**E**) is therefore the **root** of this chord.

Four-part chord recognition method and examples (contd)

The next stage is to identify the intervals from the root up to the other parts of the chord - in particular the **third** and **seventh** of the chord i.e. we need to determine whether the chord has a **major or minor third interval**, and a **major or minor seventh interval**. (We recall that the **5th** of all the four-part chords studied so far, is always a **perfect 5th** interval from the root - so this does **not** help us identify the chord in question).

Using the interval recognition techniques presented in **Chapter 2**, we can determine that the **3rd** interval in this chord (**E** up to **G#**) is a **major 3rd**, and the **7th** interval in this chord (**E** up to **D**) is a **minor 7th**. (If you're still not sure how to figure out these intervals, review **Chapter 2** as necessary - in particular **Figs. 2.18. - 2.21.** and accompanying text). Checking our four-part chord interval summary on **p160**, we note that the four-part chord with major 3rd and minor 7th intervals is a **dominant 7th** chord. The chord in example #1 is therefore an **E dominant seventh** chord, for which the correct chord symbol would be **E7**.

Figure 6.13. Four-part chord recognition example #2

(Note that we have used bass clef in this example).

The internal intervals in this chord look different to the previous example - now we have a **second** interval **between two third** intervals. This is an indication of a **second inversion** four-part seventh chord (see text following **Fig. 6.9.**). We also recall that the **root** of a second inversion four-part seventh chord is the **second note from the top** (which is also the higher note of the second interval present). In this example the second note from the top is **Bb**, which is therefore the **root** of this chord.

Again we then determine the **third** and **seventh** intervals present in the chord (i.e. the intervals between the root up to the 3rd, and the root up to the 7th, if the chord were in root position). The **third** of the above chord is the note immediately above the **root** (which we have decided is **Bb**) - this is the note **D**. We know that the **seventh** of the chord is always the **lowest** note of the internal **second interval**, within inverted four-part seventh chords - this is the note **A** in the above example. Therefore **Bb** up to **D** is the **3rd** interval we need to analyze, and **Bb** up to **A** is the **7th** interval we need to analyze. Again using the interval recognition process outlined in **Chapter 2**, we see that **Bb** up to **D** is a **major 3rd** interval and that **Bb** up to **A** is a **major 7th** interval (**D** and **A** being the 3rd and 7th degrees respectively of a **Bb major** scale). Checking our four-part chord interval summary on **p160**, we note that the four-part chord with major 3rd and major 7th intervals is a **major 7th** chord. The chord in example #2 above is therefore a **Bb major seventh** chord, for which the correct chord symbol would be **Bbma7**.

Four-part chord recognition method and examples (contd)

Figure 6.14. Four-part chord recognition example #3

Looking again at the internal intervals within this chord, now we have a **second** interval **below two third** intervals. This is an indication of a **third inversion** four-part seventh chord (see text following **Fig. 6.9.**). We also recall that the **root** of a third inversion four-part seventh chord is the **second note from the bottom** (which is also the higher note of the second interval present). In this example the second note from the bottom is **F#**, which is therefore the **root** of this chord.

Again we then determine the **third** and **seventh** intervals present in the chord (i.e. the intervals between the root up to the 3rd, and the root up to the 7th, if the chord were in root position). The **third** of the above chord is the note immediately above the **root** (which we have decided is **F#**) - this is the note **A**. We know that the **seventh** of the chord is always the **lowest** note of the internal **second interval**, within inverted four-part seventh chords - this is the note **E** in the above example. Therefore **F#** up to **A** is the **3rd** interval we need to analyze, and **F#** up to **E** is the **7th** interval we need to analyze. Again using the interval recognition process outlined in **Chapter 2**, we see that **F#** up to **A** is a **minor 3rd** interval and that **F#** up to **E** is a **minor 7th** interval. Checking our four-part chord interval summary on **p160**, we note that the four-part chord with minor 3rd and minor 7th intervals is a **minor 7th** chord. The chord in example #3 above is therefore an **F# minor seventh** chord, for which the correct chord symbol would be **F#mi7**.

We can summarize this four-part (seventh) chord recognition process as follows:-

- first of all, figure out if the chord is **root position**, or **1st**, **2nd** or **3rd** inversion
    - the chord is in **root position** if it consists of **consecutive third intervals**
    - the chord is in **1st**, **2nd**, or **3rd** inversion if there is a **second interval** on the **top**, **middle** or **bottom** of the chord respectively.
- then determine the root of the chord, which
    - the **bottom** note of a **root position** chord, or
    - the **top** note of the internal **second interval**, within an inverted chord.
- then analyze the **intervals** from the the **root** of the chord up to the **3rd** and the **7th**
    - if there are **major 3rd** and **major 7th** intervals present, the chord is a **major 7th**.
    - if there are **minor 3rd** and **minor 7th** intervals present, the chord is a **minor 7th**.
    - if there are **major 3rd** and **minor 7th** intervals present, the chord is a **dominant 7th**.

Chapter Six Workbook Questions

<u>1.</u>   **<u>*Root position four-part chord spelling*</u>**

Write the notes on the staff corresponding to the the following major 7th chord symbols:-

  1.   2.   3.   4.

  Fma7   **A♭ma7**   **Bma7**   **Gma7**

Write the notes on the staff corresponding to the the following major 6th chord symbols:-

  5.   6.   7.   8.

  E6   **E♭6**   **B♭6**   **D6**

Write the notes on the staff corresponding to the the following minor 7th chord symbols:-

  9.   10.   11.   12.

  Ami7   **Cmi7**   **F♯mi7**   **Emi7**

  13.   14.   15.   16.

  C♯mi7   **Fmi7**   **G♯mi7**   **Bmi7**

1. **_Root position four-part chord spelling (contd)_**

Write the notes on the staff corresponding to the the following dominant 7th chord symbols:-

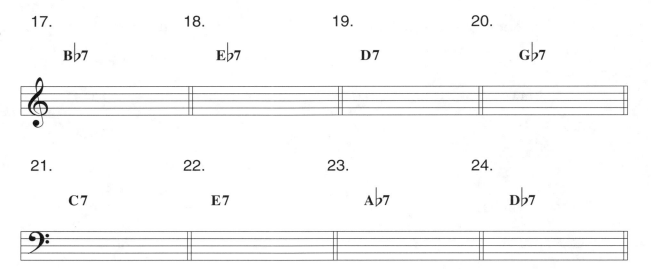

17.   18.   19.   20.

B♭7   E♭7   D7   G♭7

21.   22.   23.   24.

C7   E7   A♭7   D♭7

2. **_Root position four-part chord recognition_**

This section contains a mixture of (root-position) major 7th, major 6th, minor 7th and dominant 7th four-part chords. Write the chord symbol above the staff for each question:-

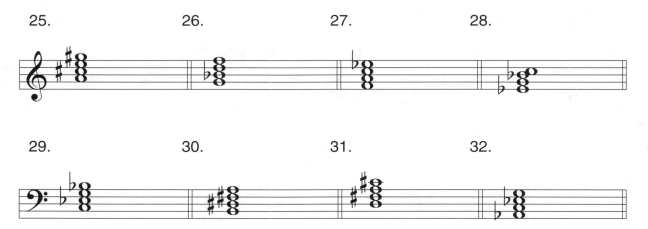

25.   26.   27.   28.

29.   30.   31.   32.

168

2. *Root position four-part chord recognition (contd)*

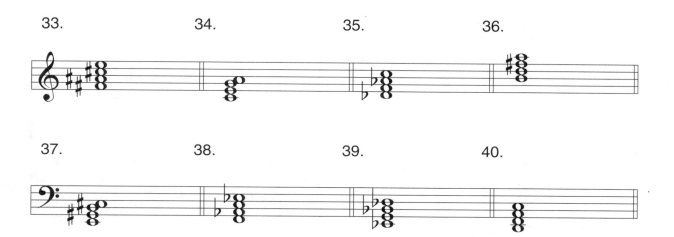

3. *Inverted four-part chord spelling*

Write the notes on the staff corresponding to the following four-part chord symbols and requested inversions. (For example, for question #41 you need to spell a 2nd inversion **Bbma7** chord).

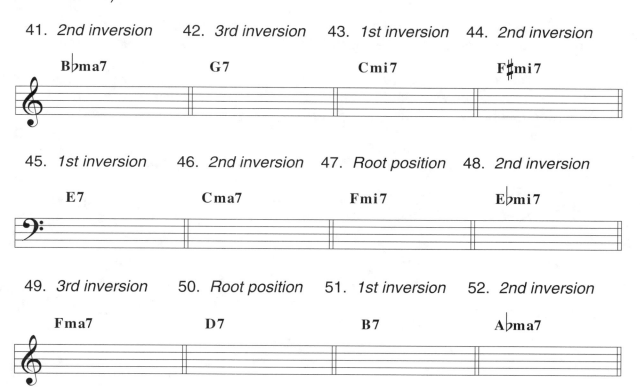

3.   *Inverted four-part chord spelling (contd)*

53. *3rd inversion* 54. *1st inversion* 55. *2nd inversion* 56. *1st inversion*

Dma7   Ama7   G♭7   A♭7

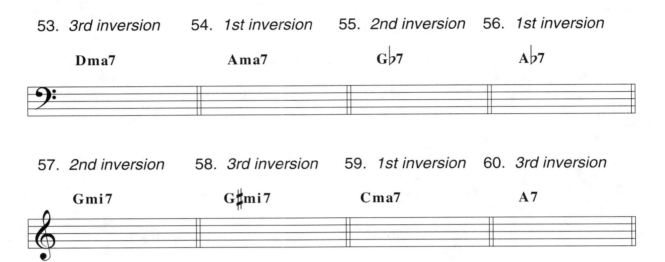

57. *2nd inversion* 58. *3rd inversion* 59. *1st inversion* 60. *3rd inversion*

Gmi7   G♯mi7   Cma7   A7

4.   *Inverted four-part chord recognition*

This section contains a mixture of major 7th, minor 7th and dominant 7th four-part chords. (For the purposes of this exercise, you are to assume that no major 6th chords are present - the major 6th chord is an inversion of the minor 7th chord, and vice versa). Each four-part chord may be in root position, 1st inversion, 2nd inversion or 3rd inversion. You are to write the chord symbol above the staff for each question.

Remember that these chords in root position will look like a succession of 3rd intervals from bottom to top, whereas the inverted four-part chords will have a 2nd interval immediately below the root of the chord.

61.   62.   63.   64.

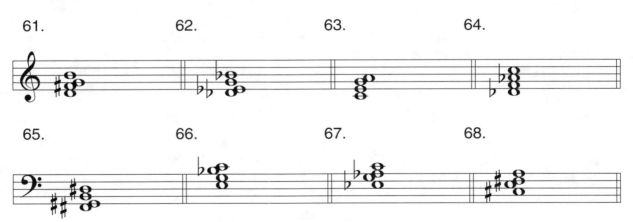

65.   66.   67.   68.

170

4. _Inverted four-part chord recognition (contd)_

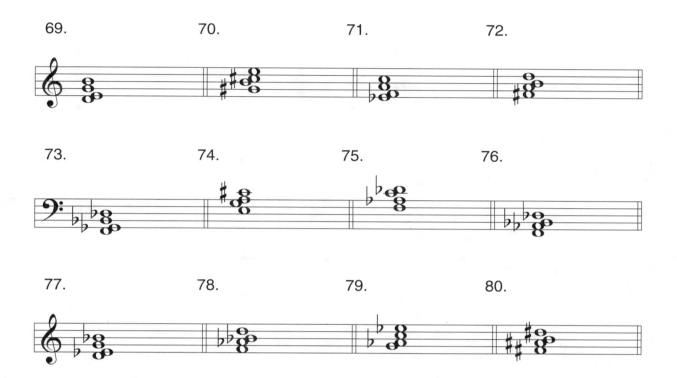

69.   70.   71.   72.

73.   74.   75.   76.

77.   78.   79.   80.

Chapter Six Workbook Answers

1. *Root position four-part chord spelling - answers*

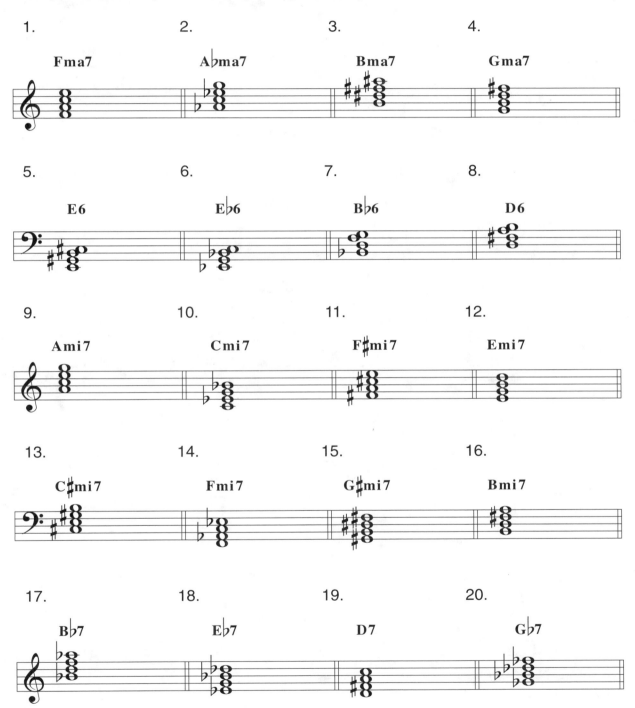

1. **_Root position four-part chord spelling - answers (contd)_**

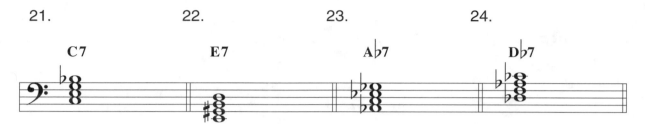

2. **_Root position four-part chord recognition - answers_**

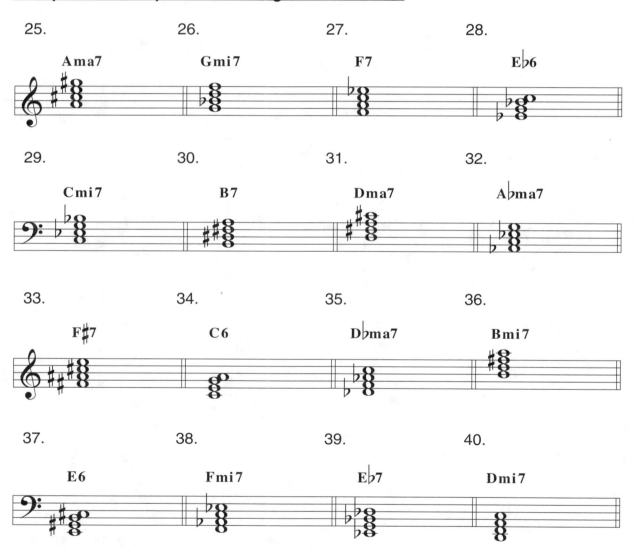

3. *Inverted four-part chord spelling - answers*

41. *2nd inversion*   42. *3rd inversion*   43. *1st inversion*   44. *2nd inversion*

45. *1st inversion*   46. *2nd inversion*   47. *Root position*   48. *2nd inversion*

49. *3rd inversion*   50. *Root position*   51. *1st inversion*   52. *2nd inversion*

53. *3rd inversion*   54. *1st inversion*   55. *2nd inversion*   56. *1st inversion*

57. *2nd inversion*   58. *3rd inversion*   59. *1st inversion*   60. *3rd inversion*

4. Inverted four-part chord recognition - answers

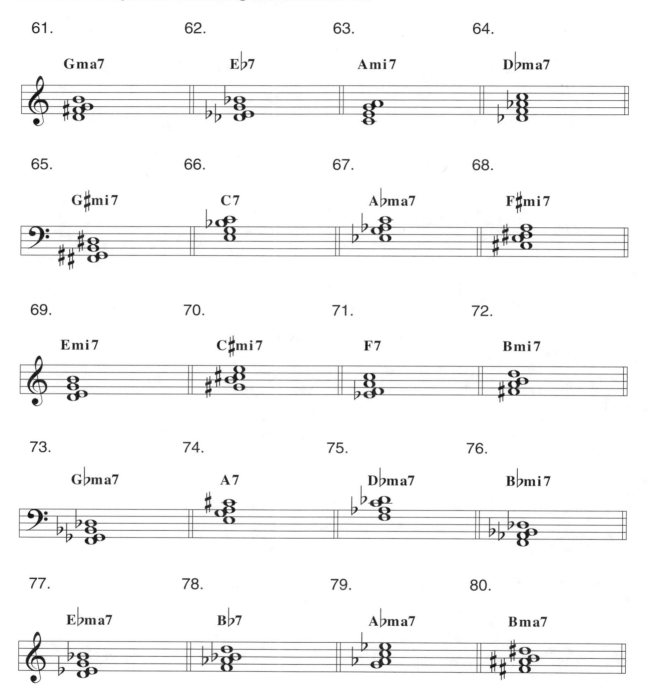

Diatonic four-part chords

Introduction

In a similar manner to our work on diatonic triads in **Chapter 4**, we will now derive all diatonic four-part chord relationships. We have seen when deriving the **major 7th** and **6th**, **minor 7th** and **dominant 7th** four-part chords in **Chapter 6**, that these chords could also be found within the major scale. Four-part chords which are wholly contained within a major scale (i.e. can be 'built from' some degree of a major scale) are termed **diatonic four-part chords**.

Building diatonic four-part chords from each degree of a major scale

We will now go through a **C major scale** and build four-part chords from each degree of the scale (while staying within the major scale restriction) to see which chord qualities (i.e. major 7th, minor 7th etc) are produced in each case:-

Figure 7.1. Four-part chord #1 built from the 1st degree of the C major scale (C major 7th)

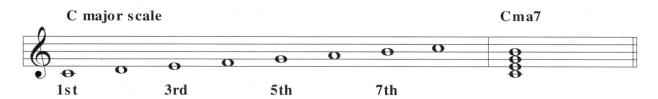

We have already seen in **Fig. 6.5.** that a **major 7th** chord is built from the **1st** degree of the major scale (i.e. when we take the 1st, 3rd, 5th and 7th degrees of the scale). Relating back to the derivation of the major 7th chord by **intervals** in **Fig. 6.1.**, we note that the interval between **C** and **E** (the **root** and **3rd** of the chord) is a **major 3rd**, the interval between **C** and **G** (the **root** and **5th** of the chord) is a **perfect 5th**, and the interval between **C** and **B** (the **root** and **7th** of the chord) is a **major 7th**.

Figure 7.2. Four-part chord #2 built from the 1st degree of the C major scale (C major 6th)

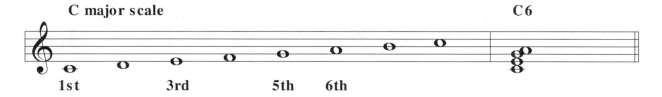

Building diatonic four-part chords from each degree of a major scale (contd)

Regarding **Fig. 7.2.** on the previous page, we have already seen in **Fig. 6.6.** that a **major 6th** chord is also built from the **1st** degree of the major scale (i.e. when we take the 1st, 3rd, 5th and 6th degrees of the scale). Relating back to the derivation of the major 6th chord by **intervals** in **Fig. 6.2.**, we note that the interval between **C** and **E** (the **root** and **3rd** of the chord) is a **major 3rd**, the interval between **C** and **G** (the **root** and **5th** of the chord) is a **perfect 5th**, and the interval between **C** and **A** (the **root** and **6th** of the chord) is a **major 6th**.

Figure 7.3. Four-part chord built from the 2nd degree of the C major scale (D minor 7th)

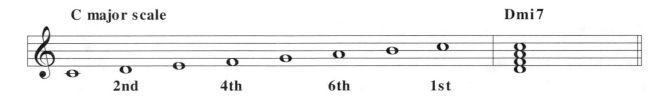

We have already seen in **Fig. 6.7.** that a **minor 7th** chord is built from the **2nd** degree of the major scale (i.e. when we take the 2nd, 4th, 6th and 1st degrees of the scale). Relating back to the derivation of the minor 7th chord by **intervals** in **Fig. 6.3.**, we note that the interval between **D** and **F** (the **root** and **3rd** of the chord) is a **minor 3rd**, the interval between **D** and **A** (the **root** and **5th** of the chord) is a **perfect 5th**, and the interval between **D** and **C** (the **root** and **7th** of the chord) is a **minor 7th.**

Figure 7.4. Four-part chord built from the 3rd degree of the C major scale (E minor 7th)

In the above example we see that a **minor 7th** chord is now also built from the **3rd** degree of the major scale (i.e. when we take the 3rd, 5th, 7th and 2nd degrees of the scale). Again considering the minor 7th chord **intervals** in **Fig. 6.3.**, we note that the interval between **E** and **G** (the **root** and **3rd** of the chord) is a **minor 3rd**, the interval between **E** and **B** (the **root** and **5th** of the chord) is a **perfect 5th**, and the interval between **E** and **D** (the **root** and **7th** of the chord) is a **minor 7th.**

Building diatonic four-part chords from each degree of a major scale (contd)

Figure 7.5. Four-part chord #1 built from the 4th degree of the C major scale (F major 7th)

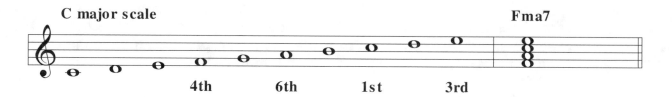

In the above example we see that a **major 7th** chord is now also built from the **4th** degree of the major scale (i.e. when we take the 4th, 6th, 1st and 3rd degrees of the scale). Again considering the major 7th chord **intervals** in **Fig. 6.1.**, we note that the interval between **F** and **A** (the **root** and **3rd** of the chord) is a **major 3rd**, the interval between **F** and **C** (the **root** and **5th** of the chord) is a **perfect 5th**, and the interval between **F** and **E** (the **root** and **7th** of the chord) is a **major 7th**.

Figure 7.6. Four-part chord #2 built from the 4th degree of the C major scale (F major 6th)

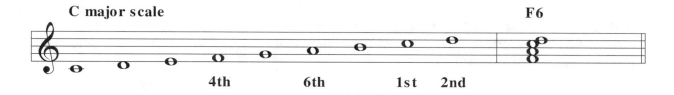

In the above example we see that a **major 6th** chord is now also built from the **4th** degree of the major scale (i.e. when we take the 4th, 6th, 1st and 2nd degrees of the scale). Again considering the major 6th chord **intervals** in **Fig. 6.2.**, we note that the interval between **F** and **A** (the **root** and **3rd** of the chord) is a **major 3rd**, the interval between **F** and **C** (the **root** and **5th** of the chord) is a **perfect 5th**, and the interval between **F** and **D** (the **root** and **6th** of the chord) is a **major 6th**.

Figure 7.7. Four-part chord built from the 5th degree of the C major scale (G dominant 7th)

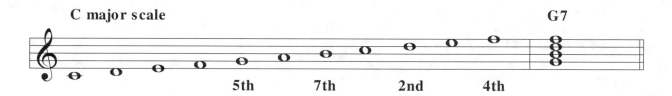

Building diatonic four-part chords from each degree of a major scale (contd)

Regarding **Fig. 7.7.** on the previous page, we see that a **dominant 7th** chord is now built from the **5th** degree of the major scale (i.e. when we take the 5th, 7th, 2nd and 4th degrees of the scale). Relating back to the derivation of the dominant 7th chord by **intervals** in **Fig. 6.4.**, we note that the interval between **G** and **B** (the **root** and **3rd** of the chord) is a **major 3rd**, the interval between **G** and **D** (the **root** and **5th** of the chord) is a **perfect 5th**, and the interval between **G** and **F** (the **root** and **7th** of the chord) is a **minor 7th**.

Figure 7.8. Four-part chord built from the 6th degree of the C major scale (A minor 7th)

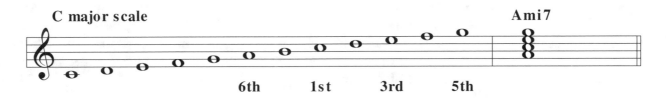

In the above example we see that a **minor 7th** chord is now also built from the **6th** degree of the major scale (i.e. when we take the 6th, 1st, 3rd and 5th degrees of the scale). Again considering the minor 7th chord **intervals** in **Fig. 6.3.**, we note that the interval between **A** and **C** (the **root** and **3rd** of the chord) is a **minor 3rd**, the interval between **A** and **E** (the **root** and **5th** of the chord) is a **perfect 5th**, and the interval between **A** and **G** (the **root** and **7th** of the chord) is a **minor 7th**.

Figure 7.9. Four-part chord built from the 7th degree of the C major scale (B minor 7th with flatted 5th)

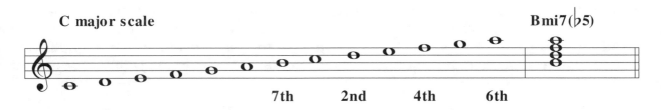

When building a diatonic four-part chord from the seventh degree of a major scale, a new chord quality is produced - the **minor 7th with flatted 5th** - which has a chord symbol suffix of '**mi7(b5)**'. If we were to construct a **minor 7th** chord from the note **B** according to the intervals defined in **Fig. 6.3.**, the resulting chord would contain the notes **B**, **D**, **F#** and **A**. If we then **flat the 5th** of this chord (i.e. change the **F#** to **F**), we would then get to the above **Bmi7(b5)** chord symbol. (Although this is technically an 'altered' chord symbol, we are still **entirely within the major scale restrictions** - we are simply 'labelling' the four-part chord built from the 7th degree). **Four-part chord symbols with 'altered fifths' will be further explained in Chapter 9.**

180

Building diatonic four-part chords from each degree of a major scale (contd)

We can summarize these **diatonic four-part chord qualities** as follows:-

- The four-part chord built from the *1st* degree of a major scale is always a *major 7th* or *major 6th*.
- The four-part chord built from the *2nd* degree of a major scale is always a *minor 7th*.
- The four-part chord built from the *3rd* degree of a major scale is always a *minor 7th*.
- The four-part chord built from the *4th* degree of a major scale is always a *major 7th* or *major 6th*.
- The four-part chord built from the *5th* degree of a major scale is always a *dominant 7th*.
- The four-part chord built from the *6th* degree of a major scale is always a *minor 7th*.
- The four-part chord built from the *7th* degree of a major scale is always a *minor 7th with flatted 5th*.

Again (as with diatonic triads studied in **Chapter 4**) it is important to realize that **all of these diatonic four-part chord qualities are simply the result of the intervals already present in the major scale** (first derived in **Fig. 1.42.**) - in other words we build the chords within the major scale restriction, and only afterwards do we then **analyze the chord qualities that the scale has 'given back to us'**. Again this confirms that it is the **scale that came first** and that the diatonic chords are simply **incomplete representations of the scale**.

*(Diatonic four-part chords in all keys are listed in **Appendix Three** at the back of this book).*

Four-part chord plurality

As already seen with diatonic triads, if the same **four-part chord quality** can be built from **more than one place** in the major scale, then it follows that a **particular four-part chord of that quality** will occur in more than one major scale. We see that the **major 7th** chord in the above table, can be built from the **1st** and **4th** degrees of a major scale. Therefore a particular major 7th chord (let's say a **C major 7th**) must occur from:-

- the **1st** degree of a major scale,
- the **4th** degree of another major scale.

To establish the major scales containing the **C major 7th** chord, you would therefore need to figure out the major scales which contained the note **C** as their **1st** and **4th** degrees i.e.:-

- which major scale do I know that contains the note **C** as its **1st** degree?
- which major scale do I know that contains the note **C** as its **4th** degree?

Four-part chord plurality (contd)

The major scale which contains **C** as its **1st** degree is of course **C major**! We already figured out which major scale has **C** as its **4th** degree, in **Chapter 4** (please refer to **Figs. 4.8. - 4.11.** and accompanying text as required) - we established then that **C** is the **4th** degree of a **G major** scale. So we can now summarize that the **C major 7th** chord occurs from:-

-       the **1st** degree of a major scale   -   this is the **C major** scale.
-       the **4th** degree of a major scale   -   this is the **G major** scale.

Now we'll look at these two occurrences of the **C major 7th** chord, within the diatonic four-part chords built from the **C major** and **G major** scales:-

Figure 7.10. C major 7th chord - built from the 1st degree of a C major scale

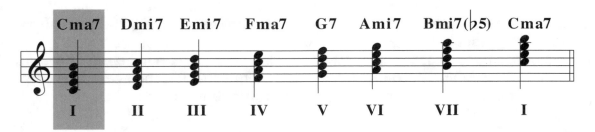

(*Note that in all of these diatonic four-part chord examples, a **major 6th** chord can also be built from the **1st** and **4th** degrees of the major scale - these chords would be **C6** and **F6** in the above **C major** scale*).

Figure 7.11. C major 7th chord - built from the 4th degree of a G major scale

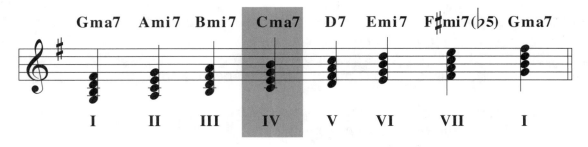

*Note that the key signature of **G major** (one sharp - see **Fig. 1.83.**) is 'in force' in this example.*

Now we'll look at a plurality example involving **minor 7th** chords. We have seen that the **minor 7th** chord can be built from the **2nd**, **3rd** and **6th** degrees of a major scale (review summary at the top of the previous page as necessary). Therefore a particular minor 7th chord (let's say a **D minor 7th**) must occur from (see following page):-

Four-part chord plurality (contd)

- the **2nd** degree of a major scale,
- the **3rd** degree of another major scale, and
- the **6th** degree of yet another major scale.

To establish the major scales containing the **D minor 7th** chord, you would therefore need to figure out the major scales which contained the note **D** as their **2nd**, **3rd** and **6th** degrees i.e.:-

- which major scale do I know that contains the note **D** as its **2nd** degree?
- which major scale do I know that contains the note **D** as its **3rd** degree?
- which major scale do I know that contains the note **D** as its **6th** degree?

Again we have already solved this problem in **Chapter 4** (please refer to **Figs. 4.19. - 4.26.** and accompanying text as required) - we established then that **D** is the **2nd** degree of a **C major** scale, the **3rd** degree of a **Bb major** scale, and the **6th** degree of an **F major** scale. So we can now summarize that the **D minor 7th** chord occurs from:-

- the **2nd** degree of a major scale - this is the **C major** scale.
- the **3rd** degree of a major scale - this is the **Bb major** scale.
- the **6th** degree of a major scale - this is the **F major** scale.

Now we'll look at these three occurrences of the **D minor 7th** chord, within the diatonic four-part chords built from the **C major**, **Bb major** and **F major** scales:-

Figure 7.12. D minor 7th chord - built from the 2nd degree of a C major scale

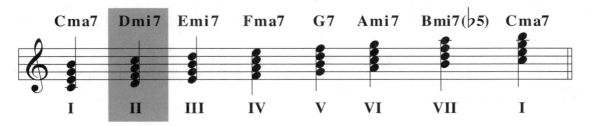

Figure 7.13. D minor 7th chord - built from the 3rd degree of a Bb major scale

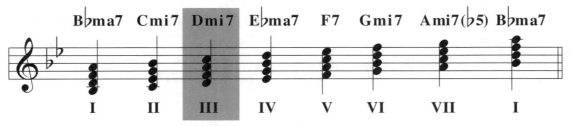

*Note that the key signature of **Bb** major (two flats - see **Fig. 1.76.**) is 'in force' in this example.*

Four-part chord plurality (contd)

Figure 7.14. D minor 7th chord - built from the 6th degree of an F major scale

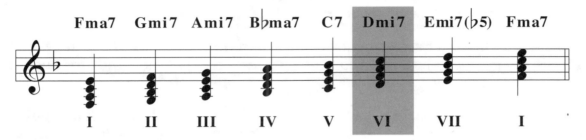

*Note that the key signature of **F** major (one flat - see **Fig. 1.74.**) is 'in force' in this example.*

Note that we have not included an example of the **dominant 7th** chord or the **minor 7th with flatted 5th** chord in these plurality examples. That is because the **dominant 7th** chord only occurs from the 5th degree of the major scale, and the **minor 7th with flatted 5th** chord only occurs from the 7th degree of the major scale. These chords will therefore never be found within (i.e. diatonic to) more than one major scale.

We can finally summarize these four-part chord plurality relationships as follows:-

- Any **major 7th** (or **major 6th**) chord can be built from the **1st** and **4th** degrees of two different major scales respectively.
- Any **minor 7th** chord can be built from the **2nd**, **3rd** and **6th** degrees of three different major scales respectively.
- Any **dominant 7th** chord can only be built from the **5th** degree of one major scale.
- Any **minor 7th with flatted 5th** chord can only be built from the **7th** degree of one major scale.

Diatonic four-part chord progressions

We will now look at some diatonic four-part chord progression examples. Again (in a similar manner as for diatonic triads in **Chapter 4**) it is important that you are able to derive diatonic four-part chords and chord symbols from all the scale degrees (**I - VII**) in any key. As we have seen in the previous examples, all diatonic four-part chord symbols consist of **two** components (see following page):-

Diatonic four-part chord progressions (contd)

- the **root** of the chord - this is the major scale degree from which the chord is built
- the chord **suffix** (the part of the chord symbol immediately following the root):-
    - '**ma7**' suffix used for **major 7th** chords (built from the **1st** and **4th** degrees)
    - '**6**' or '**ma6**' suffix used for **major 6th** chords (also built from the **1st** and **4th** degrees)
    - '**mi7**' suffix used for **minor 7th** chords (built from the **2nd**, **3rd** and **6th** degrees)
    - '**7**' suffix used for **dominant 7th** chords (built from the **5th** degree)
    - '**mi7(b5)**' suffix used for **minor 7th with flatted 5th** chords (built from the **7th** degree)

Let's say we wanted to create the diatonic four-part chords and chord symbols for a **II - V - I** progression (i.e. four-part chords built from the **2nd**, **5th** and **1st** degrees) in **E major**.

First we would spell the **E major** scale to determine that the 2nd, 5th and 1st degrees were the notes **F#**, **B** and **E** respectively. Regarding chord qualities required, we note that:-

- a **minor 7th** chord (using the chord symbol suffix '**mi7**') is built from the **2nd** degree of a major scale, so the required chord symbol in this case is **F#mi7**
- a **dominant 7th** chord (using the chord symbol suffix '**7**') is built from the **5th** degree of a major scale, so the required chord symbol in this case is **B7**
- a **major 7th** chord (using the chord symbol suffix '**ma7**') is built from the **1st** degree of a major scale, so the required chord symbol in this case is **Ema7**
    *(For the purpose of this exercise, we will assume that the **major 7th** chord - rather than the **major 6th** chord - is to be built from the **1st** degree of the scale).*

We would then build chords on the staff from each of these scale degrees as follows:-

Figure 7.15. II - V - I diatonic four-part chord progression in E major

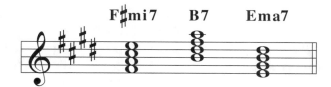

Note that the key signature of **E** major (four sharps - see **Fig. 1.87.**) is 'in force' in this example.

In styles of music using four-part chords and above (i.e. jazz & standards, latin, R'n'B etc) the **II - V - I** is seen as a very important and 'definitive' progression. Other four-part diatonic chords which we have identified in this chapter, can be viewed as **substitute** chords for either the **II**, the **V** or the **I**, which can be viewed as **primary** chords. Definitive **II - V - I** chords and their substitutes, is a major area of study in the following **Contemporary Music Theory Level 2** course - stay tuned!

Diatonic four-part chord progressions (contd)

Now we will create the diatonic four-part chords and chord symbols for a **III - VI - II** progression (i.e. four-part chords built from the **3rd**, **6th** and **2nd** degrees) in **Bb major**.

First we would spell the **Bb major** scale to determine that the 3rd, 6th and 2nd degrees were the notes **D**, **G** and **C** respectively. Regarding chord qualities required, we note that:-

- a **minor 7th** chord (using the chord symbol suffix '**mi7**') is built from the **3rd** degree of a major scale, so the required chord symbol in this case is **Dmi7**
- a **minor 7th** chord (again using the chord symbol suffix '**mi7**') is also built from the **6th** degree of a major scale, so the required chord symbol in this case is **Gmi7**
- a **minor 7th** chord (again using the chord symbol suffix '**mi7**') is also built from the **2nd** degree of a major scale, so the required chord symbol in this case is **Cmi7**.

We would then build chords on the staff from each of these scale degrees as follows:-

Figure 7.16. III - VI - II diatonic four-part chord progression in Bb major

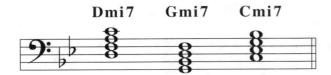

Note that the key signature of **Bb** major (two flats - see **Fig. 1.76.**) is 'in force' in this example, and that **bass clef** has been used.

Analyzing four-part chord progressions to determine the major key being used

We will now look at some four-part chord progressions to determine **which major key is being used** i.e. which major scale all of the chords are **found in**, or '**diatonic to**'. To do this we need to apply the '**four-part chord plurality**' rules as summarized on **p184**. Initially we will look at each chord in the progression, to determine which keys the chord could belong to. At the end of this process, we will then determine if there is one key 'in common' among all of the possibilities. Again this is best demonstrated by working through some examples, as follows:-

Figure 7.17. Four-part chord progression analysis example #1

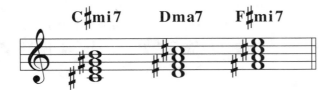

Note that there is now **no key signature in force** - any necessary accidentals are supplied directly on the staff.

Analyzing four-part chord progressions to determine the major key (contd)

We will now analyze each chord to determine which keys it could belong to, as follows:-

- **C# minor 7th** - Using the same process as outlined for the **D minor 7th** chord from the bottom of **p182** to **p183** (and **Figs. 7.12. - 7.14.**), but applied to a **C# minor 7th** chord, we see that this chord can be built from:-
  - the **2nd** degree of a **B major** scale
  - the **3rd** degree of a **A major** scale
  - the **6th** degree of an **E major** scale.

- **D major 7th** - Using the same process as outlined for the **C major 7th** chord from the bottom of **p181** to **p182** (and **Figs. 7.10. - 7.11.**), but applied to a **D major 7th** chord, we see that this chord can be built from:-
  - the **1st** degree of a **D major** scale
  - the **4th** degree of an **A major** scale.

- **F# minor 7th** - Using the same process as outlined for the **D minor 7th** chord from the bottom of **p182** to **p183** (and **Figs. 7.12. - 7.14.**), but applied to an **F# minor 7th** chord, we see that this chord can be built from:-
  - the **2nd** degree of an **E major** scale
  - the **3rd** degree of a **D major** scale
  - the **6th** degree of an **A major** scale.

Now we look at these options to see if there is a key 'in common' between the chords:-

Figure 7.18. Four-part chord progression analysis example #1 - with major key options

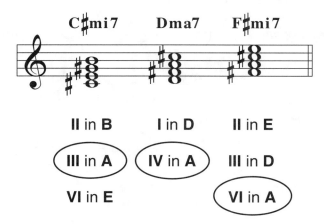

Note that all of the diatonic options above have been listed under each chord - the one key in common throughout is the **key of A** - so we conclude that the progression constitutes a **III - IV - VI** sequence in **A major**.

Analyzing four-part chord progressions to determine the major key (contd)

As with the triad progressions, you will learn to recognize certain diatonic four-part relationships more quickly, as an alternative to the rather 'step-by-step' method outlined on the previous page. For example, reviewing the diatonic four-part chord qualities at the top of **p181**, we see that the only place in the scale that a **minor 7th** is immediately followed by a **major 7th** chord (i.e. built from consecutive scale degrees), is from the **3rd** and the **4th** degrees of the major scale respectively. We could conclude therefore that the **C# minor 7th** and **D major 7th** chords in the preceding example (with roots a scale-step apart i.e. using consecutive letternames) are a **III** and **IV** in **A major**.

Figure 7.19. Four-part chord progression analysis example #2

C major 7th -
- We have seen in **Figs. 7.10. - 7.11.** that this chord can be built from:-
  - the **1st** degree of a **C major** scale
  - the **4th** degree of a **G major** scale.

G major 7th -
- We see that this major 7th chord can be built from:-
  - the **1st** degree of a **G major** scale
  - the **4th** degree of a **D major** scale.

A minor 7th -
- We see that this minor 7th chord can be built from:-
  - the **2nd** degree of a **G major** scale
  - the **3rd** degree of an **F major** scale
  - the **6th** degree of a **C major** scale.

Again we look at these options to see if there is a key 'in common' between the chords:-

Figure 7.20. Four-part chord progression analysis example #2 - with major key options

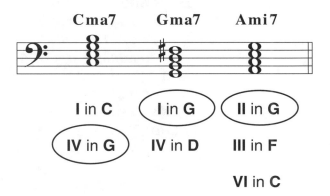

*Again all of the diatonic options above have been listed under each chord - the one key in common throughout is the **key of G** - so we conclude that the progression constitutes a **IV - I - II** sequence in **G major**.*

188

Chapter Seven Workbook Questions

_1._   **_Writing diatonic four-part chords for specified keys_**

Write the key signatures, followed by all of the diatonic four-part chords on the staff (in root position), and corresponding chord symbols above the staff, for the following major keys:-

1.   *Key of D major*

2.   *Key of Eb major*

3.   *Key of F major*

4.   *Key of A major*

5.   *Key of Ab major*

_189_

_1._   **_Writing diatonic four-part chords for specified keys (contd)_**

6.   _Key of B major_

7.   _Key of G major_

8.   _Key of Db major_

9.   _Key of E major_

10.   _Key of Bb major_

2. *Writing diatonic four-part chords for specified progressions*

Write the key signatures, followed by the diatonic four-part chords on the staff (in root position) and chord symbols above the staff, for the following diatonic progressions.

You are to write a **II - V - I(ma7)** diatonic four-part chord progression in the keys requested, for questions 11 - 14. For example, in the key of **D** you would write the D major key signature followed by the notes and chord symbols for the chords **Emi7**, **A7** and **Dma7**.

11. *Key of G Major*   12. *Key of Bb Major*

13. *Key of A Major*   14. *Key of F Major*

You are to write a **III - VI - II** diatonic four-part chord progression in the keys requested, for questions 15 - 18. For example, in the key of **F** you would write the F major key signature followed by the notes and chord symbols for the chords **Ami7**, **Dmi7** and **Gmi7**.

15. *Key of E Major*   16. *Key of Gb Major*

17. *Key of Eb Major*   18. *Key of B Major*

2. *Writing diatonic four-part chords for specified progressions (contd)*

You are to write a *IV - III - II - I(ma7)* diatonic four-part chord progression in the keys requested, for questions 19 - 22. For example, in the key of *G* you would write the G major key signature followed by the notes and chord symbols for the chords *Cma7, Bmi7, Ami7* and *Gma7*.

19. *Key of Ab Major*   20. *Key of D Major*

21. *Key of F# Major*   22. *Key of Db Major*

3. *Diatonic four-part chord key analysis*

You are to write chord symbols above the staff, and then determine the major key, for each of the following diatonic four-part chord progressions. Remember that:-
-       the major 7th chord can occur from the 1st or 4th degrees of a major key
-       the minor 7th chord can occur from the 2nd, 3rd, or 6th degrees of a major key
-       the dominant 7th chord can only occur from the 5th degree of a major key.
-       the minor 7th with flatted 5th chord can only occur from the 7th degree of a major key.

23. *Key of _____*   24. *Key of _____*

3. **_Diatonic four-part chord key analysis (contd)_**

25.   *Key of* _____

26.   *Key of* _____

27.   *Key of* _____

28.   *Key of* _____

29.   *Key of* _____

30.   *Key of* _____

193

Chapter Seven Workbook Answers

1. **Writing diatonic four-part chords for specified keys - answers**

1. *Key of D major*

Dma7   Emi7   F♯mi7   Gma7   A7   Bmi7   C♯mi7(♭5)   Dma7

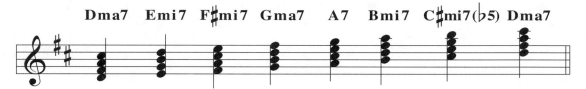

2. *Key of Eb major*

E♭ma7   Fmi7   Gmi7   A♭ma7   B♭7   Cmi7   Dmi7(♭5)   E♭ma7

3. *Key of F major*

Fma7   Gmi7   Ami7   B♭ma7   C7   Dmi7   Emi7(♭5)   Fma7

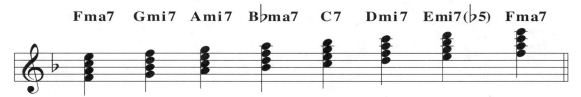

4. *Key of A major*

Ama7   Bmi7   C♯mi7   Dma7   E7   F♯mi7   G♯mi7(♭5)   Ama7

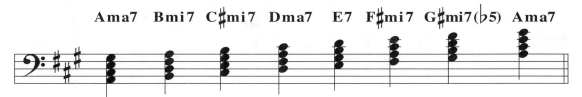

5. *Key of Ab major*

A♭ma7   B♭mi7   Cmi7   D♭ma7   E♭7   Fmi7   Gmi7(♭5)   A♭ma7

1. **_Writing diatonic four-part chords for specified keys - answers (contd)_**

6. *Key of B major*

7. *Key of G major*

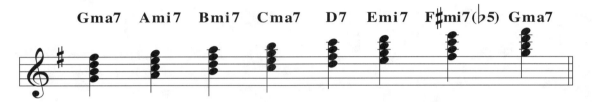

8. *Key of Db major*

9. *Key of E major*

10. *Key of Bb major*

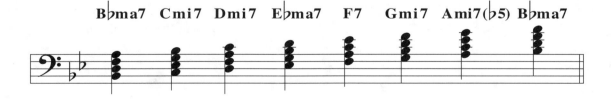

2. _Writing diatonic four-part chords for specified progressions - answers_

(**II - V - I** diatonic four-part progressions)

11. _Key of G Major_

12. _Key of Bb Major_

13. _Key of A Major_

14. _Key of F Major_

(**III - VI - II** diatonic four-part progressions)

15. _Key of E Major_

16. _Key of Gb Major_

17. _Key of Eb Major_

18. _Key of B Major_

2. **_Writing diatonic four-part chords for specified progressions - answers (contd)_**

(*IV - III - II - I* diatonic four-part chord progressions)

19.   *Key of Ab Major*   20.   *Key of D Major*

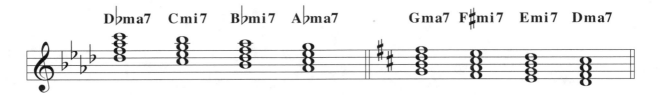

21.   *Key of F# Major*   22.   *Key of Db Major*

3. **_Diatonic four-part chord key analysis - answers_**

23.   *Key of A Major*   24.   *Key of F Major*

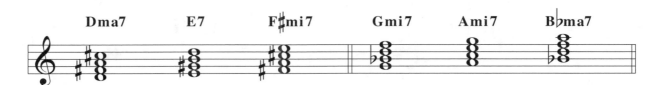

25.   *Key of G Major*   26.   *Key of Eb Major*

3. *Diatonic four-part chord key analysis - answers (contd)*

27. *Key of D Major*   28. *Key of Ab Major*

29. *Key of Bb Major*   30. *Key of E Major*

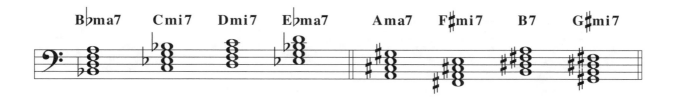

200

Minor scales and key signatures

Introduction to minor scales

In this chapter we will be introduced to three minor scales - **melodic**, **harmonic** and **natural**, and we will learn the different methods available for constructing these scales. Some of you may have encountered differing 'ascending and descending' forms of these scales within a classical music discipline - although of course relevant to classical music, this will not be a consideration in contemporary situations (i.e. pop and jazz styles).

Also in this chapter we will be deriving the **key signatures** needed for **minor keys**. You will recall that we derived all of our major scales and major key signatures in **Chapter 1**. One important distinction between major and minor key applications is that, while generally we will just be using **one major scale** within a **major key**, now we may potentially be using up to **three minor scales** (i.e. melodic, harmonic and/or natural) within a **minor key**. This means that we will sometimes need to adjust minor key signatures with additional accidentals depending on the scale required, as we will see shortly.

Deriving the minor scales using tetrachords and intervals

The first method we will use to derive the minor scales is similar to the method used to derive major scales in **Chapter 1**, where we constructed the major scale using **tetrachords** which were in turn made up of **whole-step** and **half-step intervals**. First we will define a **minor tetrachord** as having a whole-step, half-step and whole-step interval construction, as follows:-

Figure 8.1. C minor tetrachord (whole-step, half-step, whole-step)

All of the three minor scales **begin with the above intervals**, i.e. this minor tetrachord is actually the **lower tetrachord** of all the minor scales. The only difference between the scales (from an interval standpoint) is therefore in the remaining intervals, which will form part of the **upper tetrachord** in each case. We will begin with the **melodic minor** scale, using this interval and tetrachord derivation (see example on following page):-

Deriving the minor scales using tetrachords and intervals (contd)

Figure 8.2. C melodic minor scale *(showing tetrachords and intervals)*

<------- *lower tetrachord* ------>   <------- *upper tetrachord* ------>

Note in the above example that the lower tetrachord is the same as shown in **Fig. 8.1.**, and that (as with the major scale) the lower and upper tetrachords are separated by a **whole-step** interval. The **upper** tetrachord of the melodic minor scale is **identical to that of the major scale** (i.e. whole-step, whole-step and half-step intervals - review **Fig. 1.42.** as required). One other distinguishing feature of the melodic minor scale is that it contains **four consecutive whole-steps**, from the third up to the seventh scale degrees (**Eb** up to **B** in the above example).

The melodic minor scale is widely used in more sophisticated styles (jazz, latin and fusion), but is less frequently encountered in modern pop and commercial settings. Now we will look at the **harmonic minor** scale as follows:-

Figure 8.3. C harmonic minor scale *(showing tetrachords and intervals)*

<------- *lower tetrachord* ------>   <------- *upper tetrachord* ------>

Again we are using the same lower tetrachord, with the two tetrachords separated by a whole-step. Note that we now have a different **upper tetrachord**, consisting of **half-step**, **minor 3rd**, and **half-step** intervals. Distinguishing features of this scale are the **minor 3rd** interval (between the 6th and 7th scale degrees - this is the first time we have derived a scale containing an interval greater than a whole-step), and the **three half-step intervals** (between the 2nd & 3rd, 5th & 6th, and 7th & 1st scale degrees).

This harmonic minor interval structure makes the scale somewhat less useful melodically (except perhaps in certain 'ethnic' contexts) - however it is useful as a chordal 'scale source' in jazz styles - more about this in ***Contemporary Music Theory Level 2***.

Now we will finally look at the intervals and tetrachords within the **natural minor** scale (see following page):-

Deriving the minor scales using tetrachords and intervals (contd)

Figure 8.4. C natural minor scale *(showing tetrachords and intervals)*

<-------- lower tetrachord ------>   <------ upper tetrachord ------>

Again we are using the same lower tetrachord, with the two tetrachords separated by a whole-step. Note that we again have a different **upper tetrachord**, this time consisting of **half-step, whole-step**, and **whole-step** intervals. The natural minor scale is identical to an **Aeolian mode** (major scale starting from its **6th** degree - see **Figs. 5.5.** and **5.28.**), so the above **C natural minor** scale is equivalent to a **C Aeolian** mode.

The natural minor scale is widely used in contemporary pop and rock styles.

Note that (similar to the **major** scales in **Chapter 1**) these **minor scales use all the letters in the music alphabet consecutively, with no letter name used more than once**. Therefore to create any minor scale using this interval method, you simply need to write the notes on the staff corresponding to the consecutive note letternames that you need, and then qualify the notes as necessary using accidentals to achieve the required intervals (see examples later in this chapter). Now we will look at the next way of deriving the minor scales - by altering the major scale built from the same starting note.

Deriving the minor scales by altering the major scale

All of the previous minor scale examples can also be viewed from the standpoint of how a major scale (built from the same starting note) could be **altered** to produce each minor scale. We will begin by altering a **C major** scale to produce a **C melodic minor** scale, as follows:-

Figure 8.5. C melodic minor scale
(built by flatting the 3rd degree of a C major scale)

Note that in comparison to a **C major** scale (as in **Fig. 1.42.**) the **3rd** degree has been flatted i.e. the note **E** has been flatted to **Eb**, to create a **C melodic minor** scale.

Deriving the minor scales by altering the major scale (contd)

Next we will alter a **C major** scale to produce a **C harmonic minor** scale, as follows:-

Figure 8.6. C harmonic minor scale
(built by flatting the 3rd and 6th degrees of a C major scale)

Note that in comparison to a **C major** scale (as in **Fig. 1.42.**) the **3rd** and **6th** degrees have been flatted (i.e. the note **E** has been flatted to **Eb** and the note **A** has been flatted to **Ab**) to create a **C harmonic minor** scale.

Finally we will alter a **C major** scale to produce a **C natural minor** scale, as follows:-

Figure 8.7. C natural minor scale
(built by flatting the 3rd, 6th and 7th degrees of a C major scale)

Note that in comparison to a **C major** scale (as in **Fig. 1.42.**) the **3rd**, **6th** and **7th** degrees have been flatted (i.e. the note **E** has been flatted to **Eb**, the note **A** has been flatted to **Ab** and the note **B** has been flatted to **Bb**) to create a **C natural minor** scale. Don't forget that when we are flatting the various degrees of the major scale, we do not always need to use a 'flat' sign - sometimes we may be lowering a pitch which is **already sharped** (i.e. to a 'natural'), or we may even be lowering a pitch which is **already flatted** (i.e. to a 'double-flat' - review double accidentals in **Figs. 2.5. - 2.6.** as necessary).

The final method for deriving minor scales is to use the **minor key signature**, with any alterations (i.e. accidentals applied) as necessary. You will recall that I advised against deriving the **major** scales by key signature (in **Chapter 1**), as I felt that an interval-based method is more consistent with how the ear understands the scale. Knowing your intervals and tetrachords is also important when deriving the three **minor** scales (as already discussed in this chapter) - however, we will now see that when we use a minor key signature, this **only gives us one** of the three minor scales - and so we need to know how to **alter this** to get to the **other minor scales** when a **minor key signature** is used.

Minor key signatures

First we will define the concept of **minor key signatures**. You will recall that in **Chapter 1** we derived the key signatures for all of the **major** keys. What we will now see is that all of these key signatures also work for a **minor** key as well as a **major** key. Our first task is therefore to establish the relationship between a **major key** and the **minor key** which **shares the same key signature**. This minor key is known as the **relative minor** of the corresponding major key.

We have already seen that the **natural minor** scale is exactly the same as the **Aeolian mode** first derived in **Chapter 5**. Back in **Fig. 5.29.** we displaced an **Eb major** scale to start on the note **C** (creating a **C Aeolian** mode) and then notated the mode using the **Eb major key signature** (i.e. three flats). Now we can see that this process has also resulted in a **C natural minor** scale (**natural minor** being identical to **Aeolian**). It would seem reasonable therefore to **use this key signature** (i.e. three flats) **for the key of C minor**, as this key signature has at least given us **one** of the three minor scales that we might need within the **key of C minor**. Relating the key of **C minor** back to the original key of **Eb major**, we see that the note **C** is the **6th** degree of an **Eb major** scale (if you're not sure about this, review **Figs. 5.24. - 5.26.** as necessary). This leads to the following important rule:-

-       The **<u>RELATIVE MINOR</u>** (i.e. the **minor key** which shares the same key signature as the corresponding **major key**) is built from the **<u>SIXTH DEGREE</u>** of the corresponding major scale.

Now we will review how the minor key signature gives us a natural minor scale, as well as how we use extra accidentals to obtain the remaining minor scales (harmonic and melodic). A tune written in a **minor key** may need **any or all** of the **three minor scales** at different times!

Deriving the minor scales when using a minor key signature

First of all we will derive a **C natural minor** scale when using the **C minor key signature** (which we have agreed is the same as the **Eb major key signature**):-

<u>Figure 8.8. C natural minor scale</u>
*(using the C minor key signature **with no additional accidentals**)*

As mentioned above, this is identical to the **Aeolian mode** in **Fig. 5.29.** (We also see that this example produces the correct intervals for a **natural minor** scale as derived in **Fig. 8.4.**)

Deriving the minor scales when using a minor key signature (contd)

Again note that we have used no additional accidentals to obtain the **C natural minor** scale at the bottom of the previous page - we have simply used the **C minor key signature**. This leads to an important rule which we need to learn:-

-        If we build a scale (from the tonic of a minor key) with a **minor key signature** 'in force' and with **no additional accidentals**, then a **natural minor scale** is produced.

The implication therefore is that, if we need to make use of the remaining minor scales (i.e. harmonic or melodic) within a minor key, we will need to **adjust the minor key signature** using **accidentals within the music** as required. As we progressively do this to obtain the other minor scales, what we are doing is actually the **exact reverse** of the process outlined in **Figs. 8.5. - 8.7.** where we progressively altered a major scale to create the three minor scales. You will recall that (when altering the major scale) when we finally got to the natural minor scale in **Fig. 8.7.**, this represented the **most alterations** to the major scale i.e. three notes had been flatted. By contrast, when using the **minor key signature**, the natural minor scale is our **starting point** as it is the scale which results when the minor key signature is 'in force' with no additional accidentals. Deriving the remaining minor scales using a minor key signature, is equivalent to **going backwards** through the examples in **Figs. 8.5. - 8.7.** as we shall see.

Now we will take the **C natural minor** scale (which the **C minor key signature** gave us) and alter it to create a **C harmonic minor** scale, as follows:-

Figure 8.9. C harmonic minor scale
*- using the C minor key signature with the **7th** degree sharped (**Bb --> B**)*

Why have we sharped the 7th degree here? If you compare the upper tetrachord intervals of the **natural minor** scale (as in **Fig. 8.4.**) to the equivalent intervals in the **harmonic minor** scale (as in **Fig. 8.3.**), you'll see that whereas the top two intervals in the **natural minor** scale are **two whole-steps**, the top two intervals in the **harmonic minor** scale are a **minor 3rd** and a **half-step**. We have already agreed that the minor key signature with no accidentals gives us a **natural minor** scale (as in **Fig. 8.8.**)., and so the question then becomes *how do we alter this natural minor scale (i.e. using accidentals within the music) to get to the interval structure required for a harmonic minor scale?* The **7th** degree (which uses the lettername **B**) now needs to be a **minor 3rd higher** than the **6th** degree (which is **Ab**) and a **half-step lower** than the **tonic** or **1st** degree (which is **C**). We therefore need to **sharp the 7th degree** with respect

Deriving the minor scales when using a minor key signature (contd)

(Explanation of Fig. 8.9. contd)

to our starting point (the natural minor scale 'given to us' by the minor key signature). In **Fig. 8.8.** the **7th** degree was the note **Bb**, so this is now sharped to the note **B** (i.e. natural) in **Fig. 8.9.** (Again don't forget that when a pitch is 'sharped' in this way, we do not always need to use a 'sharp' sign - sometimes we may be raising a pitch which is **already flatted** (i.e. to a 'natural', as in this example), or we may even be raising a pitch which is **already sharped** (i.e. to a 'double-sharp'). This leads to the next important rule regarding minor scales and key signatures:-

- If we build a scale (from the tonic of a minor key) with a **minor key signature** 'in force' and with the **7th degree additionally sharped**, then a **harmonic minor scale** is produced.

Note that the change from **Fig. 8.8.** to **Fig. 8.9.** (i.e. sharping the **7th** degree of the **natural minor** scale 'given to us' by the minor key signature, to derive the **harmonic minor** scale) is the exact reverse of the change from **Fig. 8.6.** to **Fig. 8.7.** (i.e. flatting the **7th** degree of the **harmonic minor** scale to derive the **natural minor** scale). Another way to look at this is to see that the change from **Fig. 8.8.** to **Fig. 8.9.** is equivalent to '**moving backwards**' from **Fig. 8.7.** to **Fig. 8.6.** Now we will again take the **C natural minor** scale (which the **C minor key signature** gave us) and further alter it to create a **C melodic minor** scale, as follows:-

Figure 8.10. C melodic minor scale
- using the C minor key signature with the 6th and 7th degrees sharped (Ab --> A, Bb --> B)

Why have we sharped the 6th and 7th degrees here? If you compare the upper tetrachord intervals of the **natural minor** scale (as in **Fig. 8.4.**) to the equivalent intervals in the **melodic minor** scale (as in **Fig. 8.2.**), you'll see that whereas the top three intervals in the **natural minor** scale are a **half-step** and **two whole-steps**, the top three intervals in the **melodic minor** scale are **two whole-steps** and a **half-step**. We have already agreed that the minor key signature with no accidentals gives us a **natural minor** scale (as in **Fig. 8.8.**), and so the question then becomes *how do we alter this natural minor scale (i.e. using accidentals within the music) to get to the interval structure required for a melodic minor scale?* The **6th** degree (which uses the lettername **A**) now needs to be a **whole-step higher** than the **5th** degree (which is **G**). We therefore need to **sharp the 6th degree** with respect to our starting point (the natural minor scale 'given to us' by the minor key signature). In **Fig. 8.8.** the **6th** degree was the note **Ab**, so this is now sharped to the note **A** (i.e. natural) in **Fig. 8.10.** Similarly, the **7th** degree (which uses

Deriving the minor scales when using a minor key signature (contd)

(Explanation of Fig. 8.10. contd)

the lettername **B**) again needs to be a **whole-step higher** than the **6th** degree (which we have amended to the note **A**). We therefore need to also **sharp the 7th degree** with respect to the initial natural minor scale. In **Fig. 8.8.** the **7th** degree was the note **Bb**, so this is now sharped to the note **B** (i.e. natural) in **Fig. 8.10.** This leads to the next important rule regarding minor scales and key signatures:-

-        If we build a scale (from the tonic of a minor key) with a **minor key signature** 'in force' and with the **6th and 7th degrees additionally sharped**, then a **melodic minor scale** is produced.

        Although the **melodic minor** scale in **Fig. 8.10.** was analyzed from the standpoint of how the **natural minor** scale in **Fig. 8.8.** (resulting from the minor key signature) is altered to create this scale, we can also consider the **harmonic minor** scale derived in **Fig. 8.9.** as a 'half-way point' in this process, and we see that the **6th** degree of this **harmonic minor** scale can be sharped to get to the **melodic minor** scale shown in **Fig. 8.10.** This change is the exact reverse of the change from **Fig. 8.5.** to **Fig. 8.6.** (i.e. flatting the **6th** degree of the **melodic minor** scale to derive the **harmonic minor** scale). Another way to look at this is to see that the change from **Fig. 8.9.** to **Fig. 8.10.** is equivalent to 'moving backwards' from **Fig. 8.6.** to **Fig. 8.5.**

        In summary then, the two most recent methods discussed for deriving the minor scales:-

-        **altering the major scale** to produce the minor scales, and
-        using the **minor key signature** (with **alterations** as necessary) to produce the minor scales

        are actually **mirror-image opposites** of one another. We can take a **major scale** and:-

-        **flat** the **3rd** degree (as in **Fig. 8.5.**) to create a **melodic minor** scale
-        **flat** the **3rd** and **6th** degrees (as in **Fig. 8.6.**) to create a **harmonic minor** scale
-        **flat** the **3rd**, **6th** and **7th** degrees (as in **Fig. 8.7.**) to create a **natural minor** scale.

        However, if we **start with a natural minor scale** (as a result of using a **minor key signature** as in **Fig. 8.8.**) then we can:-

-        **sharp** the **7th** degree (as in **Fig. 8.9.**) to create a **harmonic minor** scale
-        **sharp** the **6th** and **7th** degrees (as in **Fig. 8.10.**) to create a **melodic minor** scale.

        (If we were to **sharp** the **3rd**, **6th** and **7th** degrees of the natural minor scale - we would be back to a **major scale** again - try it and see)!

Examples of creating and recognizing minor scales

We will now look at some examples of creating and recognizing minor scales, both with and without key signatures. First we will work through some examples of creating minor scales, as follows:-

> **Minor scale creation**   *- Create an Eb natural minor scale (in the bass clef)*
> **example #1**   *without a key signature.*

For this example we will use the interval method as presented in **Figs. 8.1. - 8.4.** and accompanying text. First of all we will show the letternames of the notes required on the staff, which as usual will be consecutive within the music alphabet:-

Figure 8.11. Minor scale creation example #1 stage 1 - note letternames required

What we now need to do is to adjust the notes using accidentals, to achieve the intervals required for a **natural minor** scale as shown in **Fig. 8.4.**, as follows:-

- We need a **whole-step** interval to begin with - we note that the first interval (**Eb** up to **F**) is already a **whole-step** - so we do not need to alter the note **F**.
- The next interval we need is a **half-step** - however the interval on the staff (**F** up to **G**) is a **whole-step** - so we need to flat the **G** (to **Gb**) to get the necessary **half-step** interval.
- The next interval we need is a **whole-step** - however from the previous **Gb** up to the note **A** is actually **three half-steps** (or a minor 3rd) - so we need to flat the **A** (to **Ab**) to get the necessary **whole-step** interval.
- The next interval we need is also a **whole-step** - however from the previous **Ab** up to the note **B** is again **three half-steps** (or a minor 3rd) - so we need to flat the **B** (to **Bb**) to get the necessary **whole-step** interval.
- The next interval we need is a **half-step** - however from the previous **Bb** up to the note **C** is actually a **whole-step** - so we need to flat the **C** (to **Cb**) to get the necessary **half-step** interval.
- The next interval we need is a **whole-step** - however from the previous **Cb** up to the note **D** is again **three half-steps** (or a minor 3rd) - so we need to flat the **D** (to **Db**) to get the necessary **whole-step** interval.
- The final interval we need is also a **whole-step** - however from the previous **Db** up to the note **E** is again **three half-steps** (or a minor 3rd) - so we need to flat the **E** (to **Eb**) to get the necessary **whole-step** interval (and also of course to get back to the same starting note of **Eb**).

Examples of creating and recognizing minor scales (contd)

The **Eb natural minor** scale, with accidentals applied as required by the intervals derived in **Fig. 8.4.**, is now shown as follows:-

Figure 8.12. Minor scale creation example #1 stage 2 - accidentals applied

Now we will look at another minor scale creation example as follows:-

**Minor scale creation
example #2**

- Create a D harmonic minor scale (in the treble clef) without a key signature.

For this example we will use the 'altered major scale' method as presented in **Figs. 8.5. - 8.7.** and accompanying text. This will involve building a **D major** scale, and then altering that scale to produce a **D harmonic minor** scale. First we will build a **D major** scale, using the interval and tetrachord method presented in **Chapter 1**:-

Figure 8.13. Minor scale creation example #2 stage 1 - building the D major scale

In **Fig. 8.6.** and accompanying text (and also in the summary on **p208**) we saw that a **harmonic minor** scale can be derived by **flatting** the **3rd** and **6th** degrees of a **major scale**. Applying this method to the above example, the **3rd** degree (**F#**) is flatted to **F**, and the **6th** degree (**B**) is flatted to **Bb**, finally producing the **D harmonic minor** scale as follows:-

Figure 8.14. Minor scale creation example #2 stage 2 - altering the D major scale

(The resulting intervals for the **D harmonic minor** scale, are also shown below the staff).

Examples of creating and recognizing minor scales (contd)

Note that the **D harmonic minor** scale at the bottom of the previous page, included both of the notes **Bb** and **C#**. It will occasionally be necessary to mix flats and sharps within a harmonic minor scale, as we have a larger interval (of a minor 3rd) within the upper tetrachord, and yet we still need to use consecutive note letternames within the music alphabet. In any case if you follow the methods outlined in this chapter, you will always derive your minor scales correctly!

Now we will look at some minor scale creation examples using minor key signatures:-

> ### Minor scale creation example #3
> *- Create a G# melodic minor scale (in the treble clef)* **with** *a key signature.*

As we are required to notate this scale **with a key signature**, we first of all need to figure out which **major key** shares the same **key signature** as **G# minor**. We recall from the rule on **p205** that the **relative minor** is built from the **6th** degree of the corresponding major key, and so we need to determine *what major scale has G# as its 6th degree?* - the key signature for this major key will be the one that we will also use for the key of **G# minor**.

Placing the note **G#** within the major scale interval pattern to determine which major scale it is the **6th** degree of (we have already used this technique several times in **Chapters 4** and **5** - review if necessary), we see that the note **G#** is the **6th** degree of a **B** major scale. We will therefore use the **B major** key signature (first derived in **Fig. 1.88.**) as follows:-

Figure 8.15. Minor scale creation example #3 stage 1 - finding the minor key signature

Note the key signature used (five sharps) - we now know that this is the **G# minor key signature** as well as the **B major key signature**. Now we will complete the derivation of the **G# melodic minor** scale with this key signature, using the rules defined in **Figs. 8.8. - 8.10.** and accompanying text (and summarized at the bottom of **p208**). We know that if we just leave the above example as it is (i.e. with no further adjustments) then we will get a **G# natural minor** scale - however we actually need a **G# melodic minor** scale. In **Fig. 8.10.** we saw that the **6th** and **7th** degrees (in this case, of the **G# natural minor** scale 'given to us' by the **G# minor** key signature) need to be sharped to create a melodic minor scale. Applying this method to the above example, the **6th** degree (**E**) is sharped to **E#**, and the **7th** degree (**F#**) is sharped to **Fx** (**F double-sharp**), finally producing the **G# melodic minor** scale **with a key signature** and the **necessary accidentals** (see following page):-

Examples of creating and recognizing minor scales (contd)

Figure 8.16. Minor scale creation example #3 stage 2 - adding necessary accidentals

Now we will look at a further minor scale creation example with a key signature:-

Minor scale creation example #4 — *Create an E harmonic minor scale (in the bass clef)* **with** *a key signature.*

Again we need to figure out which **major key** shares the same **key signature** as **E minor**. As the **relative minor** is built from the **6th** degree of the corresponding major key, the question is *what major scale has* **E** *as its* **6th** *degree?* - the key signature for this major key will be the one that we will also use for the key of **E minor**. Again using the major scale 'interval pattern' technique, we can determine that the note **E** is the **6th** degree of a **G** major scale. We will therefore use the **G major** key signature (first derived in **Fig. 1.83.**) as follows:-

Figure 8.17. Minor scale creation example #4 stage 1 - finding the minor key signature

Note the key signature used (one sharp) - we now know that this is the **E minor key signature** as well as the **G major key signature**. We know that if we just leave the above example as it is (i.e. with no further adjustments) then we will get an **E natural minor** scale - however we actually need an **E harmonic minor** scale. In **Fig. 8.9.** we saw that the **7th** degree (in this case, of the **E natural minor** scale 'given to us' by the **E minor** key signature) needs to be sharped to create a harmonic minor scale. Applying this method to the above example, the **7th** degree (**D**) is sharped to **D#**, finally producing the **E harmonic minor** scale **with a key signature** and the **necessary accidental**:-

Figure 8.18. Minor scale creation example #4 stage 2 - adding necessary accidental

212

Examples of creating and recognizing minor scales (contd)

Now we will look at some examples of recognizing minor scales, again with and without key signatures, as follows:-

Figure 8.19. Minor scale recognition example #1 *(no key signature provided)*

We will analyze this example using the minor scale **interval method** described in **Figs. 8.1. - 8.4.** and accompanying text. In other words we will determine each of the intervals present between successive notes in the above scale, and compare the results to the intervals already presented for each of the minor scales. Here are the intervals analyzed in the above example:-

Figure 8.20. Minor scale recognition example #1 *(intervals analyzed)*

As we would expect, the lower tetrachord of this scale consists of *whole-step/half-step/ whole-step* intervals, and the interval between the two tetrachords is a whole-step - this is the case for all of the minor scales (review **Figs. 8.2. - 8.4.** as necessary). We have already seen that it is in the **upper tetrachord** where the variations occur between the three minor scales. In the above example, we have *half-step/whole-step/whole-step* intervals in the upper tetrachord; when this is compared with the various upper tetrachords in **Figs. 8.2. - 8.4.**, we see this is the upper tetrachord for a **natural minor** scale (as in **Fig. 8.4.**). As the starting note of the above example is **G#**, this is therefore a **G# natural minor** scale.

Figure 8.21. Minor scale recognition example #2 *(no key signature provided)*

We will analyze this example using the **altered major scale method** described in **Figs. 8.5. - 8.7.** and accompanying text. In other words we will construct a major scale from the first

Examples of creating and recognizing minor scales (contd)

(Explanation of Fig. 8.21. contd)

degree of the example, and compare the major scale to the example scale to determine **which degrees of the major scale have been altered** (review summary at the bottom of **p208** as necessary). First we will derive a major scale from the starting note (in this case the note **F**), using the interval method first presented in **Chapter 1**:-

Figure 8.22. Minor scale recognition example #2 (major scale built from starting note)

In comparing this to the original example in **Fig. 8.21.**, we can see that whereas the note **A** is the **3rd** degree of the above **F major** scale, the note **Ab** is the **3rd** degree of the example scale. We can therefore consider the original example as being an **F major scale with a flatted 3rd**. We saw in **Fig. 8.5.** (and in the summary on **p208**) that a **melodic minor** scale is produced when we flat the **3rd** degree of a major scale. The correct name therefore for the example in **Fig. 8.21.** is an **F melodic minor** scale. Now we will look at some minor scale recognition examples using minor key signatures:-

Figure 8.23. Minor scale recognition example #3 (minor key signature 'in force')

First of all we should analyze the key signature provided. We recall from **Chapter 1** that this key signature (two sharps) is used for the key of **D major** (review **Fig. 1.85.** and accompanying text as necessary). We have seen from our earlier discussion of minor key signatures on **p205** that the relative minor (the minor key sharing the same key signature as the corresponding major key) is built from the **6th** degree of the major scale. We can build a **D major** scale (using intervals as in **Fig. 1.57.**) to determine that the **6th** degree is the note **B**. The above key signature is therefore also used for the key of **B minor** (as well as **D major**). Consistent with this, we can also see that **B** is the starting note in the above example - the question then becomes *which of the three B minor scales is represented above?* We know from our work earlier in this chapter that if there were no additional accidentals (to the minor key signature), then we would have a natural minor scale (review **Fig. 8.8.** and accompanying text as necessary). However we **do**

Examples of creating and recognizing minor scales (contd)

(Explanation of Fig. 8.23. contd)

have an accidental in this case - the **7th degree has been sharped**. We saw in **Fig. 8.9.** (and in the summary at the bottom of **p208**) that when the **7th** degree of the **natural minor** scale (**'given to us' by the minor key signature**) is sharped, a **harmonic minor** scale is the result. The correct name therefore for the example in **Fig. 8.23.** is a **B harmonic minor** scale.

Figure 8.24. Minor scale recognition example #4 (minor key signature 'in force')

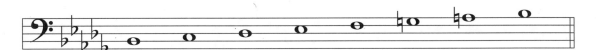

Again we should first of all analyze the key signature - we saw in **Chapter 1** that this key signature (five flats) is used for the key of **Db major** (review **Fig. 1.79.** as necessary). Building a **Db major** scale by intervals as in **Fig. 5.32.**, we see that the **6th** degree of this scale is **Bb** and therefore the relative minor which shares the same key signature is **Bb minor** (which is consistent with **Bb** being the starting note in the above example). Again the question then becomes *which of the three Bb minor scales is represented above?* We have two accidentals in this case - the **6th** and **7th degrees have been sharped**. We saw in **Fig. 8.10.** (and in the summary at the bottom of **p208**) that when the **6th** and **7th** degree of the **natural minor** scale (**'given to us' by the minor key signature**) are sharped, a **melodic minor** scale is the result. The correct name therefore for the example in **Fig. 8.24.** is a **Bb melodic minor** scale.

(All minor scales, both with and without key signatures, are listed in the **Appendices** at the back of this book).

Chapter Eight Workbook Questions

1. Writing minor scales without key signatures

You are to write the following minor scales, either by using the tetrachords/intervals method, or by constructing a major scale from the starting note and altering as required. No minor key signatures are to be written or used - instead you should write the scale **with all necessary accidentals**.

1. **C Melodic minor**

2. **E Harmonic minor**

3. **F Natural minor**

4. **G Harmonic minor**

5. **Ab Melodic minor**

6. **D Melodic minor**

7. **B Harmonic minor**

8. **F# Natural minor**

9. **Eb Melodic minor**

10. **A Harmonic minor**

2. *Writing minor scales with key signatures*

You are to write the following minor scales, preceded by the appropriate key signatures. First you should write the minor key signature required (remember that the relative minor occurs on the **sixth** degree of the corresponding major key/scale). Then, when writing the notes, you should determine if any contradictions to the key signature are needed. Remember that each harmonic minor scale requires **one** modification, and each melodic minor scale requires **two** modifications, to the minor key signature.

11. *C Natural minor*   12. *F Melodic minor*

13. *C# Melodic minor*   14. *D Harmonic minor*

15. *A# Natural minor*   16. *E Melodic minor*

17. *G# Harmonic minor*   18. *B Natural minor*

19. *G Melodic minor*   20. *F# Melodic minor*

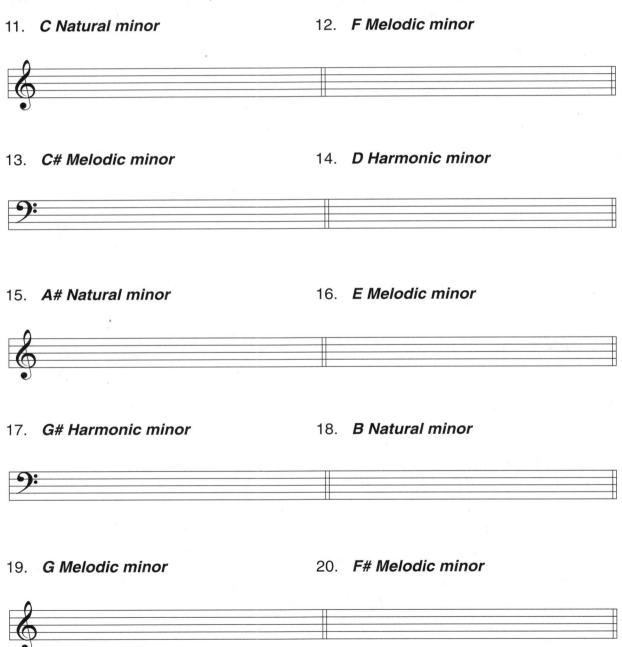

3. *Identifying minor scales without key signatures*

You are to identify the following minor scales, which are presented without key signatures. You may either:-

-   check the intervals present against the minor scale intervals and tetrachords discussed in the text (remember that the interval variations between the different minor scales will occur in the *upper* tetrachord), or
-   determine how a major scale from the same starting point would have been altered to create the minor scale in question.

Again don't forget that the scale name will have two parts - a starting note and a scale description (i.e. melodic minor, harmonic minor or natural minor).

21. ___ _____   22. ___ _____

23. ___ _____   24. ___ _____

25. ___ _____   26. ___ _____

27. ___ _____   28. ___ _____

29. ___ _____   30. ___ _____

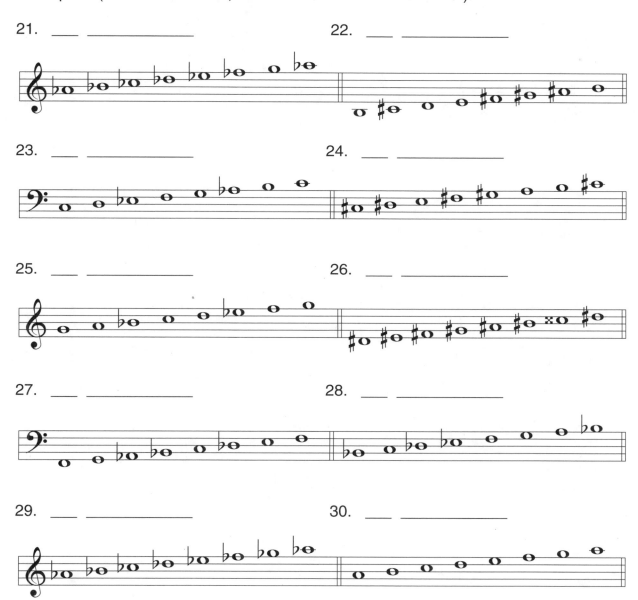

4. *Identifying minor scales with key signatures*

You are to identify the following minor scales. First use the key signature to establish the minor key, and then determine the degree to which (if any) the key signature has subsequently been modified, in order to derive the minor scale in question.

31. _____ _____   32. _____ _____

33. _____ _____   34. _____ _____

35. _____ _____   36. _____ _____

37. _____ _____   38. _____ _____

39. _____ _____   40. _____ _____

Chapter Eight Workbook Answers

1. **Writing minor scales without key signatures - answers**

1. **C Melodic minor**   2. **E Harmonic minor**

3. **F Natural minor**   4. **G Harmonic minor**

5. **Ab Melodic minor**   6. **D Melodic minor**

7. **B Harmonic minor**   8. **F# Natural minor**

9. **Eb Melodic minor**   10. **A Harmonic minor**

2. *Writing minor scales with key signatures - answers*

11. *C Natural minor*   12. *F Melodic minor*

13. *C# Melodic minor*   14. *D Harmonic minor*

15. *A# Natural minor*   16. *E Melodic minor*

17. *G# Harmonic minor*   18. *B Natural minor*

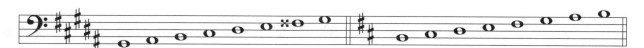

19. *G Melodic minor*   20. *F# Melodic minor*

3. *Identifying minor scales without key signatures - answers*

21. *Ab Harmonic minor*	22. *B Melodic minor*	23. *C Harmonic minor*
24. *C# Natural minor*	25. *G Natural minor*	26. *D# Melodic minor*
27. *F Harmonic minor*	28. *Bb Melodic minor*	29. *Ab Natural minor*
30. *A Natural minor*		

4. *Identifying minor scales with key signatures - answers*

31. *F# Harmonic minor*	32. *D Natural minor*	33. *A Melodic minor*
34. *Eb Harmonic minor*	35. *C# Harmonic minor*	36. *C Melodic minor*
37. *D Melodic minor*	38. *G# Natural minor*	39. *E Natural minor*
40. *F Melodic minor*		

More four-part chords, suspended chords, and altered chords

Introduction

This chapter is really a collection of 'loose ends' that we need to tie up, prior to working on the next level of our harmony study (*Contemporary Music Theory Level 2*). The following areas are covered in this chapter:-

- The **minor major seventh** and **minor sixth** chords which are now available from the **melodic minor** scales (as derived in **Chapter 8**).
- **Suspensions** of the **major** (and **minor**) **triad**, and of the **dominant seventh** chord.
- **Alterations** of **major** and **minor triads**.
- **Alterations** of **major seventh**, **minor seventh** and **dominant seventh** four-part chords.

The minor major seventh chord

The first new four-part chord to be studied is the **minor major 7th** chord. It is derived by placing **minor 3rd**, **perfect 5th** and **major 7th** intervals above the root, as follows:-

Figure 9.1. C minor major seventh chord - interval construction

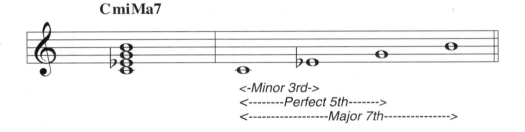

```
<-Minor 3rd->
<--------Perfect 5th------->
<-------------------Major 7th--------------->
```

This chord can also be derived by taking the minor triad (first derived in **Fig. 3.2.**) and adding the note which creates a **major 7th** interval from the root of the chord (i.e. the note **B** in the above example).

Note the chord symbol used in the above example ('**CmiMa7**'). The suffix '**miMa7**' indicates a **minor major seventh chord** built from the root i.e. in this case a **C minor major seventh chord**. In this case the '**mi**' in the chord suffix refers to the **minor 3rd** interval present, and the '**Ma**' in the chord suffix refers to the **major 7th** interval present. Although using the suffix '**miMa7**' is the preferred way to write this chord symbol, you will sometimes encounter other suffixes for the minor major seventh chord, as detailed on the following page:-

The minor major seventh chord (contd)

- 'mima7', 'minmaj7', 'minMaj7', i.e. as in the chord symbols **Cmima7, Cminmaj7, CminMaj7** etc. These would be acceptable variations, however I feel that the 'miMa7' suffix is the clearest and most explicit.
- 'miΔ7' i.e. as in the chord symbol **CmiΔ7**. As previously discussed, the 'triangle symbol' is sometimes used in older charts and fake books to indicate a major quality (in this case a major 7th interval within the chord) - again I feel this can be confusing, particularly in the context of the minor major 7th chord.
- '-ma7', '-maj7', etc. as in the chord symbols **C-ma7, C-maj7** etc. Again as previously discussed, the '-' suffix is often used in older charts and fake books to signify a minor quality (in this case a minor 3rd interval within the chord) - again I feel this can be confusing, particularly in the context of the minor major 7th chord.
- '-Δ7' i.e. as in the chord symbol **C-Δ7**. A combination of the above problems - there is even more potential for confusion with this chord symbol!
- 'mM7' i.e. as in the chord symbol **CmM7**. We have already seen that the use of the single upper case 'M' to signify major, and of the single lower-case 'm' to signify minor, can cause difficulty if the difference between the upper-case and lower-case is unclear. This chord symbol I believe rather compounds that problem!

So - when writing your minor major seventh chord symbols, use the 'miMa7' suffix - but again **be prepared to recognize** the alternatives listed above!

The **minor major 7th** chord can now also be derived from the **1st, 3rd, 5th** and **7th** degrees of the **melodic minor** scale (first constructed in **Chapter 8**), as follows:-

Figure 9.2. Deriving the C minor major 7th chord from a C melodic minor scale

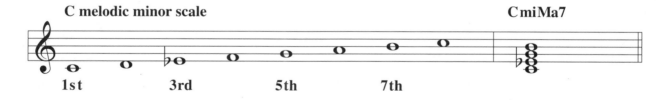

Resulting from this, we might reasonably expect the **CmiMa7** chord to 'function' as a **I** or **tonic** chord in the key of **C minor**, much as a **Cma7** chord will function as a **I** or **tonic** chord in the key of **C major** (as in **Fig. 7.1.**) - much more about this in **Contemporary Music Theory Level 2!**

Another way we can derive the **minor major 7th** chord is to take the **major 7th** chord (first derived in **Fig. 6.1.**) and flat the **3rd** of the chord (by half-step), as in the example on the following page:-

The minor major seventh chord (contd)

Figure 9.3. Deriving the C minor major 7th chord by altering a C major 7th chord

Here we have started with the **C major 7th** chord on the left, and **flatted the 3rd** (the note **E** has been altered to **Eb**) to produce the **C minor major 7th** chord on the right. Bearing in mind our previous derivation of the **minor major 7th** chord from the melodic minor scale, the above example is consistent with the fact that the melodic minor scale can be produced by taking a major scale (the source of the **Cma7** chord as in **Fig. 7.1.**) and **lowering the 3rd degree by half-step**, as in **Fig. 8.5.**

We can now summarize the three ways to derive a **minor major 7th** chord as follows:-

- build **minor 3rd**, **perfect 5th** and **major 7th** intervals from the root, as in **Fig. 9.1.**
- take the **1st**, **3rd**, **5th** and **7th** degrees of a **melodic minor** scale, as in **Fig. 9.2.**
- take a **major 7th** chord and **lower the 3rd by half-step**, as in **Fig. 9.3.**

The minor sixth chord

The next new four-part chord to be studied is the **minor 6th** chord. It is derived by placing **minor 3rd**, **perfect 5th** and **major 6th** intervals above the root, as follows:-

Figure 9.4. C minor sixth chord - interval construction

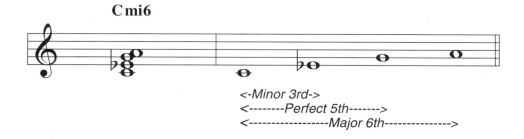

```
<-Minor 3rd->
<--------Perfect 5th------->
<-----------------Major 6th--------------->
```

This chord can also be derived by taking the minor triad (first derived in **Fig. 3.2.**) and adding the note which creates a **major 6th** interval from the root of the chord (i.e. the note **A** in the above example). I believe that in this case it is especially important to 'keep straight' the

The minor sixth chord (contd)

distinction between the **interval description** of the largest interval in this chord (a **major 6th** interval) and the **chord description** (a **minor 6th** chord). To summarize - **the largest interval within a minor 6th chord is a major 6th interval**! Make sure you take the time to learn and understand this, as in my experience students sometimes find this confusing!

Note the chord symbol used in the example at the bottom of the previous page ('**Cmi6**'). The suffix '**mi6**' indicates a **minor sixth chord** built from the root i.e. in this case a **C minor sixth chord**. In this case the '**mi**' in the chord suffix refers to the **minor 3rd** interval present. Although using the suffix '**mi6**' is the preferred way to write this chord symbol, you will sometimes encounter other suffixes for the minor sixth chord, as follows:-

- '**min6**' i.e. as in the chord symbol **Cmin6**. Unnecessary as the suffix '**mi6**' already explicitly defines a minor 6th chord.
- '**m6**' i.e. as in the chord symbol **Cm6**. Again we see a potential confusion between the lower-case '**m**' and the upper-case '**M**' when used to signify a minor and major quality respectively. Use '**mi6**' to be explicit.
- '**-6**' i.e. as in the chord symbol **C-6**. See earlier comments regarding my reservations about using the '**-**' suffix to signify minor.

So - when writing your minor sixth chord symbols, use the '**mi6**' suffix - but again **be prepared to recognize** the alternatives listed above!

The **minor 6th** chord can now also be derived from the **1st**, **3rd**, **5th** and **6th** degrees of the **melodic minor** scale (first constructed in **Chapter 8**), as follows:-

Figure 9.5. Deriving the C minor 6th chord from a C melodic minor scale

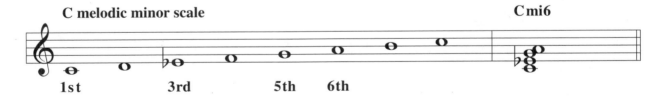

As previously discussed for the **CmiMa7** chord, we might reasonably expect the **Cmi6** chord to 'function' as a **I** or **tonic** chord in the key of **C minor** - again more about this in *Contemporary Music Theory Level 2*.

Another way we can derive the **minor 6th** chord is to take the **major 6th** chord (first derived in **Fig. 6.3.**) and flat the **3rd** of the chord (by half-step), as in the example on the following page:-

226

The minor sixth chord (contd)

Figure 9.6. Deriving the C minor 6th chord by altering a C major 6th chord

Here we have started with the **C major 6th** chord on the left, and **flatted the 3rd** (the note **E** has been altered to **Eb**) to produce the **C minor 6th** chord on the right. Bearing in mind our previous derivation of the **minor 6th** chord from the melodic minor scale, the above example is again consistent with the fact that the melodic minor scale can be produced by taking a major scale (the source of the **Cma6** chord as in **Fig. 7.2.**) and **lowering the 3rd degree by half-step**, as in **Fig. 8.5.**

We can now summarize the three ways to derive a **minor 6th** chord as follows:-

- build **minor 3rd**, **perfect 5th** and **major 6th** intervals from the root, as in **Fig. 9.4.**
- take the **1st**, **3rd**, **5th** and **6th** degrees of a **melodic minor** scale, as in **Fig. 9.5.**
- take a **major 6th** chord and **lower the 3rd by half-step**, as in **Fig. 9.6.**

When we derived the first group of four-part chords (**major 7th** and **6th**, **minor 7th** and **dominant 7th**) in **Chapter 6**, we concluded (in the table on **p160**) that it was the **3rd** and **7th/6th** intervals present in the chords which determined the particular **chord quality** in question. We can now add the preceding **minor major 7th** and **minor 6th** chords to that analysis, resulting in an updated version of the table originally found on **p160** as follows:-

Type of chord	*Third interval contained in chord*	*Seventh (or sixth) interval contained in chord*
Major 7th	*Major 3rd*	*Major 7th*
Minor major 7th	*Minor 3rd*	*Major 7th*
Major 6th	*Major 3rd*	*Major 6th*
Minor 6th	*Minor 3rd*	*Major 6th*
Minor 7th	*Minor 3rd*	*Minor 7th*
Dominant 7th	*Major 3rd*	*Minor 7th*

Suspended chords

A 'suspended' chord is one in which the **3rd** has been **replaced** by the note which is a **perfect 4th interval from the root of the chord**. We will first look at this idea applied to a **C major** triad, as follows:-

Figure 9.7. Deriving a C suspended triad by replacing the 3rd of a C major triad with the note which is a perfect 4th interval above the root of the chord

Note the chord symbol used for the second chord in the above example ('**Csus**').The suffix '**sus**' indicates a **suspended triad** built from the root (in this case a **C suspended triad**). The note **F** in the **C suspended** triad which has replaced the note **E** in the **C major** triad, is of course also the **4th** degree of a **C major** scale. Generally the **4th** degree of the scale will want to resolve back to the **3rd** degree (representing an 'active-to-resting' resolution - see my **Contemporary Eartraining Level 1** book) - although of course depending upon the musical style or context, this 'resolution' may or may not actually occur. The chord suffix '**sus4**' (i.e. as in the chord symbol **Csus4**) is also a correct way to notate this chord.

You may sometimes encounter other variations of the 'sus' chord, where the intention is to replace the **3rd** with some other scale degree (as opposed to the **4th** outlined above). An example of this is a symbol such as **Csus2** which is sometimes found on contemporary charts. The intention behind this chord symbol is that the '**2nd**' (which really is more correctly termed the **9th** - see earlier comments on **p159**) has replaced the **3rd** of the chord. Strictly speaking I feel that this is an incorrect usage of a suspended symbol, as the movement between the '2nd' (**9th**) to the **3rd** does not represent the 'active-to-resting' resolution described above. However, some musicians do find the '**sus2**' suffix convenient, and so it is important that you know what is intended by this symbol.

*[The preferred alternative to 'Csus2' would be to use the symbols **Cadd9(omit3)** or **Cadd9(no3)** - more on this in **Contemporary Music Theory Level 2**].*

If we replace the **3rd** of a **C minor** triad with the note which is a perfect **4th** interval above the root, the resulting suspended triad also consists of the notes **C**, **F** and **G**, as in the example on the following page:-

Suspended chords (contd)

Figure 9.8. Deriving a C (minor) suspended triad by replacing the 3rd of a C minor triad with the note which is a perfect 4th interval above the root of the chord

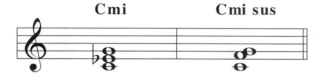

Note the chord symbol used for the second chord in the above example which is '**Cmisus**'. The note **F** in the **C** (minor) **suspended** chord has now replaced the note **Eb** in the **C minor** triad. (Again depending upon the musical context, the note **F** in the suspended chord may then resolve back to the note **Eb** which is the 3rd of the C minor chord). We can see that this '**Cmisus**' chord is identical to the '**Csus**' chord shown in **Fig. 9.7.** - both suspended chords contain the notes **C**, **F** and **G**. So you may be wondering - *why do we need to use the **Cmisus** chord symbol when **Csus** gives us the same result?* Well, depending upon the key and musical context, it may be desirable to indicate that the **3rd** of a **minor chord** (as opposed to the **3rd** of a **major** chord) has been replaced with the **4th** - this is what the '**Cmisus**' chord symbol tells us. The chord suffix '**misus4**' (i.e. as in the chord symbol **Cmisus4**) is also a correct way to notate this chord.

We will now examine the intervals present in the **C suspended** triad (which as we have seen will be the same as in the **C minor suspended** triad), as follows:-

Figure 9.9. C suspended triad - interval construction

Again we see that the note **F** (which has replaced the note **E** within a **C major** triad, or the note **Eb** within a **C minor** triad) is a **perfect 4th** interval above the root of **C**.

This suspended triad is also found within a major scale, as shown in the example on the following page:-

Suspended chords (contd)

Figure 9.10. Deriving a C suspended triad from a C major scale

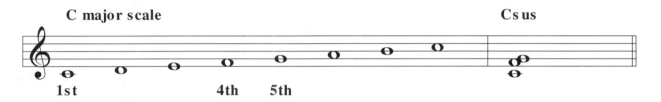

Again this further reinforces the principle that the **4th** degree has replaced the **3rd** in a suspended chord - **do not think of the suspension as having a raised or sharped 3rd** - the **3rd** has been **replaced** by the **4th** degree of the scale.

One other suspension that we need to consider at this stage is the **suspended dominant seventh** chord. Again like the suspended triads previously discussed, the **3rd** of the chord has been replaced by the note which is a perfect **4th** interval from the root of the chord, as in the following example of a **C suspended dominant seventh** chord:-

Figure 9.11. Deriving a C suspended dominant seventh chord by replacing the 3rd of a C dominant seventh with the note which is a perfect 4th interval above the root

*(The **C7** chord was first derived in* ***Fig. 6.4.*** *- review as necessary).*

Note the chord symbol in the above example which is '**C7sus**'. The suffix '**7sus**' indicates a **suspended dominant seventh chord** built from the root (in this case a **C suspended dominant seventh chord**). Although this is the the correct way to write this chord symbol, you may sometimes see this 'switched around' i.e. written as '**Csus7**'. This I believe is confusing, as we have already seen that a number written **after** the '**sus**' in the chord symbol (as in the chord **Csus4**) is representing a scale degree which is **replacing the 3rd** of the chord - and it is unlikely that we want to replace the **3rd** with the **7th** of the chord. So if you encounter the chord symbol '**Csus7**', assume that a **suspended dominant 7th** (as derived above) is intended!

We can also examine the intervals present in the **suspended dominant seventh** chord, as in the example on the following page:-

Suspended chords (contd)

Figure 9.12. C suspended dominant seventh chord - interval construction

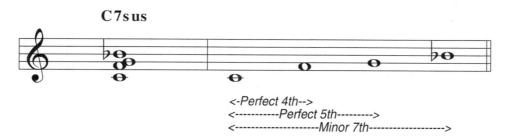

C7sus

```
<-Perfect 4th-->
<-----------Perfect 5th--------->
<--------------------Minor 7th-------------------->
```

Again we see that the note **F** (which has replaced the note **E** within the **C dominant seventh** chord) is a **perfect 4th** interval above the root of **C**.

We have already seen in **Chapter 7** (**Fig. 7.7.**) that a **G dominant 7th** chord was built from the **5th** degree of a **C major** scale. We might therefore also expect a **G suspended dominant 7th** chord to be available from the **5th** degree of a **C major** scale, as in the following example:-

Figure 9.13. Deriving a G suspended dominant 7th chord from a C major scale

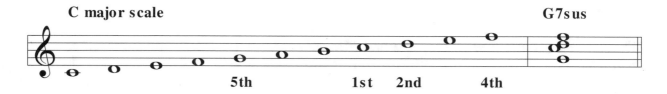

C major scale   G7sus

5th   1st   2nd   4th

We will defer a complete discussion of dominant chord function and harmonic implication until **Contemporary Music Theory Level 2** - however we can briefly say now that the (regular) **dominant 7th** chord as in **Fig. 7.7.**, and the above **suspended dominant 7th** chord, both function as 'leading' chords which generally resolve to a **I** or **tonic** chord of a key. The quality of the suspended dominant chord is however rather less 'leading' or 'active' than the 'regular' dominant chord, which makes the suspended chord more suitable in pop styles for example - much more about this later on!

Altered chords

In this chapter we will use the term '**altered chord**' to describe a chord in which the **fifth has been flatted or sharped by a half-step**. You will recall from the table on **p227** that we have already analyzed the **3rd** and **7th** intervals (or in some cases, the **3rd** and **6th** intervals) present in the four-part chords derived so far. Referring to this table, you can see that if we took a **major 7th chord** and reduced the **major 7th interval** within it to a **minor 7th interval**, this would then result in a **dominant 7th chord** being produced (i.e. we would then have **major 3rd** and **minor 7th intervals** present, which we know is the interval structure of a **dominant 7th chord**). You might therefore be tempted to think of this as an 'altered' chord - didn't we just alter a **major 7th** chord to become a **dominant 7th** chord?

Well - no, not really - not from a **functional** standpoint. The **major 7th** and **dominant 7th** chords have completely **different functions**. One clue to this is given by our work in **Chapter 7** where we discovered that the **major 7th** chord is built from the **1st** degree of a major scale (as in **Fig. 7.1.**) and therefore functions as a **I** or **tonic** chord in a major key, whereas the **dominant 7th** chord is built from the **5th** degree of a major scale (as in **Fig. 7.7.**) and therefore functions as a **V** chord, which in this case typically 'leads back' to a **I** or **tonic** chord. *(The 'functionality' of these four-part chords will be extensively discussed in **Contemporary Music Theory Level 2**).*

The point is that, while technically we could manipulate the intervals of a major 7th chord to create a dominant 7th chord as described at the top of this page, what we have actually done is **created a brand-new chord** - there is no way that a dominant 7th chord would be considered an 'altered' version of a major 7th chord, and vice-versa. Each **unique combination** of **3rd** and **7th** intervals (or in some cases, **3rd** and **6th** intervals) in the chord summary table on **p227**, **creates an entirely new and different chord in each case** - and we have already agreed that it is the **combination of the 3rd and 7th** (or **6th**) **intervals** which is giving the '**vertical quality**' to the each of these different chords, as in the discussion on **p159-160**. This leads to the following conclusions regarding four-part (or larger) chord forms:-

- The **third** and **seventh** (or sixth) intervals within a chord, together define the **basic chord quality** (i.e. major, dominant etc) of that chord.
- If any of these basic 'definitive' tones of a chord are **changed**, the result is <u>never</u> an 'altered' version of the original chord - instead an **entirely new chord** has been created.
- However, **other parts** of the chord (i.e. the **5th**) which do not contribute to this basic definition of the chord, may be altered (i.e. flatted or sharped) and the result will **still be** considered as an 'altered' version of the original chord - as we will see in this chapter.
- **Any chord symbol which refers to an 'altered' 3rd or 7th** (or **6th**) **is <u>completely incorrect</u>**. Occasionally you may encounter **horrific** chord symbols like '**C7(b3)**' for a **Cmi7** chord, or '**Cma7(b3)**' for a **CmiMa7** chord - beware!!

Altered chords (contd)

We will first of all consider some alterations (i.e. modifications to the **5th** of the chord) to triads. We have already seen in **Fig. 3.3.** that if we raise the **5th** of a **major** triad by half-step, we get an **augmented** triad. The **diminished** triad first seen in **Fig. 3.4.** could also be derived by lowering the **5th** of a **minor** triad by half-step. Now we will see what happens when we **lower** the **5th** of a **major** triad by half-step, and **raise** the **5th** of a **minor** triad by half-step.

First of all we will lower the **5th** of a **C major** triad by half-step as follows:-

Figure 9.14. Deriving a 'C major triad with flatted 5th' from a C major triad

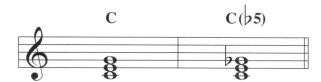

Note the chord symbol in the above example which is **C(b5)**. This is telling us to **flat the 5th of the C major triad by half-step**. Note that parentheses are used either side of the 'b5' in the chord symbol - **ensure that you always place parentheses around alterations in chord symbols**. In the above example, the chord symbol without parentheses would have looked like '**Cb5**' - we would think that the root of the chord was actually **Cb**!

We can also examine the intervals present in the above altered triad, as follows:-

Figure 9.15. C major triad with flatted 5th - interval construction

<---Major 3rd---->
<-----------Diminished 5th----------->

In the above example we see that the note **Gb** (the result of altering the note **G** within a **C major** triad) is a **diminished 5th** interval above the root of **C**.

Next we will raise the **5th** of a **C minor** triad by half-step as in the example on the following page:-

Altered chords (contd)

Figure 9.16. Deriving a 'C minor triad with sharped 5th' from a C minor triad

Note the chord symbol in the above example which is **Cmi(#5)**. This is telling us to **sharp the 5th of the C minor triad by half-step**. This altered minor triad is actually equivalent to a **first inversion major triad** - if we enharmonically rename the top note (**G#**) to **Ab**, from bottom to top we have the notes **C**, **Eb** and **Ab** which constitutes a first inversion **Ab major** triad. For this reason, when you see '**mi(#5)**' chord symbol in charts, it often signifies that a major triad has been inverted in this way.

We can also examine the intervals present in the above altered triad, as follows:-

Figure 9.17. C minor triad with sharped 5th - interval construction

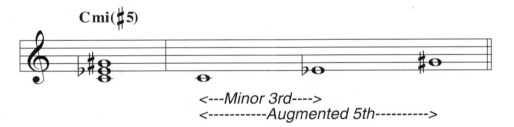

<---Minor 3rd---->
<-----------Augmented 5th---------->

In the above example we see that the note **G#** (the result of altering the note **G** within a **C minor** triad) is an **augmented 5th** interval above the root of **C**.

Now we will consider **altered 5ths** on the four-part chords first derived in **Chapter 6** - **major 7th**, **major 6th**, **minor 7th** and **dominant 7th** chords. Again in each case the basic chord type (as defined by the **3rd** and **7th/6th**) stays the same. We will see that the **5th** can be both **flatted** and **sharped** on the major 7th, minor 7th and dominant 7th chords, but can only be **flatted** on the major 6th chord.

First we will look at the possible alterations to the **5th** of a **C major 7th** chord, as shown in the example on the following page:-

Altered chords (contd)

Figure 9.18. Deriving a 'C major 7th with flatted/sharped 5th' from a C major 7th chord

Note the chord symbols in the above examples which are **Cma7(b5)** and **Cma7(#5)**. This is telling us to **flat** or **sharp** the **5th** of the **C major 7th chord** respectively. We can also analyze the intervals present in these **altered major 7th** chords as follows:-

Figure 9.19. C major 7th with flatted 5th - interval construction

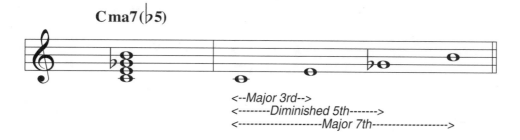

In the above example, we see that the note **Gb** (the result of flatting the note **G** within a **C major 7th** chord) is a **diminished 5th** interval above the root of **C**.

Figure 9.20. C major 7th with sharped 5th - interval construction

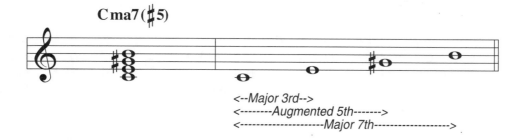

In the above example, we see that the note **G#** (the result of sharping the note **G** within a **C major 7th** chord) is an **augmented 5th** interval above the root of **C**.

Altered chords (contd)

We can also **flat** the **5th** of a **C major 6th** chord, as shown in the following example:-

Figure 9.21. Deriving a 'C major 6th with flatted 5th' from a C major 6th chord

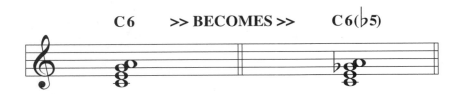

Note the chord symbol in the above example which is **C6(b5)**. This is telling us to **flat** the **5th** of the **C major 6th chord**. Another correct way to write this chord symbol would be **Cma6(b5)** - see original comments concerning **major 6th** chord symbols on **p157**.

We can also analyze the intervals present in this **altered major 6th** chord as follows:-

Figure 9.22. C major 6th with flatted 5th - interval construction

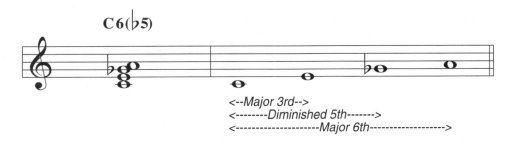

```
<--Major 3rd-->
<--------Diminished 5th------->
<---------------------Major 6th-------------------->
```

In the above example, we see that the note **Gb** (the result of flatting the note **G** within a **C major 6th** chord) is a **diminished 5th** interval above the root of **C**.

You may be wondering why we don't have a '**major 6th chord with sharped 5th**' chord - after all, we did sharp the **5th** on the **major 7th** chord, and we know that the major 7th and major 6th chords are functionally similar. Well, the **sharped 5th** on a **C major 6th** chord would be **G#**, which would only be a half-step away from the **6th** of the chord (the note **A**), resulting in an undesirable dissonance.

*(This potential '**C major 6th with sharped 5th**' chord - containing the notes **C, E, G#** and **A** from bottom to top - is actually a first inversion **A minor major 7th** chord - see if you can figure this out by reviewing four-part inversion concepts on **p162**, and the derivation of the minor major seventh chord on **p223-225**, as necessary)!*

Altered chords (contd)

A final word on the '**major 6th with flatted 5th**' chord - it is itself an **inversion** - of a '**minor 7th with flatted 5th**' chord, which we first encountered in **Fig. 7.9.** and which we are about to look at in more detail. For example, the **C6(b5)** chord shown in **Figs. 9.21. and 9.22.** is equivalent to a second inversion **F#mi7(b5)** chord, assuming that we enharmonically rename the note **Gb** to an **F#**.

Next we will look at the possible alterations to the **5th** of a **C minor 7th** chord, as shown in the following example:-

Figure 9.23. Deriving a 'C minor 7th with flatted/sharped 5th' from a C minor 7th chord

Note the chord symbols in the above examples which are **Cmi7(b5)** and **Cmi7(#5)**. This is telling us to **flat** or **sharp** the **5th** of the **C minor 7th chord** respectively. We can also analyze the intervals present in these **altered minor 7th** chords as follows:-

Figure 9.24. C minor 7th with flatted 5th - interval construction

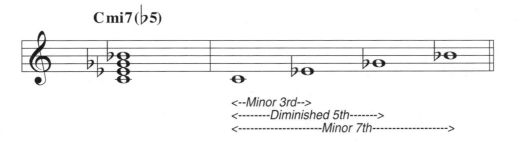

In the above example, we see that the note **Gb** (the result of flatting the note **G** within a **C minor 7th** chord) is a **diminished 5th** interval above the root of **C**.

*(You will recall that our first encounter with the '**minor 7th with flatted fifth**' chord was in the context of diatonic four-part chord relationships - we discovered that this chord occurred 'naturally' from the **7th** degree of a **major** scale - see **Fig. 7.9.**).*

Altered chords (contd)

Figure 9.25. C minor 7th with sharped 5th - interval construction

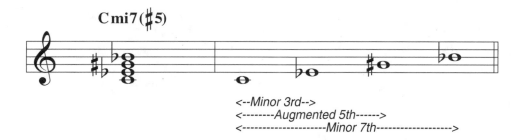

<--Minor 3rd-->
<--------Augmented 5th------>
<-------------------Minor 7th-------------------->

In the above example, we see that the note **G#** (the result of sharping the note **G** within a **C minor 7th** chord) is an **augmented 5th** interval above the root of **C**.

Before we leave the topic of **altered minor 7th** chords, you should be aware that the '**minor 7th with flatted 5th**' chord is sometimes referred to as a '**half-diminished**' or '**half-diminished 7th**' chord. I will do my best to explain how this alternate chord description has evolved! If we were to take the '**minor 7th with flatted 5th**' chord in **Fig. 9.24.** and **further flat** the top note of **Bb** to **Bbb** (as in the diminished 7th interval example in **Fig. 2.9.**), we would actually produce a '**diminished 7th chord**' - more about this in *Contemporary Music Theory Level 2*. The '**half**-diminished' description reflects the fact that the **7th** of the chord has only been flatted **once** or **half-way** (i.e. from a major 7th to a minor 7th interval as in **Fig. 2.8.**) and not **twice** or the **rest of the way** (i.e. from a minor 7th interval to a diminished 7th interval as in **Fig. 2.9.**) as would be required by a ('fully') **diminished 7th chord**.

I personally feel that the 'half-diminished' label is misleading, because the '**minor 7th with flatted 5th**' chord still has the definitive **minor 3rd** and **minor 7th** intervals within it, which make it a **minor 7th-type chord** (see table on **p227**), not a diminished chord. However, the term 'half-diminished' is in fairly common usage, and so you need to know what it means. The corresponding chord symbol suffix - the circle with a diagonal line through it (as in the symbols **Cø** or **Cø7**) is also frequently seen, particularly in older fakebooks. Be careful not to confuse this with either a **diminished triad** (as in **Fig. 3.4.**) or the above-mentioned **diminished 7th** chord!

So, my advice is - use the '**minor 7th with flatted 5th**' chord description instead of '**half-diminished**' and use the '**mi7(b5)**' chord suffix instead of '**ø**' - but as usual be prepared to recognize these other ways of presenting the chord!

Altered chords (contd)

Finally we will look at the possible alterations to the **5th** of a **C dominant 7th** chord, as shown in the following example:-

Figure 9.26. Deriving a 'C dominant 7th with flatted/sharped 5th' from a C dominant 7th chord

Note the chord symbols in the above examples which are **C7(b5)** and **C7(#5)**. This is telling us to **flat** or **sharp** the **5th** of the **C dominant 7th chord** respectively. We can also analyze the intervals present in these **altered dominant 7th** chords as follows:-

Figure 9.27. C dominant 7th with flatted 5th - interval construction

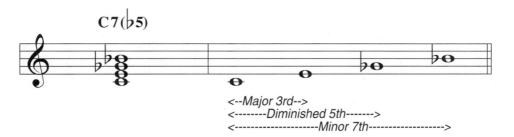

In the above example, we see that the note **Gb** (the result of flatting the note **G** within a **C dominant 7th** chord) is a **diminished 5th** interval above the root of **C**.

Figure 9.28. C dominant 7th with sharped 5th - interval construction

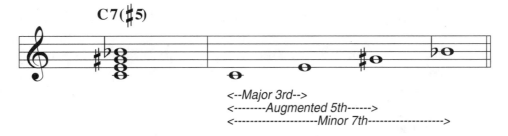

In the above example, we see that the note **G#** (the result of sharping the note **G** within a **C dominant 7th** chord) is an **augmented 5th** interval above the root of **C**.

Altered chords (contd)

A final word on the '**dominant 7th with sharped 5th**' chord - you may encounter the chord symbol suffix '**+7**' (i.e. as in '**C+7**') and the description '**augmented seventh**' (i.e. as in '**C augmented 7th**') used for this chord. This is an acceptable chord symbol and description, **provided you remember that the '+' and the '7' in the chord symbol** (corresponding to the '**augmented**' and the '**7th**' in the chord description) **have absolutely NO CONNECTION with one another** - in other words we are **NOT** raising the 7th of the chord! (see **p232** comments). The '**+**' suffix in this chord symbol indicates that the **5th has been raised by half-step**, as already discussed in the context of the **augmented triad** (see **Fig. 3.3.** and accompanying text). We already know that the chord symbol '**C7**' indicates a **C dominant 7th** chord - and so the addition of the '**+**' in the chord symbol (as in '**C+7**') therefore indicates a **C dominant 7th chord with sharped 5th**. Although the symbol '**C+7**' is a correct chord symbol, I do sometimes find that it is misinterpreted by less experienced musicians, due to the potential problems outlined above. You might therefore want to stick with the '**7(#5)**' suffix for this chord, as it is arguably more explicit!

More examples of recognizing four-part chords

This section of the chapter can be viewed as a follow-up to the four-part chord recognition examples in **Chapter 6**, where we were learning how to recognize **major 7th**, **minor 7th** and **dominant 7th** chords. Now we will see how to recognize the following new four-part chords (in root position) introduced in this chapter:-

- **Minor major 7th** and **minor 6th** chords, as in **Figs. 9.1. - 9.6.**
- **Suspended dominant 7th** chords, as in **Figs. 9.11. - 9.13.**
- **Altered major 7th** chords, as in **Figs. 9.18. - 9.20.**
- **Altered major 6th** chords, as in **Figs. 9.21. - 9.22.**
- **Altered minor 7th** chords, as in **Figs. 9.23. - 9.25.**
- **Altered dominant 7th** chords, as in **Figs. 9.26. - 9.28.**

The method to use is to first determine the nature of the **3rd** and **7th intervals** (or in some cases the **3rd** and **6th intervals**) on the chord. This will tell us the 'basic four-part chord type' (from the table on **p227**). Also we now know that certain 'basic four-part chord types' can have **altered 5ths**, and so we will determine the nature of the **5th interval** within the chord if necessary, to determine whether the chord is **altered**.

*(One exception to the above process will be in the case of the **suspended dominant 7th** chord, which is the only chord in the above list which does not have a **3rd** - in this case we will be looking for **perfect 4th** and **minor 7th** intervals above the root of the chord, as shown in **Fig. 9.12.**).*

240

More examples of recognizing four-part chords (contd)

All the following chord recognition examples will be presented in root position, and in all cases when determining the interval between two notes (for example, in order to find out what type of **3rd** or **7th** is in the chord) you are to use the interval recognition method outlined in **Chapter 2** - review as necessary!

Figure 9.29. Four-part chord recognition example #1

First of all we note that the chord has **3rd**, **5th** and **7th intervals** present. We then analyze the **3rd** and **7th** intervals as follows:-

- the **3rd** interval (**G** up to **Bb**) is a **minor 3rd**, and
- the **7th** interval (**G** up to **F#**) is a **major 7th**.

Checking in the chord/interval table on **p227**, we note that the four-part chord containing **minor 3rd** and **major 7th intervals** is a **minor major 7th chord**. (We recall from **Fig. 9.1.** that this chord also contains a **perfect 5th** interval, and the above **5th** interval of **G** up to **D** is also a **perfect 5th**). The chord in example **#1** is therefore a **G minor major 7th** chord, for which the correct chord symbol would be **GmiMa7**.

Figure 9.30. Four-part chord recognition example #2

First of all we note that the chord has **3rd**, **5th** and **6th intervals** present. We then analyze the **3rd** and **6th** intervals as follows:-

- the **3rd** interval (**C#** up to **E**) is a **minor 3rd**, and
- the **6th** interval (**C#** up to **A#**) is a **major 6th**.

Checking in the chord/interval table on **p227**, we note that the four-part chord containing **minor 3rd** and **major 6th intervals** is a **minor 6th chord**. (We recall from **Fig. 9.4.** that this chord also contains a **perfect 5th** interval, and the above **5th** interval of **C#** up to **G#** is also a **perfect 5th**). The chord in example **#2** is therefore a **C# minor 6th** chord, for which the correct chord symbol would be **C#mi6**.

More examples of recognizing four-part chords (contd)

Figure 9.31. Four-part chord recognition example #3

First of all we note that the chord has **4th, 5th** and **7th intervals** present. Within the current range of chord options, this is therefore likely to be a **suspended dominant 7th** chord. We can further verify the intervals as follows:-

- the **4th** interval (**E** up to **A**) is a **perfect 4th**,
- the **5th** interval (**E** up to **B**) is a **perfect 5th**, and
- the **7th** interval (**E** up to **D**) is a **minor 7th**.

Checking the above against the intervals derived in **Fig. 9.12.**, we note that this is indeed the interval construction for a **suspended dominant 7th** - so the chord in example #3 is therefore an **E suspended dominant 7th** chord, for which the correct chord symbol would be **E7sus**.

Figure 9.32. Four-part chord recognition example #4

First of all we note that the chord has **3rd, 5th** and **7th intervals** present. We then analyze the **3rd** and **7th** intervals as follows:-

- the **3rd** interval (**Bb** up to **D**) is a **major 3rd**, and
- the **7th** interval (**Bb** up to **A**) is a **major 7th**.

Checking in the chord/interval table on **p227**, we note that the four-part chord containing **major 3rd** and **major 7th intervals** is a **major 7th chord**. We recall from **Figs. 9.18. - 9.20.** that the **major 7th** chord may also have an **altered 5th**, and so we also need to analyze the **5th interval** in the above example, as follows:-

- the **5th** interval (**Bb** up to **F#**) is an **augmented 5th**.

The chord in example #4 is therefore a **Bb major 7th with sharped 5th** chord, for which the correct chord symbol would be **Bbma7(#5)**.

More examples of recognizing four-part chords (contd)

Figure 9.33. Four-part chord recognition example #5

First of all we note that the chord has **3rd**, **5th** and **7th intervals** present. We then analyze the **3rd** and **7th** intervals as follows:-

- the **3rd** interval (**F** up to **A**) is a **major 3rd**, and
- the **7th** interval (**F** up to **Eb**) is a **minor 7th**.

Checking in the chord/interval table on **p227**, we note that the four-part chord containing **major 3rd** and **minor 7th intervals** is a **dominant 7th chord**. We recall from **Figs. 9.26. - 9.28.** that the **dominant 7th** chord may also have an **altered 5th**, and so we also need to analyze the **5th interval** in the above example, as follows:-

- the **5th** interval (**F** up to **Cb**) is a **diminished 5th**.

The chord in example **#5** is therefore an **F dominant 7th with flatted 5th** chord, for which the correct chord symbol would be **F7(b5)**.

Figure 9.34. Four-part chord recognition example #6

First of all we note that the chord has **3rd**, **5th** and **7th intervals** present. We then analyze the **3rd** and **7th** intervals as follows:-

- the **3rd** interval (**D** up to **F**) is a **minor 3rd**, and
- the **7th** interval (**D** up to **C**) is a **minor 7th**.

Checking in the chord/interval table on **p227**, we note that the four-part chord containing **minor 3rd** and **minor 7th intervals** is a **minor 7th chord**. We recall from **Figs. 9.23. - 9.25.** that the **minor 7th** chord may also have an **altered 5th**, and so we also need to analyze the **5th interval** in the above example, as follows:-

- the **5th** interval (**D** up to **A#**) is an **augmented 5th**.

More examples of recognizing four-part chords (contd)

(Explanation of example #6 contd)

The chord in example **#6** is therefore a **D minor 7th with sharped 5th** chord, for which the correct chord symbol would be **Dmi7(#5)**.

Figure 9.35. Four-part chord recognition example #7

First of all we note that the chord has **3rd**, **5th** and **6th intervals** present. We then analyze the **3rd** and **6th** intervals as follows:-

- the **3rd** interval (**F#** up to **A#**) is a **major 3rd**, and
- the **6th** interval (**F#** up to **D#**) is a **major 6th**.

Checking in the chord/interval table on **p227**, we note that the four-part chord containing **major 3rd** and **major 6th intervals** is a **major 6th chord**. We recall from **Figs. 9.21. - 9.22.** that the **major 6th** chord may also have a **flatted 5th**, and so we also need to analyze the **5th interval** in the above example, as follows:-

- the **5th** interval (**F#** up to **C**) is a **diminished 5th**.

The chord in example **#7** is therefore an **F# major 6th with flatted 5th** chord, for which the correct chord symbol would be **F#6(b5)**.

Chapter Nine Workbook Questions

1.   *Altered and suspended triad spelling*

Write the notes on the staff corresponding to the following altered and suspended triad chord symbols:-

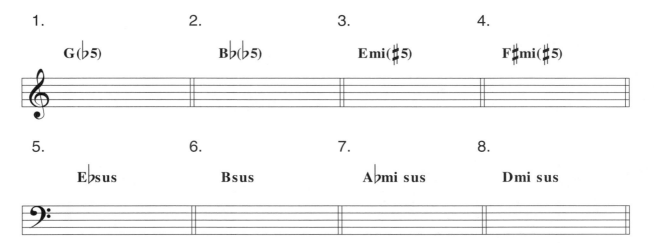

1.	2.	3.	4.
G(♭5)	B♭(♭5)	Emi(♯5)	F♯mi(♯5)

5.	6.	7.	8.
E♭sus	Bsus	A♭mi sus	Dmi sus

2.   *'Minor major 7th' and 'minor 6th' chord spelling*

Write the notes on the staff corresponding to the following minor major 7th and minor 6th chord symbols:-

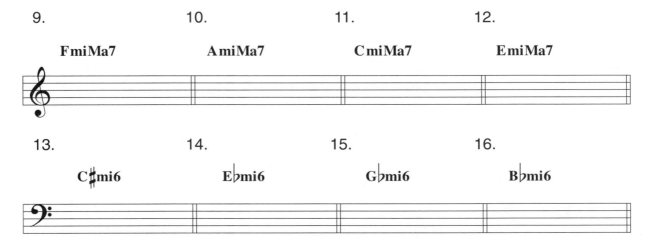

9.	10.	11.	12.
FmiMa7	AmiMa7	CmiMa7	EmiMa7

13.	14.	15.	16.
C♯mi6	E♭mi6	G♭mi6	B♭mi6

3. _Altered 'minor 7th' chord spelling_

Write the notes on the staff corresponding to the following altered minor 7th chord symbols:-

17.   18.   19.   20.

Ami7(♯5)   E♭mi7(♯5)   Fmi7(♭5)   Bmi7(♭5)

21.   22.   23.   24.

Gmi7(♭5)   C♯mi7(♯5)   A♭mi7(♯5)   Cmi7(♭5)

4. _Altered and suspended 'dominant 7th' chord spelling_

Write the notes on the staff corresponding to the following altered and suspended dominant 7th chord symbols:-

25.   26.   27.   28.

E7(♯5)   D♭7(♭5)   D7sus   B♭7(♯5)

29.   30.   31.   32.

A7(♭5)   G♭7(♯5)   C♯7(♯5)   G7sus

5.   *Altered 'major 7th' and 'major 6th' chord spelling*

Write the notes on the staff corresponding to the following altered major 7th and major 6th chord symbols:-

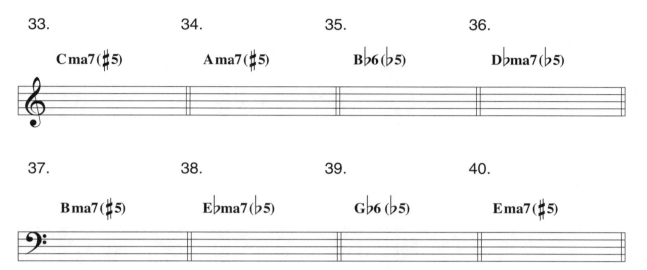

33.   34.   35.   36.

Cma7(♯5)   Ama7(♯5)   B♭6(♭5)   D♭ma7(♭5)

37.   38.   39.   40.

Bma7(♯5)   E♭ma7(♭5)   G♭6(♭5)   Ema7(♯5)

6.   *Four-part chord recognition - part 1*

This section contains a mixture of (root-position) minor major 7th, minor 6th, major 7th, major 6th, minor 7th, and dominant 7th chords. Write the chord symbol above the staff for each question:-

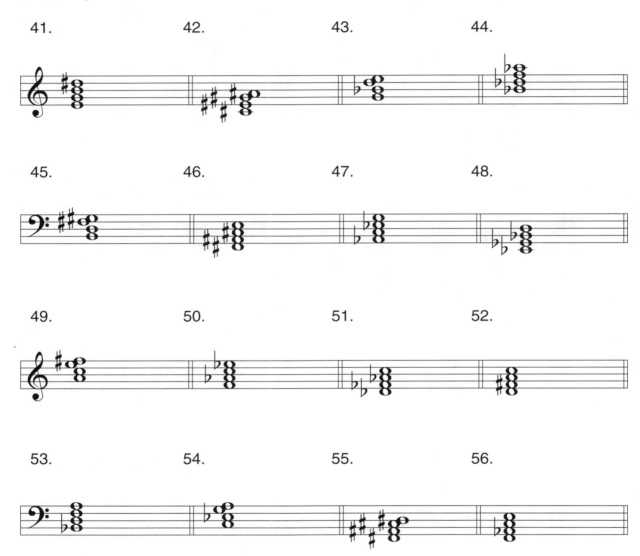

6. ***Four-part chord recognition - part 2***

This section contains a mixture of the following chords in root position:-
- altered major 7th (sharped or flatted 5th)
- altered major 6th (flatted 5th)
- altered minor 7th (sharped or flatted 5th)
- altered dominant 7th (sharped or flatted 5th)
- suspended dominant 7th.

Write the chord symbol above the staff for each question:-

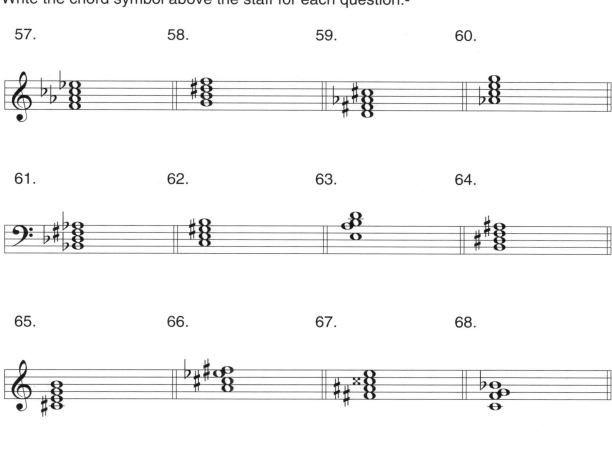

57.   58.   59.   60.

61.   62.   63.   64.

65.   66.   67.   68.

69.   70.   71.   72.

6. *Four-part chord recognition - part 2 (contd)*

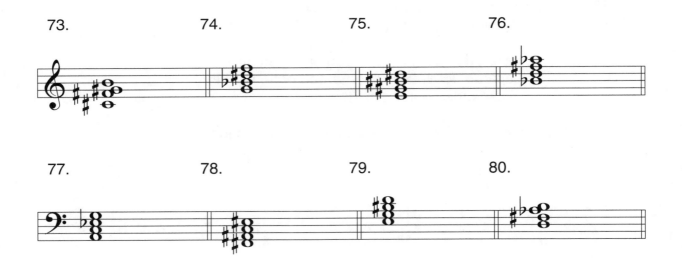

73.　　　　　74.　　　　　75.　　　　　76.

77.　　　　　78.　　　　　79.　　　　　80.

Chapter Nine Workbook Answers

1. *Altered and suspended triad spelling - answers*

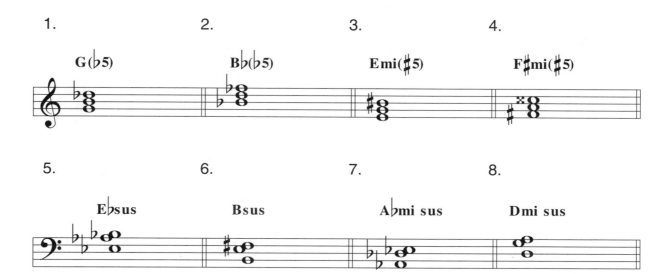

2. *'Minor major 7th' and 'minor 6th' chord spelling - answers*

3. **Altered 'minor 7th' chord spelling - answers**

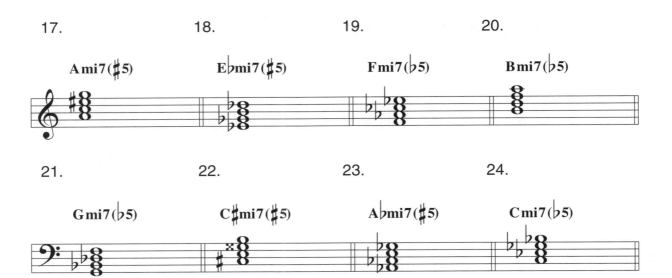

4. **Altered and suspended 'dominant 7th' chord spelling - answers**

5. *Altered 'major 7th' and 'major 6th' chord spelling - answers*

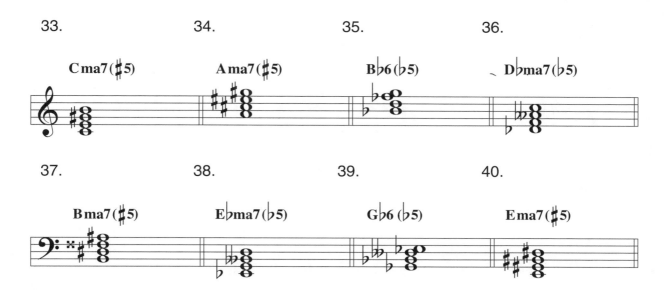

33.   34.   35.   36.

Cma7(♯5)   Ama7(♯5)   B♭6(♭5)   D♭ma7(♭5)

37.   38.   39.   40.

Bma7(♯5)   E♭ma7(♭5)   G♭6(♭5)   Ema7(♯5)

6.   *Four-part chord recognition part 1 - answers*

6. **_Four-part chord recognition part 2 - answers_**

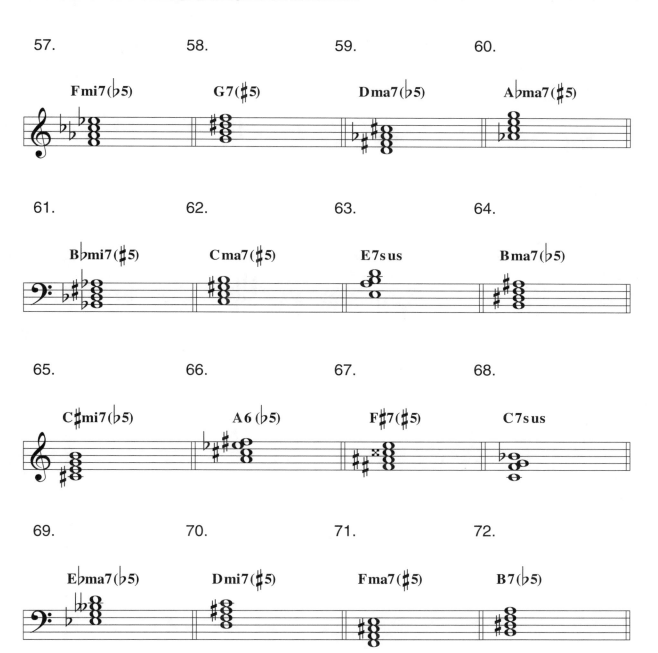

6. **_Four-part chord recognition part 2 - answers (contd)_**

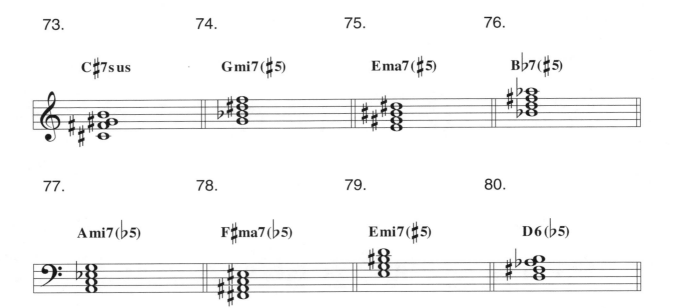

Major and minor scales (with key signatures)

Major scales with key signatures

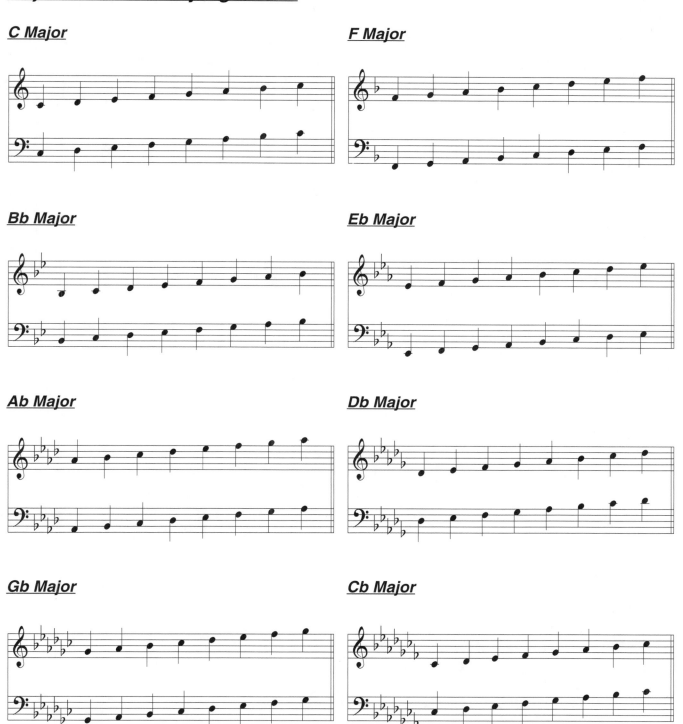

Major scales with key signatures (contd)

G Major

D Major

A Major

E Major

B Major

F# Major

C# Major

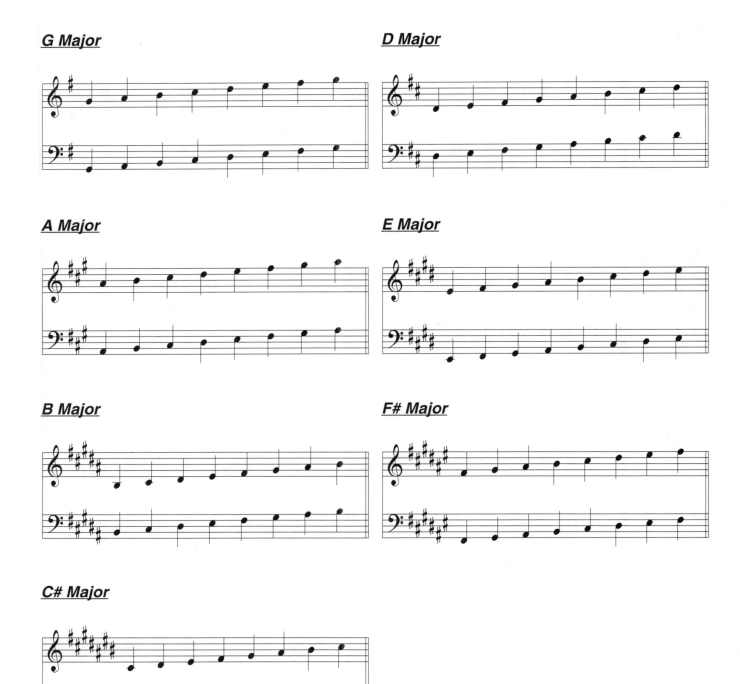

Natural Minor scales with key signatures

A Natural Minor

D Natural Minor

G Natural Minor

C Natural Minor

F Natural Minor

Bb Natural Minor

Eb Natural Minor

Ab Natural Minor

Natural Minor scales with key signatures (contd)

E Natural Minor

B Natural Minor

F# Natural Minor

C# Natural Minor

G# Natural Minor

D# Natural Minor

A# Natural Minor

Harmonic Minor scales with key signatures

A Harmonic Minor

D Harmonic Minor

G Harmonic Minor

C Harmonic Minor

F Harmonic Minor

Bb Harmonic Minor

Eb Harmonic Minor

Ab Harmonic Minor

Harmonic Minor scales with key signatures (contd)

E Harmonic Minor

B Harmonic Minor

F# Harmonic Minor

C# Harmonic Minor

G# Harmonic Minor

D# Harmonic Minor

A# Harmonic Minor

Melodic Minor scales with key signatures

A Melodic Minor

D Melodic Minor

G Melodic Minor

C Melodic Minor

F Melodic Minor

Bb Melodic Minor

Eb Melodic Minor

Ab Melodic Minor

Melodic Minor scales with key signatures (contd)

E Melodic Minor

B Melodic Minor

F# Melodic Minor

C# Melodic Minor

G# Melodic Minor

D# Melodic Minor

A# Melodic Minor

Major and minor scales (without key signatures)

Major scales without key signatures

C Major

F Major

Bb Major

Eb Major

Ab Major

Db Major

Gb Major

Cb Major

265

Major scales without key signatures (contd)

G Major

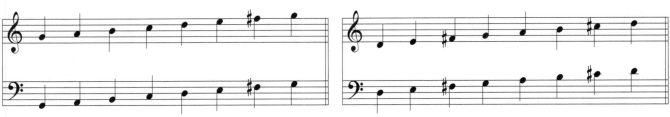

D Major

A Major

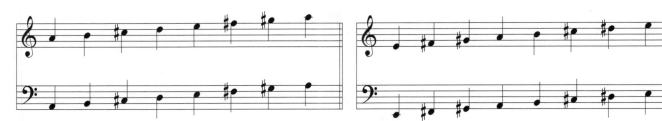

E Major

B Major

F# Major

C# Major

Natural Minor scales without key signatures

C Natural Minor

F Natural Minor

Bb Natural Minor

Eb Natural Minor

Ab Natural Minor

Db Natural Minor

Gb Natural Minor

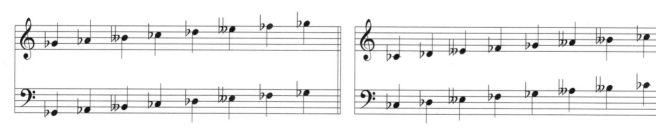

Cb Natural Minor

Natural Minor scales without key signatures (contd)

G Natural Minor

D Natural Minor

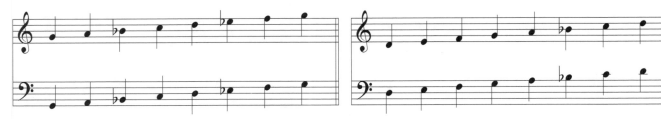

A Natural Minor

E Natural Minor

B Natural Minor

F# Natural Minor

C# Natural Minor

Harmonic Minor scales without key signatures

C Harmonic Minor

F Harmonic Minor

Bb Harmonic Minor

Eb Harmonic Minor

Ab Harmonic Minor

Db Harmonic Minor

Gb Harmonic Minor

Cb Harmonic Minor

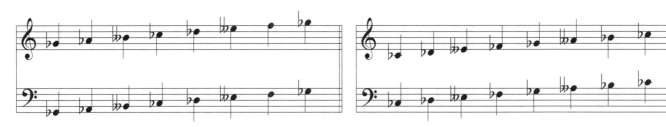

Harmonic Minor scales without key signatures (contd)

G Harmonic Minor

D Harmonic Minor

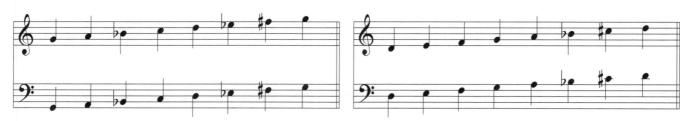

A Harmonic Minor

E Harmonic Minor

B Harmonic Minor

F# Harmonic Minor

C# Harmonic Minor

Melodic Minor scales without key signatures

C Melodic Minor

F Melodic Minor

Bb Melodic Minor

Eb Melodic Minor

Ab Melodic Minor

Db Melodic Minor

Gb Melodic Minor

Cb Melodic Minor

Melodic Minor scales without key signatures (contd)

G Melodic Minor

D Melodic Minor

A Melodic Minor

E Melodic Minor

B Melodic Minor

F# Melodic Minor

C# Melodic Minor

Diatonic triads and four-part chords

Diatonic triads in all major keys

Key of C Major

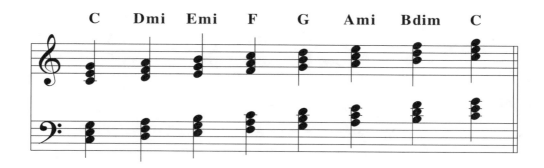

Key of F Major

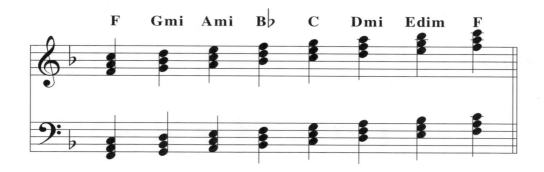

Key of Bb Major

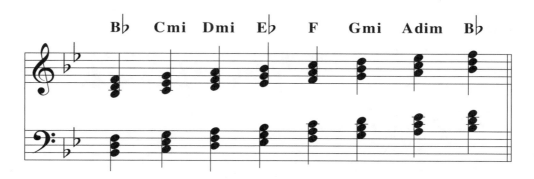

Diatonic triads in all major keys (contd)

Key of Eb Major

Key of Ab Major

Key of Db Major

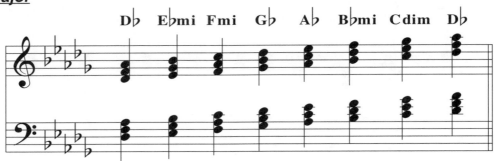

Key of Gb Major

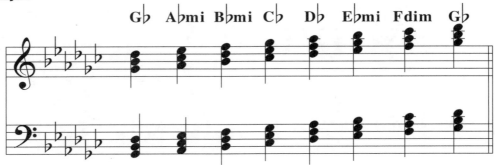

Diatonic triads in all major keys (contd)

Key of Cb Major

Key of G Major

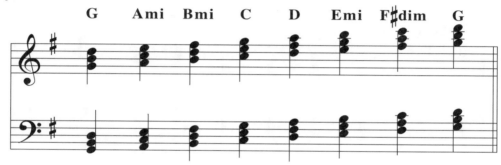

Key of D Major

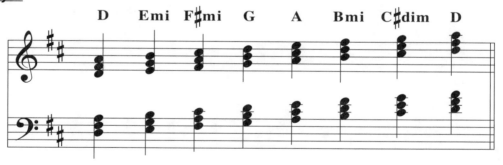

Key of A Major

Diatonic triads in all major keys (contd)

Key of E Major

Key of B Major

Key of F# Major

Key of C# Major

Diatonic four-part chords in all major keys

Key of C Major

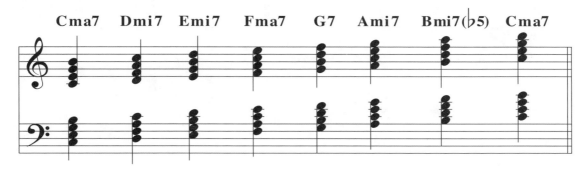

Key of F Major

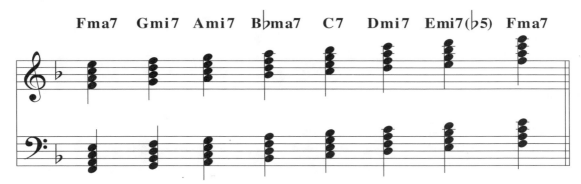

Key of Bb Major

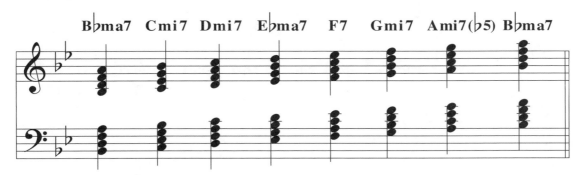

Diatonic four-part chords in all major keys (contd)

Key of Eb Major

Key of Ab Major

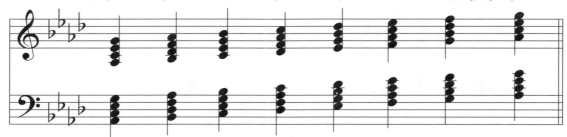

Key of Db Major

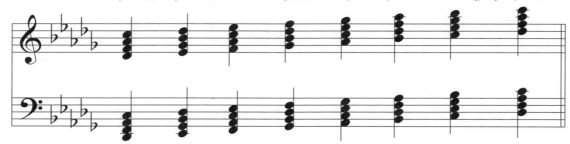

Key of Gb Major

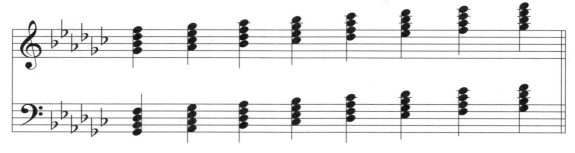

Diatonic four-part chords in all major keys (contd)

Key of Cb Major

C♭ma7 D♭mi7 E♭mi7 F♭ma7 G♭7 A♭mi7 B♭mi7(♭5) C♭ma7

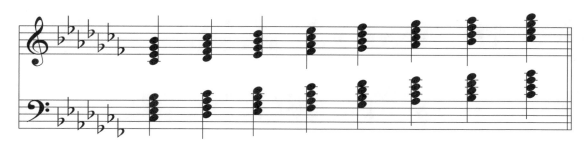

Key of G Major

Gma7   Ami7   Bmi7   Cma7   D7   Emi7   F♯mi7(♭5) Gma7

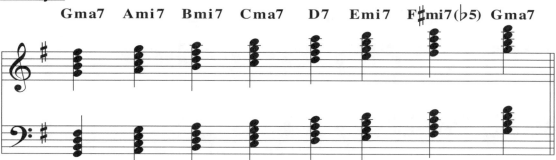

Key of D Major

Dma7   Emi7   F♯mi7   Gma7   A7   Bmi7   C♯mi7(♭5) Dma7

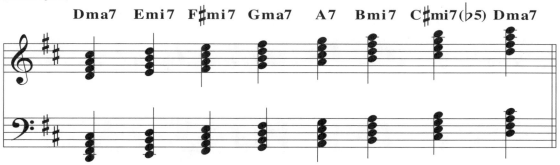

Key of A Major

Ama7   Bmi7   C♯mi7   Dma7   E7   F♯mi7   G♯mi7(♭5) Ama7

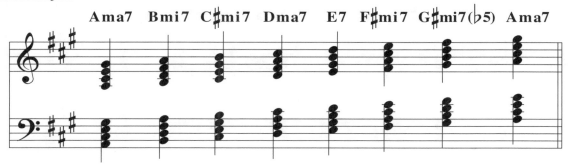

Diatonic four-part chords in all major keys (contd)

Key of E Major

Key of B Major

Key of F# Major

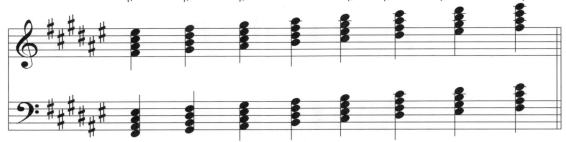

Key of C# Major

Glossary of terms used in this book

Accidental Collective term for prefixes such as sharps, flats, and natural signs placed to the left of music noteheads.

Aeolian (mode) The mode created when a major scale is displaced to start on its **6th** degree (first seen in **Fig. 5.5.**) - also equivalent to a natural minor scale.

Alphabet - See *'music alphabet'*.

Altered This is a general term applied to a triad or four-part chord, which signifies that the **5th** of the chord has been **flatted** or **sharped** by **half-step** - see **Chapter 9** and in particular the text on **p232**. (Later in *Contemporary Music Theory Level Two* we will see that other chordal extensions, such as the 9th, can also be 'altered').

Altered chord See above comments regarding the term *'altered'*.

Altered fifth See above comments regarding the term *'altered'*.

Altered minor triad - See *'minor triad with sharped 5th'*.

Altered minor 7th chord - See *'minor 7th with flatted 5th chord'* and *'minor 7th with sharped 5th chord'*.

Altered major triad - See *'major triad with flatted 5th'*.

Altered major 6th chord - See *'major 6th with flatted 5th chord'*.

Altered major 7th chord - See *'major 7th with flatted 5th chord'* and *'major 7th with sharped 5th chord'*.

Augmented interval A **major** or **perfect interval** which has been **increased** by a **half-step** (see **Figs. 2.9.** and **2.11.**).

Augmented triad A triad consisting of **major 3rd** and **augmented 5th** intervals (measured from the root of the chord - see **Fig. 3.3.**) - can also be derived by taking a major triad and raising the **5th** by a **half-step**.

Bass clef	The bass clef staff is typically used in contemporary music to notate pitches which are in the 'lower half' of the overall musical range i.e. from around the **Middle C** area downwards (see **Fig. 1.6.**). Instruments using the bass clef would include the bass guitar and the piano (left hand part). The first leger line above the bass clef staff represents **Middle C**.
Beat	A unit of rhythmic duration i.e. as in "a half note lasts for two beats". The **beat** will also be equivalent to the **pulse** or point of rhythmic emphasis in the measure, if the bottom number of the time signature is **four** - signifying that the **pulse** is felt on the **quarter-note** (as in **four/four** time which is used in the vast majority of contemporary applications) - see **p11** comments.
Chart	A written representation of a tune which typically contains the melody and chord symbols, which is then **interpreted** by the musicians according to their understanding of the style. (Specific instrument parts and rhythmic figures may also be indicated). See also *Fake Book*.
Chord	Term generally used to describe the harmony created when three or more pitches are used simultaneously, in a vertical 'stack'. Most contemporary styles are harmonically organized around 'chords'.
Chord progression	A series of chords used in sequence during a piece of music (as indicated on a chart for the particular tune).
Chord quality	The vertical sound created by the chord in question i.e. major, minor, suspended etc.
Chord symbol	The symbol used on the chart to indicate the chord required. See the various chord symbol definitions in **Chapters 3**, **6**, **7** and **9**.
Chromatic interval	An interval in which the top note does not belong within the major scale built from the bottom note - see **Fig. 2.4.** and accompanying text.
Circle-of-fifths	A succession of major scales and keys based on a series of 'five-to-one' relationships - see **Chapter 1 p23-31**.
Circle-of-fourths	A succession of major scales and keys based on a series of 'four-to-one' relationships - see **Chapter 1 p23-31**.

Common time Another way to describe **4/4** time - see **Fig. 1.24.**

Cut time Another way to describe **2/2** time - see **Fig. 1.26.**

Diatonic interval An interval in which the top note belongs within the major scale built from the bottom note - see **Fig. 2.3.** and accompanying text.

Diatonic triads Triads which belong to, or occur naturally within, the major scale or key in question. See **Chapter 4** and **Appendix 3.**

Diatonic four-part chords Four-part chords which belong to, or occur naturally within, the major scale or key in question. See **Chapter 7** and **Appendix 3.**

Diminished interval A diminished interval occurs when a **minor** interval is reduced by a **half-step** (as in **Fig. 2.8.**), or when a **perfect** interval is reduced by a **half-step** (as in **Fig. 2.10.**).

Diminished triad A triad consisting of **minor 3rd** and **diminished 5th** intervals (measured from the root of the chord - see **Fig. 3.4.**) - can also be derived by taking a major triad and lowering the **3rd** and **5th** by a **half-step**.

Displaced scale A scale beginning on a note other than the normal starting note or 'tonic'. For example, the modal scales derived in **Chapter 5** are all displaced major scales.

Dominant 7th chord A four-part chord consisting of **major 3rd**, **perfect 5th** and **minor 7th** intervals (measured from the root of the chord - see **Fig. 6.4.**). This chord is built from the **5th** degree of a major scale (see **Fig. 7.7.**) and generally needs to resolve back to the 'tonic' or **I** chord of the key.

Dominant 7th with flatted 5th chord A dominant 7th chord in which the **5th** has been flatted - see **Figs. 9.26. and 9.27.**

Dominant 7th with sharped 5th chord A dominant 7th chord in which the **5th** has been sharped - see **Figs. 9.26. and 9.28.**

Dorian (mode) The mode created when a major scale is displaced to start on its **2nd** degree (first seen in **Fig. 5.1.**).

Dotted eighth note A note with duration lasting for three-quarters of a beat (see **Fig. 1.13.**).

Dotted eighth note rest	A rest with duration lasting for three-quarters of a beat (see **Fig. 1.21.**).
Dotted half note	A note with duration lasting for three beats (see **Fig. 1.9.**).
Dotted half note rest	A rest with duration lasting for three beats (see **Fig. 1.17.**).
Dotted quarter note	A note with duration lasting for one-and-a-half beats (see **Fig. 1.11.**).
Dotted quarter note rest	A rest with duration lasting for one-and-a-half beats (see **Fig. 1.19.**).
Eighth (8th) interval	Another term for **octave** (see **Fig. 2.5.**).
Eighth note	A note with duration lasting for one-half of a beat (see **Fig. 1.12.**).
Eighth note rest	A rest with duration lasting for one-half of a beat (see **Fig. 1.20.**).
Eleventh (11th) interval	An interval derived by increasing a **fourth interval** by one **octave**. All possible versions of the **fourth** interval *(see glossary entry for fourth interval)* are also possible for the **eleventh** interval.
Enharmonic	A term used to describe alternative note names for the same pitch - for example, **C#** and **Db** are considered enharmonic equivalents (see **Figs. 1.2. - 1.3.** and accompanying text).
Extensions	Upper tones added to chords (beyond the basic root, 3rd and 5th of the chord).
Fake book	A book which contains **charts** of tunes (rather than written-out arrangements). The musician is left to create their own arrangement based on the melody and chord symbols provided, and on their understanding of the harmony and style.
Fifth (5th) interval	- A **perfect 5th** interval occurs between the tonic (**1st** degree) and the **5th** degree of a major scale i.e. **G** is the **5th** degree of **C major**, therefore **C** up to **G** is a **perfect 5th** interval (see **Fig. 2.5.**). - A **diminished 5th** interval occurs when a **perfect 5th** interval is reduced by a half-step i.e. **C** up to **G** is a **perfect 5th** interval, therefore **C** up to **Gb** is a **diminished 5th** interval (see **Fig. 2.10.**). - An **augmented 5th** interval occurs when a **perfect 5th** interval is increased by a half-step i.e. **C** up to **G** is a **perfect 5th** interval, therefore **C** up to **G#** is an **augmented 5th** interval.

First inversion   A three- or four-part chord is in first inversion when the root has been moved up an octave and has become the highest note - see **Figs. 3.10. - 3.13.** and **6.9. - 6.11.**

Five-to-one   A relationship created between successive stages around the **circle-of-5ths**, implying a movement from the **5th** degree to the **1st** degree of a major scale - see **Figs. 1.62. - 1.63.** and **1.66.**

Flashcards   A set of flashcards contains one card for each note, with the note shown (on the treble or bass clef) on the front, and the note name (and keyboard location) on the back. A highly recommended tool for learning the notes on the staff!

Flat   A flat sign prefixed to a note requires that note to be lowered in pitch by one half-step. May also form part of a key signature.

'Flat' keys   A name sometimes given to those major keys which contain flats in the key signature - see **Chapter 1.**

Four-four (4/4) time   A time signature with four 'pulses' per measure, with the quarter note 'getting the beat' i.e. the pulse is felt on the quarter note (see **Fig. 1.23.**).

Four-part chords   A four-note chord consisting of **3rd**, **5th** and **7th** (or **3rd**, **5th** and **6th**) intervals, measured from the root of the chord - see **Chapters 6**, **7** and **9**.

Fourteenth (14th) interval   An interval derived by increasing a **seventh interval** by one **octave**. All possible versions of the **seventh** interval *(see glossary entry for seventh interval)* are also possible for the **fourteenth** interval.

Fourth (4th) interval   - A **perfect 4th** interval occurs between the tonic (**1st** degree) and the **4th** degree of a major scale i.e. F is the **4th** degree of **C major**, therefore **C** up to **F** is a **perfect 4th** interval (see **Fig. 2.5.**).
- An **augmented 4th** interval occurs when a **perfect 4th** interval is increased by a half-step i.e. **C** up to **F** is a **perfect 4th** interval, therefore **C** up to **F#** is an **augmented 4th** interval (see **Fig. 2.11.**).

Four-to-one   A relationship created between successive stages around the **circle-of-4ths**, implying a movement from the **4th** degree to the **1st** degree of a major scale - see **Figs. 1.64. - 1.66.**

285

Grand staff   A combination of **treble** and **bass** clef staffs, typically used to notate piano music (first seen in **Fig. 1.4.**).

'Half-diminished' or 'Half-diminished 7th'   These terms are sometimes used as alternative names for the **minor 7th with flatted 5th** chord - see comments on **p238**.

Half note   A note with duration lasting for two beats (see **Fig. 1.8.**).

Half note rest   A rest with duration lasting for two beats (see **Fig. 1.16.**).

Half-step   The smallest unit of interval measurement in conventional Western tonal music. There are twelve half-steps in one octave.

Harmonic minor scale   One of the three minor scales in common usage. A harmonic minor scale can be derived in the following ways:-
- using the required tetrachords as in **Fig. 8.3.**
- taking a major scale and flatting the **3rd** and **6th** degrees as in **Fig. 8.6.**
- using the minor key signature and sharping the **7th** degree as in **Fig. 8.9.**

Interval   The distance in pitch between two notes. (See **Chapter 2** and the individual glossary entries for the different types of intervals).

Inversion, inverted   An inversion of a chord occurs when the normal sequence of notes from bottom to top is changed, typically by moving one or more notes up an octave. See **Figs. 3.10. - 3.13.** and **6.9. - 6.11.**

Ionian (mode)   The mode name given to a major scale which is NOT displaced, i.e. still starting on the normal tonic (see **p130**).

Key   Term used to indicate tonality or the 'home base' for a piece of music. For example, in the keys of **C major** and **C minor**, the note **C** will be heard as the tonic or 'home base'. However, a tune in the key of **C major** will use a **C major scale** (subject to any accidentals being used), whereas a tune in the key of **C minor** may use any of the **C minor scales** (i.e. melodic, harmonic, and/or natural) as required.

Key signature   A group of sharps or flats placed at the beginning of a tune to indicate the key. (See **Figs. 1.74. - 1.90.** for major key signatures). Each key signature can also be used for a 'relative' minor key, built from the **6th** degree of the major key - see **p205**.
(All major and minor key signatures are also shown in **Appendix 1**).

'Landing point'	A term used to refer to a stage around the **circle-of-5ths** (when moving in a **five-to-one** manner) or the **circle-of-4ths** (when moving in a **four-to-one** manner) - see explanation in **Chapter 1 p23-31**.
Leger line	A short horizontal line used either above or below the staff, used to notate a pitch which would otherwise be beyond the normal range of the particular staff (first seen in **Fig. 1.4.**).
Lettername	A letter within the music alphabet (**A - G**) used for a note name.
Locrian mode	The mode created when a major scale is displaced to start on its **7th** degree (first seen in **Fig. 5.6.**).
Lower tetrachord	The lower or left-hand portion of a scale created using tetrachords. The lower tetrachord contains the **1st** (tonic), **2nd**, **3rd** and **4th** scale degrees - see **Fig. 1.42.** (for a major scale) and **Figs. 8.2. - 8.4.** (for the minor scales).
Lydian mode	The mode created when a major scale is displaced to start on its **4th** degree (first seen in **Fig. 5.3.**).
Major interval	The term **major** is applied to all **2nd**, **3rd**, **6th** and **7th** intervals (and octave displacements) which are diatonic i.e. in which the top note is within the major scale built from the bottom note - see **Fig. 2.5.**
Major key	- See *'key'*.
Major key signature	- See *'key signature'*.
Major scale	A set of interval relationships (*whole-step, whole-step, half-step, whole-step, whole-step, whole-step & half-step*) constituting the basic tonality or 'reference point' for most Western music (first seen in **Fig. 1.42.**).
Major tetrachord	A 'scalewise grouping' of four notes containing the intervals *whole-step, whole-step* and *half-step* - used to construct the major scale as in **Fig. 1.42.**
Major triad	A triad consisting of **major 3rd** and **perfect 5th** intervals (measured from the root of the chord - see **Fig. 3.1.**) - can also be derived by taking the 1st, 3rd & 5th degrees of a major scale.
Major triad with flatted 5th	A major triad in which the **5th** has been flatted - see **Figs. 9.14. - 9.15**.

Major 2nd (second) interval — See *'second interval'*.

Major 3rd (third) interval — See *'third interval'*.

Major 6th (sixth)

This term can be applied to a chord and an interval:-

Major 6th chord — A four-note chord consisting of **major 3rd**, **perfect 5th**, and **major 6th** intervals (measured from the root of the chord - see **Fig. 6.2.**).

Major 6th interval - See *'sixth interval'*.

Major 6th with flatted 5th chord

A major 6th chord in which the **5th** has been flatted - see **Figs. 9.21. - 9.22**.

Major 7th (seventh)

This term can be applied to a chord and an interval:-

Major 7th chord — A four-note chord consisting of **major 3rd**, **perfect 5th**, and **major 7th** intervals (measured from the root of the chord - see **Fig. 6.1.**).

Major 7th interval - See *'seventh interval'*.

Major 7th with flatted 5th chord

A major 7th chord in which the **5th** has been flatted - see **Figs. 9.18. - 9.19**.

Major 7th with sharped 5th chord

A major 7th chord in which the **5th** has been sharped - see **Figs. 9.18. and 9.20**.

Melodic minor scale

One of the three minor scales in common usage. A melodic minor scale can be derived in the following ways:-
- using the required tetrachords as in **Fig. 8.2.**
- taking a major scale and flatting the **3rd** degree as in **Fig. 8.5.**
- using the minor key signature and sharping the **6th** and **7th** degrees as in **Fig. 8.10.**

Middle C

The note **C** which is in the middle of the piano keyboard, generally considered to be a central 'reference point' in Western music.

Minor interval

A **major interval** which has been **reduced** by a **half-step** (see **Fig. 2.7.**).

Minor key	- See *'key'*.
Minor key signature	- See *'key signature'*.
Minor scale	There are three minor scales in common usage - melodic, harmonic and natural. See **Chapter 8** and individual glossary entries.
Minor tetrachord	A 'scalewise grouping' of four notes containing the intervals *whole-step*, *half-step* and *whole-step* - used to construct the minor scales as in **Figs. 8.1. - 8.4.**
Minor triad	A triad consisting of **minor 3rd** and **perfect 5th** intervals (measured from the root of the chord - see **Fig. 3.2.**) - can also be derived by taking the 2nd, 4th & 6th degrees of a major scale.
Minor triad with sharped 5th	A minor triad in which the **5th** has been sharped - see **Figs. 9.16. - 9.17.**
Minor 2nd (second) interval	- See *'second interval'*.
Minor 3rd (third) interval	- See *'third interval'*.
Minor 6th (sixth)	This term can be applied to a chord and an interval:-

	Minor 6th chord	A four-note chord consisting of **minor 3rd**, **perfect 5th**, and **major 6th** intervals (measured from the root of the chord - see **Fig. 9.4.**).
	Minor 6th interval	- See *'sixth interval'*.

Minor major 7th (seventh) chord	A four-note chord consisting of **minor 3rd**, **perfect 5th** and **major 7th** intervals (measured from the root of the chord - see **Fig. 9.1.**).
Minor 7th (seventh)	This term can be applied to a chord and an interval:-

	Minor 7th chord	A four-note chord consisting of **minor 3rd**, **perfect 5th**, and **minor 7th** intervals (measured from the root of the chord - see **Fig. 6.3.**).
	Minor 7th interval	- See *'seventh interval'*.

Minor 7th with flatted 5th chord	A minor 7th chord in which the **5th** has been flatted - see **Figs. 9.23. - 9.24.**

Minor 7th with sharped 5th chord	A minor 7th chord in which the **5th** has been sharped - see **Figs. 9.23.** and **9.25**.
Mixolydian (mode)	The mode created when a major scale is displaced to start on its **5th** degree (first seen in **Fig. 5.4.**).
Mode, modal scale	Terms used to describe a 'displaced' scale i.e. a scale starting from a note other than the normal tonic or first note of the scale. This concept is most frequently applied to major scales - see **Chapter 5** and in particular **Figs. 5.1. - 5.6.**
Music alphabet	The letters **A**, **B**, **C**, **D**, **E**, **F** and **G** which are used for note names. See **Chapter 1**.
Music notation	A convention of written symbols indicating musical pitch and rhythm.
Natural	A natural sign attached to a note cancels out a previously applied sharp or flat (from an earlier accidental, or from a key signature).
Natural minor scale	One of the three minor scales in common usage. A natural minor scale can be derived in the following ways:- - using the required tetrachords as in **Fig. 8.4.** - taking a major scale and flatting the **3rd, 6th** and **7th** degrees as in **Fig. 8.7.** - using the minor key signature **without** additional alterations as in **Fig. 8.8.**
Nine-eight (9/8) time	A time signature with nine 'pulses' per measure, each of which consists of an eighth note (see **Fig. 1.29.**).
Ninth (9th) interval	An interval derived by increasing a **second interval** by one **octave**. All possible versions of the **second** interval *(see glossary entry for second interval)* are also possible for the **ninth** interval.
Notation	- See *'music notation'*.
Octave	The interval created between notes with the same name. For example, the interval between middle **C** and the next **C** in either direction is one octave - see **Fig. 2.5**.
Perfect interval	The term **perfect** is applied to all **4th** and **5th** intervals (and octave displacements thereof) which are diatonic i.e. in which the top note is within the major scale built from the bottom note - see **Fig. 2.5**.

Phrygian (mode)

The mode created when a major scale is displaced to start on its **3rd** degree (first seen in **Fig. 5.2.**).

Plural, plurality

A chord which occurs diatonically in different keys is said to be **plural** to those keys. See *'triad plurality'* section in **Chapter 4** and *'four-part chord plurality'* section in **Chapter 7**.

Progression

- See *'chord progression'*.

Pulse, pulses

This term is used in **Chapter 1** in the context of time signatures, to describe the points of rhythmic emphasis (i.e. 'where you would tap your foot') during the measure. The **bottom** number of the time signature tells you which rhythmic unit (i.e. quarter note, half note, eighth note etc.) this will occur on.

Quarter note

A note with duration lasting for one beat (see **Fig. 1.10.**).

Quarter note rest

A rest with duration lasting for one beat (see **Fig. 1.18.**).

Relative major

This term can be used in two contexts:-

- in a **modal** context, the relative major scale is the major scale which has been displaced to create the mode in question - see discussion on **p131.**
- in a **key signature** context, the relative major is the key which shares the same key signature as the minor key in question. For example, from the discussion on **p205** we see that the keys of **Eb major** and **C minor** share the same key signature - so **Eb major** can be considered the **relative major** of **C minor.**

Relative minor

The minor key which shares the same key signature as the major key in question. For example, **C minor** is the **relative minor** of **Eb major** - see discussion on **p205.**

Rhythm

The organization of music in respect to time. See **Chapter 1 Figs. 1.7. - 1.22.** for a summary of the common rhythmic 'durations' used in music notation.

Rhythmic value

The number of beats (units of 'rhythmic duration') that a note or rest may last for - see **Chapter 1**.

Root
A term normally used in the context of a chord - the root of a chord is the fundamental tone of the chord, as contained in the chord symbol i.e. the root of a **Bmi** triad is the note **B**.

Root position
A chord in which the notes appear in their normal vertical sequence i.e. root, 3rd, 5th etc. (as opposed to an inversion, in which case this sequence is modified). A **root position** chord will therefore have the **root** on the bottom of the chord. See **Figs. 3.10. - 3.13.** and **6.9. - 6.11.**

Scale
A sequence of notes (typically considered in ascending order) governed by a specific interval relationship. For example, the major scale illustrated in **Fig. 1.42.** is created via the series of whole-steps and half-steps as indicated.

Scale source
A scale from which a particular chord can be derived. For example, diatonic triads can be derived from modal scale sources - see **Figs. 5.1. - 5.6.** and accompanying text.

Scalewise
A movement occurring either up or down a scale by adjacent scale steps.

Second (2nd) interval
- A **major 2nd** interval occurs between the tonic (**1st** degree) and the **2nd** degree of a major scale i.e. **D** is the **2nd** degree of **C major**, therefore **C** up to **D** is a **major 2nd** interval (see **Fig. 2.5.**).
- A **minor 2nd** interval occurs when a **major 2nd** interval is reduced by a half-step i.e. **C** up to **D** is a **major 2nd** interval, therefore **C** up to **Db** is a **minor 2nd** interval.
- An **augmented 2nd** interval occurs when a **major 2nd** interval is increased by a half-step i.e. **C** up to **D** is a **major 2nd** interval, therefore **C** up to **D#** is an **augmented 2nd** interval.

Second inversion
A triad or four-part chord is in second inversion when the root and third have been moved up an octave, the third becoming the highest note - see **Figs. 3.10. - 3.13.** and **6.9. - 6.11.**

Seventh (7th) interval
- A **major 7th** interval occurs between the tonic (**1st** degree) and the **7th** degree of a major scale i.e. **B** is the **7th** degree of **C major**, therefore **C** up to **B** is a **major 7th** interval (see **Fig. 2.5.**).
- A **minor 7th** interval occurs when a **major 7th** interval is reduced by a half-step i.e. **C** up to **B** is a **major 7th** interval, therefore **C** up to **Bb** is a **minor 7th** interval (see **Fig. 2.7.**).

Seventh (7th) interval (contd)	- A **diminished 7th** interval occurs when a **minor 7th** interval is reduced by a half-step i.e. **C** up to **Bb** is a **minor 7th** interval, therefore **C** up to **Bbb** (**B double-flat**, equivalent to the note **A**) is a **diminished 7th** interval - see **Fig. 2.8.** This interval has the same span as a **major 6th** interval.
Sharp	A sharp sign prefixed to a note requires that note to be raised in pitch by one half-step. May also form part of a key signature.
'Sharp' keys	A name sometimes given to those major keys which contain sharps in the key signature - see **Chapter 1**.
Six-eight (6/8) time	A time signature with six 'pulses' per measure, each of which consists of an eighth note (see **Fig. 1.28.**).
Sixteenth note	A note with duration lasting for one-quarter of a beat (see **Fig. 1.14.**).
Sixteenth note rest	A rest with duration lasting for one-quarter of a beat (see **Fig. 1.22.**).
Sixth (6th) interval	- A **major 6th** interval occurs between the tonic (**1st** degree) and the **6th** degree of a major scale i.e. **A** is the **6th** degree of **C major**, therefore **C** up to **A** is a **major 6th** interval (see **Fig. 2.5.**). - A **minor 6th** interval occurs when a **major 6th** interval is reduced by a half-step i.e. **C** up to **A** is a **major 6th** interval, therefore **C** up to **Ab** is a **minor 6th** interval. - An **augmented 6th** interval occurs when a **major 6th** interval is increased by a half-step i.e. **C** up to **A** is a **major 6th** interval, therefore **C** up to **A#** is an **augmented 6th** interval.
Staff	A set of horizontal lines used in music notation. The lines (and spaces in between) are used to denote pitches, depending upon the **clef** (for example, bass clef or treble clef) being used.
Suffix	The part of the chord symbol following the root note name. For example, the chord symbol **Cma7** has a suffix of **'ma7'**.
Sus, suspended	A suspended chord is one in which the **3rd** is replaced by the **4th** (i.e. the note which is a **perfect 4th** interval above the root of the chord). See **Figs. 9.7. - 9.13.** and accompanying text.
Suspended triad	- See above comments, and **Figs. 9.7. - 9.10**.
Suspended dominant 7th chord	- See above comments, and **Figs. 9.11. - 9.13**.

293

Tenth (10th) interval	An interval derived by increasing a **third interval** by one **octave**. All possible versions of the **third** interval *(see glossary entry for third interval)* are also possible for the **tenth** interval.
Tetrachord	A group of four notes arranged in a 'scalewise' sequence - used as a building block for major and minor scales.
Third (3rd) interval	- A **major 3rd** interval occurs between the tonic (**1st** degree) and the **3rd** degree of a major scale i.e. **E** is the **3rd** degree of **C major**, therefore **C** up to **E** is a **major 3rd** interval. - A **minor 3rd** interval occurs when a **major 3rd** interval is reduced by a half-step i.e. **C** up to **E** is a **major 3rd** interval, therefore **C** up to **Eb** is a **minor 3rd** interval.
Third inversion	A four-part chord is in third inversion when the root, third and fifth have all been moved up an octave (or when the 6th or 7th has been moved down an octave) - see **Figs. 6.9. - 6.11.**
Thirteenth (13th) interval	An interval derived by increasing a **sixth interval** by one **octave**. All possible versions of the **sixth** interval *(see glossary entry for sixth interval)* are also possible for the **thirteenth** interval.
Three-four (3/4) time	A time signature with three 'pulses' per measure, each of which consists of a quarter note (see **Fig. 1.27.**).
Time signature	A pair of numbers (placed one above the other, at the beginning of the music staff) which indicates how many 'pulses' occur in each measure, and on which rhythmic unit (i.e. quarter note, eighth note etc.) this 'pulse' falls - see **p11**.
Tonic	The first degree of the scale or key in question. For example, the tonic of **C major** is the note **C**.
Treble clef	The treble clef staff is typically used in contemporary music to notate pitches which are in the 'upper half' of the overall musical range i.e. from around the **Middle C** area upwards (see **Fig. 1.6.**). Instruments using the treble clef would include the guitar and the piano (right hand part). The first leger line below the treble clef staff represents **Middle C**.
Triad	A three-note chord consisting of **3rd** and **5th** intervals, measured from the root of the chord - see **Chapter 3**.

Twelve-eight (12/8) time

A time signature with twelve 'pulses' per measure, each of which consists of an eighth note (see **Fig. 1.30.**).

Twelfth (12th) interval

An interval derived by increasing a **fifth interval** by one **octave**. All possible versions of the **fifth** interval *(see glossary entry for fifth interval)* are also possible for the **twelfth** interval.

Two-two (2/2) time

A time signature with two 'pulses' per measure, each of which consists of a half note (see **Fig. 1.25.**) - also known as **cut time**.

Upper extensions

See *'extensions'*.

Upper tetrachord

The upper or right-hand portion of a scale created using tetrachords. The upper tetrachord contains the **5th**, **6th**, **7th** and **1st** (tonic) scale degrees - see **Fig. 1.42.** (for a major scale) and **Figs. 8.2. - 8.4.** (for the minor scales).

Whole note

A note with duration lasting for four beats (see **Fig. 1.7.**).

Whole note rest

A rest with duration lasting for four beats (see **Fig. 1.15.**).

Whole-step

An interval measurement equivalent to two **half-steps**. Together the whole-step and half-step intervals are the building blocks for most conventional scales (i.e. the major scale - see **Fig. 1.42.**). The whole-step is also equivalent to a **major 2nd** interval.

'Wrap around'

This term is used in the context of the music alphabet - if we are sequentially ascending through the alphabet, after the lettername **G** we 'wrap around' to the lettername **A**, i.e. we go back to the beginning of the music alphabet (see **p1**).

295